MASSACHUSETTS

A Pictorial History

Massachusetts

Walter Muir Whitehill
and Norman Kotker

CHARLES SCRIBNER'S SONS

New York

Library of Congress Cataloging in Publication Data

Whitehill, Walter Muir, 1905-
    Massachusetts: a pictorial history.

    Bibliography: pp. 327-28.
    Includes index.
    1. Massachusetts—History—Pictorial works.
I. Kotker, Norman, joint author.   II. Title.
F65.W62   974.4   76-28586
ISBN 0-684-14358-5

1 3 5 7 9 11 13 15 17 19   M/D   20 18 16 14 12 10 8 6 4 2

Printed in the United States of America

Title Page
Orthodox Congregational Church, Manchester.
HABS, LC

Pages xii–xiii
Map of Massachusetts, from *A New General Atlas,* Anthony Finley, Philadelphia, 1824

Editor   NORMAN KOTKER

Editorial Assistant   PATRICIA LUCA

Art Director   RONALD FARBER

Contents

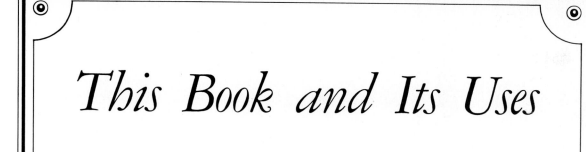

This Book and Its Uses

One picture, as the saying has it, is worth a thousand words. If that is true, then this book, with its 750 or so pictures, illustrating innumerable aspects of Massachusetts life from the seventeenth century to the present, is equivalent to a massive volume on the history of the state, a volume much more comprehensive than any available at present. The aim of this book is to make the folk saying valid, to provide authoritative and thorough documentation of the rich and varied pictorial material that has evolved in the centuries of Massachusetts history and, by the inclusion of an extensive and unique index, to enable the reader and the reference librarian to find in the pictures themselves hundreds of facts which are unavailable elsewhere, or, if available, very difficult of access.

In this work, as in Scribner's notable *Album of American History* which has proven so useful as a book of historical reference, the pictures themselves contain the history, and the text, except for Walter Muir Whitehill's informative introduction, assumes a subordinate role. The captions aim merely to identify the pictures within a historical context, without intending to be in any sense a complete, however brief, narrative history of the state. In this book, we have a thread of text which explains the pictures, instead of scattered pictures which only scantily illustrate a text.

The plan of the book has been to reproduce only pictures which are contemporary with the events they illustrate. As a result, each picture is a primary source of historical information, a rich repository of facts about the period in which it was made. Most of us are not accustomed to looking at pictures in this way. We generally look at them aesthetically and as illustrations of

a story, scene, or event, rather than as aggregates of historical facts. This book is designed to alter that balance, to enable the reader to "milk" the pictures, as it were, of the historical or factual information they contain, and to provide, through a comprehensive index, an instrument of reference and research.

An example will show the system by which this is done. *The Kitchen,* reproduced on the next page and on page 268, is a chromolithograph showing a typical kitchen in 1874. It was made by the Boston lithographer Louis Prang, who is probably best known today as the man who popularized the custom of exchanging Christmas cards. The picture shows the following facts:

1. Cast iron coal stoves were in general use by this time for cooking and baking.
2. There are two faucets on the sink; therefore, by 1874, hot and cold running water were generally available.
3. Water was heated in a hot water heater connected with the stove.
4. Hot water for a bath could be drawn directly from the hot water heater by turning the faucet at the bottom.
5. Roller towels were in use.
6. A lifter—seen on the rack beside the stove—was required to lift the hot stove lid.
7. A small broom and dust pan were at hand in the kitchen to clean up ashes. Next to the stove there is also a shaker for shaking ashes out of the grate.
8. Eggs were stored in baskets.

Not all these facts are in the caption, and some may not be readily apparent to the reader. The

comprehensive index, which indicates the subjects which are illustrated but not discussed in the captions, is designed to provide these facts, to supply a key to each of the hundreds of pictures in the book. The index entries give the reader and researcher ready access to visual information that contains answers to a multitude of questions.

A typical entry will read:

Water, hot, heater for, 19c. (attached to stove by copper pipe), 268–69:1

The entry contains a picture number (1) as well as a page (268–69), indicating that the object is illustrated but not discussed in the caption. The century in which the object was made (19c.) is indicated. Further information about it—in this case that its piping was made of copper—is provided for the reader. Some indication of its location in the picture is given when necessary. And finally, the page on which the subject appears and the picture number are given. Anyone interested in learning about the subject will find an informative illustration of it which is incorporated within an illustration of an entirely different subject. Thus, a book designed to document pictorially the history of one state—one volume in a series devoted to the pictorial history of all the states—has broader application, becoming, in effect, a distinguished pictorial ref-

erence library, encompassing numerous aspects of the varied life of America.

The Kitchen is cross-indexed under the following entries:

basket, for eggs
bathing:
    hot water for in water heater
broom, for ashes, 19c.
bucket
clock, kitchen
coal scuttle
coal stove, 19c.
cooking
cooking, utensils for
costume, female, 1874
cupboard, kitchen, 19c.
dishpan, 19c.
dustpan, 19c.
egg basket
faucets:
    for drawing bath water from water heater
    for hot and cold water
heating
interiors, kitchen, 1874
kitchens
occupations:
    housewife
pie, apple, preparing
pitcher
Prang, Louis, *The Kitchen,* 1874

scuttle, coal
sink, kitchen
stove, cast iron, coal burning, 19c.
    implements related to use of (these implements will be listed)
table, kitchen
towel, roller
water, hot, heater for
women

Since the book contains other illustrations of cooking utensils, heating devices, female costume, etc., elsewhere, the index will lead the reader to a wide range of information on the subject of his interest—kitchen utensils and their use throughout the centuries of Massachusetts history.

This book is part of a series of volumes on the American states. The series will bring together an unequalled library of pictures devoted to American history, some 35,000 pictures in all, each different and each contemporary with the events described, ensuring its trustworthiness as a historical document. Eventually, a comprehensive index will be published for the entire series, providing on a national scale the same sort of reference documentation contained in individual volumes.

Acknowledgments

In the production of this book, the authors have drawn on the resources of a great many people and institutions. The notes on picture sources on page 329 contain a list of the institutions whose cooperation made the task of gathering pictures possible. Numerous individuals—some affiliated with institutions and others unaffiliated—were also of help, and great thanks are extended for their assistance. They are: Malcolm Freiberg, Winifred V. Collins, Massachusetts Historical Society; Abbott L. Cummings, Daniel M. Lohnes, Society for the Preservation of New England Antiquities; Sinclair Hitchings, Boston Public Library; Marcus McCorison, Georgia B. Bumgardner, American Antiquarian Society; Elton W. Hall, Richard C. Kugler, Old Dartmouth Historical Society; Elaine Zetes, Museum of Fine Arts; Ernest Dodge, Philip C. F. Smith, Catherine Flynn, Peabody Museum; Gordon Abbott, Jr., John Marksbury, The Trustees of Reservations, Milton; Helena Wright, Merrimack Valley Textile Museum; Rodney Armstrong, Jack Jackson, Boston Athenaeum; Margaret L. Nelson, Essex Institute; Francis Carpenter, Museum of the American China Trade; Reverend Thomas V. Daily, Archdiocese of Boston; George E. Ryan, *The Pilot;* Richard Weisberg, Newtonville; Rowland Cox, Groton School; Lawrence D. Geller, Pilgrim Society; Joan Irish, Massachusetts Audubon Society; Joe Fitzgerald, West Roxbury; George J. Gloss, Brattle Book Shop; Leo Flaherty, Archives of the Commonwealth of Massachusetts; James J. Keeney, Division of Tourism, Massachusetts Department of Commerce and Development; Wesley J. Christenson, College of the Holy Cross; John F. Waters, Chatham; Helen Constant, Arlington; Harriet Ropes Cabot, Bostonian Society; Ruth A. Woodbury, Wakefield Historical Society; Dorothy C. Haywood, Lynn Public Library; Mary K. Shaw, Historic Deerfield, Inc.; John I. Taylor, *Boston Globe;* Stanley F. Chyet, American Jewish Archives, Cincinnati; Governor Michael S. Dukakis; Reverend Msgr. Matthew P. Stapleton, St. Columbkille's Church, Brighton; Joseph G. Weisberg, *The Jewish Advocate;* Reverend Philip S. Gialopsos, Holy Trinity Church, Lowell; Reverend J. Thomas Leamon, First Congregational Church, Williamstown; Nicholas J. Minadakis, Chelsea Public Library; Ethel I. Newell, M.I.T.; Elizabeth Bidula, Kosciusko Foundation, New York; Oscar Handlin, Cambridge; Jean C. Hickcox, South Yarmouth; George M. Cushing, Boston; James Anagnostos, *Hellenic Chronicle;* Peggy Buchwalter, New York; Fan Smith, New York; Bertram K. Little, Brookline. Special thanks go to Irv Shaffer of Framingham, who took many fine photographs especially for use in this book.

Massachusetts—1824

An 1824 map of Massachusetts was made before the mill towns of Lowell and Lawrence were established and before the name of South Freetown was changed to Fall River. The map shows the Middlesex Canal reaching from Medford to Chelmsford and the roads that carried most of the Commonwealth's traffic before the building of the railroads. The boundary with Rhode Island has been modified since this map was published. In 1862 the area which now makes up the city of Pawtucket was handed over to Rhode Island in exchange for lands which now form the southern section of the city of Fall River.

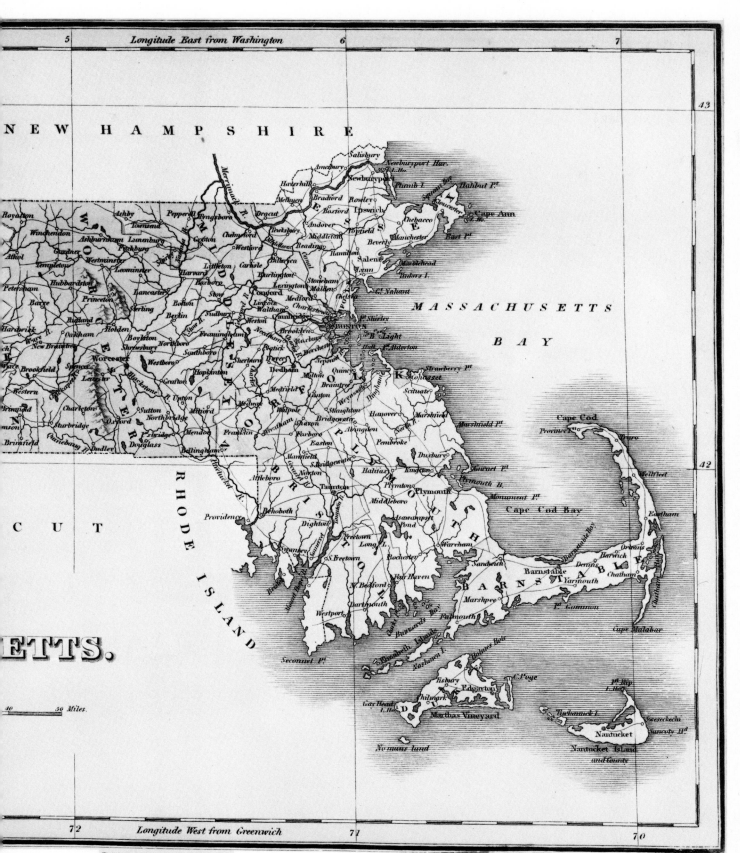

5   6   7

43

NEW HAMPSHIRE

Royalston
Winchendon
Athol
Templeton
Ashby
Ashburnham Lunenburg
Gardner
Westminster
Fitchburg
Leominster
Peterham
Hubbardston
Princeton
Barre
Lancaster
Hardwick
Rutland
Holden
Oakham
New Braintree
Boylston
Worcester
Shrewsbury
Northboro
Southboro
Westboro
Brookfield
Leicester
Spencer
Western
Charlton
Sutton
Northbridge
Grafton
Millbury
Sturbridge
Oxford
Upton
Brimfield
Charleton
Douglass
Mendon
Milford
Bellingham
Brimfield
Sturbridge
Dudley

Townsend
Pepperell
Groton
Shirley
Harvard
Littleton
Carlisle
Westford
Chelmsford
Dracut
Tewksbury
Billerica
Reading
Stoneham
Maldon
Lexington
Concord
Medford
Lincoln
Waltham
Weston
Framingham
Natick
Needham
Sudbury
Sherborn
Holliston
Hopkinton
Medway
Medfield
Walpole
Sharon
Wrentham
Franklin
Norton
Mansfield
Attleboro
Rehoboth
Dighton
Swansey
S. Freetown
Freetown
Long I.

Merrimack R.
Haverhill
Methuen
Bradford
Andover
Amesbury
Salisbury
Newburyport
Newburyport Har.
Plum I.
Rowley
Ipswich
Boxford
Topsfield
Hamilton
Thebacco
Beverly
Manchester
Salem
Marblehead
Lynn
Nahant I.
C. Nahant
Chelsea
P.t Shirley
BOSTON
B. Light
Roxbury
Hull P.t Alderton
Dorchester
Quincy
Braintree
Weymouth
Hingham
Cohasset
Strawberry P.t
Scituate
North R.
Hanover
Marshfield
Marshfield P.t
Abington
Bridgewater
Pembroke
Duxbury
E. Bridgewater
Halifax
Kingston
Gurnet P.t
Plympton
Plymouth
Yarmouth H.
Middleboro
Assawampsett Pond
Monument P.t
Taunton
Wareham
Rochester
Sandwich
Marshpee
New Bedford
Fairhaven
Dartmouth
Westport
Acushnet
Providence

Haddut P.t
Gloucester
Cape Ann
C. Ann
East P.t

MASSACHUSETTS
BAY

Cape Cod
Province T.n
Truro
Wellfleet
Eastham
Orleans
Barwick
Dennis
Chatham
Yarmouth
Barnstable
Js. Common
Cape Malabar

Cape Cod Bay

Seconnet P.t
Elizabeth Islands
Nashaun I.
Buzzards Bay
Falmouth
Holmes Hole
C. Poge
Tisbury
Edgarton
Chilmark
Gay Head L. Ho.
D U K E S
Martha's Vineyard
No mans land
Nantucket
Sankoty H.d
P.t Bay L. Ho.
Nantucket I.
Nantucket Island
and County

RHODE ISLAND

CUT

40   50 Miles.

42

72   71   70

Published by A. Finley Philad.a

MASSACHUSETTS

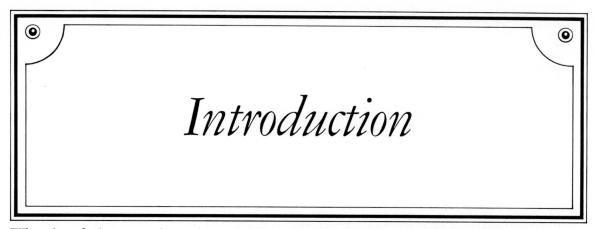

Introduction

When introducing an earlier volume in this series, Parke Rouse, Jr., observed that "the key to Virginia's history is a love for the land—for land and the power which it confers on men and nations. It was a desire for land that brought the first 104 settlers across the wintry Atlantic from London to Jamestown in 1607." The histories of Virginia and Massachusetts diverge at the moment when they begin, for it was religion rather than land that brought Englishmen to Plymouth in 1620 and to Boston in 1630. The respective religious preoccupations of those two very different Massachusetts groups acquired an importance in American history exceeding that achieved by land or other material possessions.

The record of the first group is best read in *Of Plymouth Plantation 1620–1647 by William Bradford Sometime Governor Thereof.* That classic narrative tells how a little group of English Puritans, who wished to separate from—rather than to reform—the Church of England, went first to Holland and eventually to the New England wilderness. In describing their departure from Leyden, Bradford wrote, "So they left that goodly and pleasant city which had been their resting place near twelve years; but they knew they were pilgrims, and looked not much on those things, but lifted up their eyes to the heavens, their dearest country, and quieted their spirits." From that passage, with its evocation of the Epistle of Paul the Apostle to the Hebrews, the company of the *Mayflower,* who came ashore at Plymouth on December 21, 1620, has come to be known as the Pilgrim Fathers. While still at sea the previous month, they had drawn up the Mayflower Compact, which Samuel Eliot Morison has described as "simply an agreement made by Englishmen who, finding themselves on English soil without any specified powers of government, agreed to govern themselves until the king's pleasure should be signified." Although the Pilgrims knew that they had to support themselves in the wilderness by whatever means they could, it was their religious conviction, rather than a hope for land or profit, that brought them there.

Ten years later another group of Englishmen, organized as the Massachusetts Bay Company, chartered by the Crown ostensibly for commercial purposes, came to New England. They too were Puritans, but of a different stamp from the Pilgrim Fathers, for they wished not to separate from, but to purify and reform, the Church of England. Their governor, John Winthrop, was a Suffolk gentleman of good standing and property. The members of the Massachusetts Bay Company had more ample resources than the Pilgrims, as well as good relations with Puritans at home who would later hold high places in the government of the Cromwellian Commonwealth. Their motives in emigrating were to found a church and state in which they might live according to their interpretation of the Word of God. In the spring of 1630, during the Atlantic passage of the Massachusetts Bay Company in the *Arbella* to New England, Winthrop wrote a lay sermon, entitled *A Modell of Christian Charity,* in which he said, "Wee must Consider that we shall be as a Citty upon a Hill, the eies of all people are upon us."

The elevated religious purpose of this migration is indicated by the founding of Harvard College in 1636, only six years after the arrival of the Massachusetts Bay Company at Boston. A tract entitled *New Englands First Fruits,* published in London in 1643, thus describes this remarkable act of literate faith: "After God had carried us safe to New England, and wee had built our houses, provided necessaries for our liveli-hood, rear'd convenient places for Gods worship, and setled the Civill Government: One of the next things we longed for, and looked after was to advance Learning and perpetuate it to Posterity; dreading to leave an illiterate Ministery to the Churches, when our present Ministers shall lie in the Dust." As the Reverend Thomas Shepard, minister of the church at Cambridge, put it, "Thus the Lord was pleased to direct the harts of the magistrates (then keeping court ordinarily in our town because of the stirs at Boston) to thinke of erecting a Schoole or Colledge, and that speedily to be a nursery of knowledge in these deserts and supply for posterity."

The going was not easy, yet the response of farming towns to requests for gifts toward the support of the college indicates how completely men and women who had scant means for their own maintenance respected the principle of a "nursery of knowledge." When an appeal was received in Andover in November 1653, the constable called the inhabitants together. His touching reply, admirably expressed, stated that the Andover farmers "well approved of the care of the Court for the advancement of Learning and are willing to be helpfull according to their ability; but by reason our Towne is very small consisting of about 20 poore familyes (few whereof have corne for their owne necesseity) they found themselves unable to give any considerable sum to the use aforesaid. Yet to show their willingness to forward so good a worke they have generally agreed to give a pecke of wheat this year for the least family, others two, some a bushell, what it will exactly come to I cannot yet tell. We hope God will enable us to doe the like hereafter, or to agree upon a certain somme for the whole as wee shall finde may best sute the occasion of the Colledge and our abilityes." In the end, those "20 poore familyes" gave Harvard College two pounds' worth of wheat, a performance as creditable to their good feeling as Constable Daniel Poore's letter was to his literacy. With such a tradition early established, it is not difficult to understand why education in the nineteenth and twentieth centuries became one of the principal occupations of Massachusetts.

The climate of Massachusetts, with long snowy winters, hot summers, and a growing season curtailed by late spring and early autumn frosts, must have proved a rude shock to settlers accustomed to the mildness of England. As the region was a glacial dump-heap, there was a pleasing variety to the landscape. Near the coast, in relatively close proximity, one finds harbors, granite cliffs, sand dunes and beaches, salt marshes, river valleys, and isolated hills; farther west the Berkshires are a segment of the Appalachian mountain chain. Massachusetts is better to look at than to try to cultivate; the land provided an uncertain economic base for the Puritan "City upon a Hill."

By 1650 there were forty settlements, in addition to Plymouth, in what is now Massachusetts. The year 1630 saw the founding of Boston; the adjacent towns of Charlestown, Dorchester, Roxbury, and Watertown just up the Charles River; and the formal establishment of Salem on the coast to the northeast. In 1631 a "new town" was settled between Boston and Watertown that became Cambridge. Marblehead and Scituate date from 1633, and Ipswich from 1634. 1635 saw the settlement of Lynn, Newbury, Concord, Weymouth, and Hingham. Dedham was settled in 1636, Duxbury in 1637, Barnstable and Sandwich, both on Cape Cod, in 1638; Rowley, Sudbury, Taunton, and Yarmouth in 1639. Salisbury, Braintree, and Marshfield date from 1640; Haverhill and Springfield from 1641; Gloucester and Woburn from 1642; Wenham from 1643; Reading and Hull from 1644; Manchester and Rehoboth from 1645; Andover from 1646; Topsfield from 1648; Malden from 1649; Natick and Medfield from 1650. Most of these settlements were within a day's sail along the coast, or a day's march inland through the woods, with the conspicuous exception of Springfield, which was a hundred miles west on the Connecticut River. The names almost entirely echo those of English places, but in an unfamiliar sequence, for Plymouth in Devonshire is a far greater distance away from Boston in Lincolnshire than their Massachusetts namesakes are from each other. Ipswich in Suffolk is northeast of London, while Andover in Hampshire is southwest, yet in Essex County in Massachusetts towns of those names are only a few miles apart. That often startles and confuses British visitors to New England today.

The first comers of the Massachusetts Bay Company had sold their farms in England to meet the expense of the voyage and their first years in America. During the 1630s large numbers of

English Puritans migrated to the Massachusetts Bay, bringing English goods with them but requiring food. Those new emigrants were ready purchasers for the corn and cattle raised by earlier comers. As the Puritan cause began to triumph in England, the stream of new arrivals dwindled to a trickle; sellers found no buyers and economic depression ensued. Governor John Winthrop noted in his journal for June 2, 1641, that political changes at home "caused all men to stay in England in expectation of a new world, so as few coming to us, all foreign commodities grew scarce, and our own of no price. Corn would buy nothing; a cow which cost last year £20 might now be bought for 4 or £5. etc., and many gone out of the countey, so as no man could pay his debts, nor the merchants make return into England for their commodities, which occasioned many there to speak evil of us. These straits set our people on work to provide fish, clapboards, plank, etc., and to sew hemp and flax (which prospered very well) and to look out to the West Indies for a trade for cotton." So from sheer necessity rather than choice, Massachusetts Puritans became shipbuilders, seamen, merchants, and fishermen. The sea before them, teeming with fish, and the forests behind, which could be converted into ship timber, masts, and lumber, offered the only solution. For the next 175 years maritime commerce was the mainstay of Massachusetts. The story has been told with consummate skill by Samuel Eliot Morison in *The Maritime History of Massachusetts,* a classic of American historical writing that first appeared in 1921.

The peninsula upon which Boston was settled was ideal for a seaport, for it fronted on a deep protected harbor; the considerable extent of shoreline, only a few minutes' walk from any part of the peninsula, provided excellent space for wharves and shipyards. Boston was, as William Wood had described it in 1634 in his promotional tract *New Englands Prospect,* "fittest for such as can Trade into England, for such commodities as the Country wants, being the chiefe place for shipping, and Merchandize." So it became, and so it remained well into the nineteenth century. Along the Massachusetts shore, from Newburyport and Cape Ann on the north to Cape Cod and Buzzards Bay on the south, were other seaports that developed thriving specialties of their own.

During the years of Puritan triumph in England, from the execution of Charles I in 1649 to the restoration of Charles II in 1660, as commerce increased, men went back and forth across the Atlantic in considerable numbers. Because of the close ties of family and trade that linked Boston and London, Boston evolved from a wilderness settlement to being an English town, a microcosm of the city of London. By the end of the seventeenth century, Boston's fleet of seagoing vessels ranked third in size in the English-speaking world, exceeded only by those of London and Bristol. The owners of these vessels lived as prosperous Englishmen might have at home. Thus Daniel Neal, in his *History of New England,* published in London in 1725, wrote, "Conversation in Boston is as polite as in most of the Cities and Towns in England, many of their Merchants having travell'd into Europe, and those that stay at home having the advantage of free Conversation with Travellers; so that a Gentleman from London would almost think himself at home at Boston, when he observes the numbers of people, their Houses, their Furniture, their Tables, their Dress and Conversation, which, perhaps, is as splendid and showy, as that of the most considerable Tradesmen in London." In the first half of the eighteenth century Boston was the largest place in British North America. It had a population of 16,282 in 1743, at a time when Philadelphia had 13,000 and New York 11,000 inhabitants. By 1760, however, the roles were reversed, for Philadelphia had grown to 23,750, New York to 18,000, while Boston had declined slightly to 15,361.

Although the chief prosperity of colonial Massachusetts came from the sea, some men moved to the westward, clearing in the wilderness and establishing new settlements. In the century following 1650, twenty-two towns were established in what is today Worcester County; that is, the area running from the northern to the southern borders of Massachusetts to the westward of Middlesex and Norfolk counties, which were settled earlier because they were nearer Boston and the sea. Lancaster was settled in 1653, Mendon in 1667, Brookfield in 1673, Worcester in 1684, and Oxford in 1693. In the first quarter of the eighteenth century, five more towns were established in this area; in the second quarter twelve more were organized.

West of Worcester County came the Connecticut River valley, subdivided today into the counties of Franklin, Hampshire, and Hampden. Although farther from Boston, the region attracted settlers, for the land close to the river was fertile, while the river itself gave access to Connecticut settlements to the south. Springfield had been established here in 1641. In the second half of the seventeenth century, five towns were settled upriver—Northampton (1656), Hadley (1661), Westfield (1669), Hatfield (1670), and Deerfield (1677)—but only five more were organized in the first half of the eighteenth century. The mountainous Berkshire County, at the extreme west of Massachusetts, was naturally enough the last to be settled; only in 1733 was the town of Sheffield established, and in 1739 Stockbridge. In the colonial period, Worcester County and points west were less prosperous and populous than regions nearer the coast; the development of central and western Massachusetts came in the nineteenth century with factories and railroads.

In spite of the title of John Winthrop's *A Modell of Christian Charity,* the Massachusetts Puritan "Citty upon a Hill" included no tolerance for persons of other religious opinions. When the peace of the community was disturbed in the first decade by religious controversy, the dissenters and troublemakers were given short shrift. Roger Williams moved on to Rhode Island; Anne Hutchinson, the ringleader of the Antinomian controversy, was banished from the colony. Quakers, who in the seventeenth century were often disturbers of the peace, were chased out and, if they persistently returned, hanged. The first president of Harvard College, the Reverend Henry Dunster, resigned under fire in 1654 because he held Baptist principles; he moved to Scituate, in the Plymouth Colony, where a small Baptist congregation was tolerated. Although a group of Baptists, organized in Charlestown in 1665, was allowed to build a meetinghouse in Boston in 1679, Boston in the first half-century was a theocracy in which the town's three Puritan churches accounted for almost all the organized religion.

That undisputed religious hegemony was rudely interrupted in 1686, when a clergyman of the Church of England arrived in Boston in the wake of a royal governor. The Massachusetts Bay Company had been chartered by Charles I ostensibly for commercial purposes, like the East India, the Muscovy, and other trading companies. It was assumed by the Crown that its headquarters would be in London. But the company, led by its gov-

ernor, John Winthrop, had quietly moved to New England in 1630—lock, stock, and barrel—bringing along its charter, which it proceeded to regard as authorization to set up a self-governing community in the wilderness. During the first two decades, the settlement was too insignificant to attract the notice of government at home, for Charles I had more immediate problems to worry him. During the Protectorate, friends of Boston's Puritans were at the helm in England, but after the Restoration the growing prosperity of Boston trade made the place the subject of greater interest in London than it had been earlier. Charles II declared the charter of Massachusetts Bay null and void in 1684; two years later royal authority was definitely established in Boston. On December 20, 1686, Sir Edmund Andros took office as the first royal governor of the newly constituted Territory and Dominion of New England, which included the colonies of the Massachusetts Bay and of New Plymouth. With him came a chaplain, the Reverend Robert Ratcliffe, M.A., appointed by the Bishop of London to officiate according to the Book of Common Prayer. Anglican services were held first in the Town House, then—to the disgust of its congregation—in the Third (Old South) Church. Finally in 1689 a modest King's Chapel, built in a corner of the old burying ground at the corner of Tremont and School streets, was opened for Anglican worship. The growth of the Church of England during the first half of the eighteenth century is indicated by the establishment of two new parishes—Christ Church in the North End in 1723 and Trinity Church in the South End in 1733—and by the need in midcentury of replacing the 1689 King's Chapel with the present stone building, designed by Peter Harrison. Although the Puritan clergy, particularly the Mathers, still made themselves heard, the lines of authority had altered with a royal governor in residence and the Church of England on the scene.

The memory of those first fifty-four years when the Massachusetts Bay Company did what it had a mind to, without let or hindrance from London, died hard. They were, in a sense, the seedbed of future revolution and independence. On April 18, 1689, when the news reached Boston of the "Glorious Revolution" that had deposed James II and placed his son-in-law and daughter, William and Mary, upon the throne, the citizens quickly responded by a revolution of their own. They captured and locked up Governor Andros and most of his officials! The new charter of the Province of the Massachusetts Bay, granted by William and Mary in 1691, incorporated into Massachusetts the Plymouth Colony and the province of Maine. Maine continued to be governed from Boston until 1820, when it was detached from Massachusetts and admitted as the twenty-third state in the Union; its history is not considered in this book.

Eighty-six years and one day after Boston militia men jailed a British royal governor, other militia men at Lexington and Concord attacked the king's troops, spilling the first blood of the American Revolution. One of them, Captain Levi Preston, was interviewed sixty-seven years later by a young student of history, Mellen Chamberlain, later in life librarian of the Boston Public Library. Chamberlain, age twenty-one, confidently asked the ninety-one-year-old veteran why he had gone to the Concord fight on April 19, 1775. "The old man, bowed beneath the weight of years, raised himself upright, and turning to me said: 'Why did I go?' 'Yes,' I replied; 'my histories tell me that you men of the Revolution took up arms against "intolerable oppressions." ' 'What were they? Oppressions? I didn't feel them.' 'What, were you not oppressed by the Stamp Act?' 'I never saw one of those stamps, and always understood that Governor Bernard put them all in Castle William. I am certain I never paid a penny for one of them.' 'Well, what then about the tea-tax?' 'Tea-tax! I never drank a drop of the stuff; the boys threw it all overboard.' 'Then I suppose you had been reading Harrington or Sidney and Locke about the eternal principles of liberty.' 'Never heard of 'em. We read only the Bible, the Catechism, Watts's Psalms and Hymns and the Almanack.' 'Well, then, what was the matter? and what did you mean in going to the fight?' 'Young man, what we meant in going for those red-coats was this: we always had governed ourselves, and we always meant to. They didn't mean we should.' "

Old Captain Preston's final remark, Mellen Chamberlain claimed, is "the ultimate philosophy of the American Revolution." It was also, I suspect, grounded in the memory of the years 1630 to 1684, and the one-day Revolution of April 18, 1689. New Englanders are an opposite-minded crew; when on foot they still have a lordly disregard for crosswalks governed by traffic lights and other minor forms of regulation generally accepted elsewhere. They never took kindly to navigation acts or similar attempts of the British government to regulate, and derive some revenue from, maritime trade; consequently they developed considerable agility in evading them. The use of writs of assistance to facilitate the enforcement of such commercial restrictions raised a great hullabaloo in Boston in 1761, as did the passage of the Stamp Act in 1765.

A carefully instigated Boston mob on August 14, 1765, hanged in effigy at the Liberty Tree Andrew Oliver, who had been appointed stamp officer. In the evening they razed a building thought to have been intended for the stamp office, and ransacked Oliver's house. Taking the hint, Oliver wisely resigned his post the next day, but the mob, having tasted the joys of hoodlumism, attacked the house of his brother, Chief Justice Peter Oliver, and that of Lieutenant Governor Thomas Hutchinson. The repeal of the Stamp Act in March 1766 removed one ground of complaint, but dissident Bostonians were fertile in finding excuses for riots. The seizure by customs officials of John Hancock's sloop *Liberty* in June 1768 for false entry raised another, which caused officials to flee to Castle William, in the harbor, for protection. In October of that year British troops arrived in Boston. Their presence led to the brawl on the evening of March 5, 1770, grandiloquently dubbed the Boston Massacre, in which three men were killed and eight wounded.

A tax upon tea became another *casus belli*. When ships containing tea arrived in Boston, citizens disguised as Indians boarded them on December 16, 1773, dumping 342 chests into the harbor. The Boston Tea Party was too much for government in London to swallow. In March 1774, Parliament passed the Boston Port Bill, closing it to the import and export of all goods except food or fuel, and passed also an act for better regulating the government of Massachusetts, which greatly increased the power of the governor by virtually revoking the 1691 charter. General Thomas Gage, commander in chief of the British Army forces in North America, was appointed governor of Massachusetts. The Boston Port Bill went into operation on June 1, 1774. Gage, who had landed in Boston on May 17, made military preparations for trouble.

That chain of events led to the assembly of the Continental Congress in Philadelphia on September 5, 1774. Much sympathy was shown for the plight of Boston, so when fighting broke out at Lexington and Concord on April 19, 1775, and at Bunker Hill in Charlestown on June 17, the die was cast. This was more than a local quarrel; the other colonies were in the act. Sympathizers with the patriot cause mostly left Boston to join the militia based across the river in Cambridge; those troops were adopted as the American Continental Army, of which George Washington of Virginia took command on July 3, 1775. Thereafter General Gage's troops and those Bostonians who remained loyal to the Crown were virtually besieged.

On March 4, 1776, General Washington occupied Dorchester Heights, placing there cannon dragged overland from Fort Ticonderoga by General Henry Knox. As those cannon were in range of Boston, the British troops evacuated the town on March 17. With them left many Loyalists, some of whom never returned. Immediately after the evacuation of Boston. Washington's army marched off to New York. The theater of military operations of the Revolution thus left Massachusetts.

Fifteen years of agitation had greatly reduced the population and impaired the commerce of Boston. During the Revolution many Massachusetts shipowners fitted out their vessels as privateers; some profited by that, while others lost their shirts. The Derby family of Salem were prosperous shipowners both before and after the Revolution, but in many ports merchants who had been successful before the war came to grief because of it, while new men, like Captain Joseph Peabody of Salem, who got his start through privateering prize-money, came to fill their places. It was an era of great social mobility, for there were places left by the departed Loyalists that were filled by energetic men who had risen from the obscurity of the farm by way of revolutionary military or political service, as well as by successful ventures at sea.

Independence completely altered the pattern of Massachusetts trade, for it transformed American merchants from colonists to foreigners so far as trade with ports of the British Empire was concerned. Most familiar routes of commerce were automatically closed to them. Survival in the postwar period depended upon the discovery

of wholly new channels of trade. Just as the economic depression of the 1640s had sent Massachusetts men to sea, so the crisis of the 1780s drove their ships to distant and hitherto unfamiliar parts of the world. The development of trade with China, with its ramifications on the Northwest Coast of North America and in the Hawaiian Islands, with India, and along other new routes never attempted before the Revolution, solved the post-Revolutionary crisis. That commercial expansion, which raised Massachusetts to greater prosperity than it had hitherto known, was largely the achievement of the new men, who had moved in from country obscurity to fill Loyalist shoes. Through the end of the eighteenth century, maritime commerce was still the mainstay of Massachusetts, although in a new, far-flung, and more profitable direction.

The population of Massachusetts remained overwhelmingly English in origin through the end of the eighteenth century. The first census, in 1790, reported a total population of 378,556 in the state. Of those 373,187 were white and 5,369 "colored" (presumably Indians and blacks); to each 100 white inhabitants, there were only 1.4 "colored." Of the 373,187 white residents, 354,528 (95 percent) were of English origin; 3.6 percent were Scots and 1 percent Irish, making a total of 99.6 percent from the British Isles. French amounted to only 0.2 percent, Dutch to 0.1 percent. Germans, "Hebrews," and all other nationalities were represented by less than one tenth of 1 percent.

It must be remembered that nationalities were determined in the first census by inspection of the names of the heads of families as they appeared upon the schedules; there was then no question concerning the place of birth of residents or their parents. As the silversmith Apollos Rivoire, who arrived in Boston from France via Guernsey about 1716, anglicized his name "merely on account that the Bumpkins should pronounce it easier," his son, the patriot Paul Revere (1735–1818), was undoubtedly counted in 1790 with the English majority. Although there were probably other instances of this kind, the English character of Massachusetts in 1790 is apparent. The 700 French names reported were scattered around the state in all regions, save for Nantucket and Martha's Vineyard. Of the 428 Dutch, 203 were in Berkshire County—having presumably wandered across the hills from

Albany and the Hudson River valley—and 135 were in Plymouth County for reasons less obviously apparent. Some 36 of the 53 Germans were in Essex County; some of those were doubtless the shipowning Crowninshields, who in changing their names from von Kroninschilt had not completely obscured their Leipzig origin. Of the 49 Hebrews listed, 17 were in Barnstable, and 17 in Essex County, with 15 in Worcester; none were identified in Boston.

As to population, Boston was growing again after the decline brought about by years of Revolutionary agitation; the 18,038 inhabitants reported in 1790, however, seem a modest increase over the 1743 peak of 16,182, when the town was the largest in British North America. The census reported forty towns in the state with populations in excess of 2,000; those were almost evenly divided between the coast and inland areas. The four of these forty that exceeded 5,000 were, however, all seaports: Boston, Salem (7,921), Gloucester (5,137), and Marblehead (5,061).

The situation was about to change radically and rapidly. In 1800 the population of Boston had increased to 24,397, although it was still a relatively simple and homogeneous seaport whose residents were of obvious British extraction. A century later, other things than ships were the mainstay of its 560,892 inhabitants, of whom 197,129 were foreign-born. Among the latter group were 70,147 natives of Ireland, 47,374 of English Canada, 14,995 of Russia, 13,378 of Italy, 13,174 of England, and 10,523 of Germany. The numbers were even greater when one considers the native-born children of immigrants. Nearly half of the 1900 population of Boston was Irish, for when one adds to the 70,147 persons actually born in Ireland, 156,650 first-generation children of Irish-born parents, and 19,305 born here with one Irish and one native parent, the total amounts to 246,101. Boston was thus not only a half-Irish city but also the unacknowledged capital of the Maritime Provinces, for it could muster, between actual immigrants and first-generation children, 112,269 residents hailing from English Canada—another fifth of the population. The 1900 census could discover in Boston only 68,717 native-born residents of native parents of unknown origin, but as 9,646 of these were blacks, the number of white Bostonians who might be considered

descendants of 1800 residents amount to 59,071, less than 11 percent of the city's population.

The 1900 census gives a similar picture for the state of Massachusetts. Of a total population of 2,751,852, 2,276,096 were white. The designation *colored* of 1790 was subdivided to show in 1900 32,192 blacks, 587 Indians, and 2,977 Mongolians. To each 100 white inhabitants, there were 1.2 blacks. Within the state as a whole there were 846,324 foreign-born persons. Immigration and industrialization brought about those dramatic changes, altering the face of Massachusetts and the way of life of its inhabitants. Because of their diversity and importance, the nineteenth century, in which they occurred, is given a generous proportion of the illustrations in this book. One must, however, remember that pictorial histories are of necessity shaped by the availability of material. The earlier the period, the greater is the scarcity of authentic illustration. With the appearance of lithography and of photography in the nineteenth century, pictures proliferate.

Until the Civil War, when the depredations of Confederate raiders dealt a heavy blow to American shipping, maritime commerce continued to produce substantial fortunes for Massachusetts merchants. As the nineteenth century progressed, however, other fortunes were made in mercantile and manufacturing pursuits without recourse to the sea. A Bostonian importer and exporter, Francis Cabot Lowell (1775–1817), while traveling in England shortly before the War of 1812, studied observantly the new textile machinery in use in Lancashire; on his return home he determined to start a cotton mill. With his brother-in-law, Patrick Tracy Jackson (1780–1847), and an inventive genius from Byfield, Paul Moody (1779–1831), Lowell started the Boston Manufacturing Company at Waltham in 1813 with an authorized capital of $400,000. That pioneering plant—deriving its power from the Charles River and combining all the processes of converting raw cotton into woven cloth—represented the expansion of capital gained from maritime trade into the new field of large-scale manufacturing. It was also a step toward economic independence for the United States, for it eliminated the need of shipping raw cotton to England for manufacture and bringing the finished product back across the Atlantic.

In the first flush of enthusiasm it was thought

that Boston, while retaining its traditional character as a seaport, would become a major industrial city. To bring this about, Uriah Cotting (circa 1766–1819), an incorporator of the Boston Manufacturing Company who had been responsible for major improvements in the wharves and warehouses of the Boston waterfront, undertook to provide water power for factories by means of a mill dam in the Back Bay of the Charles River. Those plans envisioned harnessing the tides that flowed from the harbor in and out of the Charles River. Although the dam was built and a few modest mills constructed, Cotting's death eliminated the chief driving force. The flow of water was not great enough for large-scale operations; moreover, Boston had no substantial labor force at that time. Patrick Tracy Jackson, who had become head of the Boston Manufacturing Company in 1817, after the death of Francis Cabot Lowell, was looking north for expansion along the Merrimack River, where there was an abundance of water power, and where farm girls from northern New England could more easily be induced to come to operate the new machines. In 1820 Jackson and his associates chose East Chelmsford on the Merrimack, where they created a wholly new manufacturing city, named Lowell in honor of the founder of their enterprise. As the advent of railroads in the 1830s brought once-distant places miraculously close to Boston, it was soon evident that large-scale factories could be established where the best water power was to be found, and still be controlled by their Boston owners. The brothers Amos and Abbott Lawrence, who had come from a Groton farm to Boston in the first decade of the nineteenth century, after developing a substantial business as importers of English dry goods, eventually became not only agents for the newly competing local products, but also active promoters of Massachusetts manufacturing. Thus Abbott Lawrence in 1845 initiated the creation of another new mill city, down the Merrimack from Lowell, carved out of Andover and Methuen farmland, and named after his family.

Although capital and initiative for much manufacturing came from Boston, the actual factories were usually many miles away rather than in the city itself. In some parts of Massachusetts, however, enterprising men turned from farming to manufacturing, building mills in their own towns and living within sight of their operations. During the War of 1812, Nathaniel Stevens, whose family had been farming in the north parish of Andover since the settlement of the town in 1646, started a woolen textile mill there.

The report of Massachusetts manufacturers, town by town, prepared by the Secretary of the Commonwealth in 1845, presents an incredible variety of industrial activity, large and small. Salem, a seaport with the second largest population of any town in 1790—7,921—still had a few ships in 1845, but it had many other things as well. It had grown to 15,802, and was thus described: "The manufactures of Salem consisted of gold, silver, and brass wares, chemical preparations, chronometers, watches, saddles, harnesses, trunks, upholstery, cordage, cars and other carriages, lead, oil, sperm and tallow candles, chairs, tin and cabinet-wares, white lead, gums, leather, boots, shoes, knives, tobacco, &c. There were four whale ships belonging to this place, and three cod and mackerel vessels."

Worcester, with 2,095 inhabitants in 1790, had grown to 7,497 in 1840. Here are its manufactures: "Three cotton mills, with 4,800 spindles; six woolen mills, with eleven sets of machinery; one carpet factory, one paper-mill, and establishments for the manufacture of hollow-ware, and castings; cotton, woolen, and other machinery; card wire, cotton carpeting, saddlery, trunks, cars and other carriages, locks, ploughs, brass and tin-wares; hats, caps, cordage, cards, soap, candles, chairs, cabinet-ware, boots, shoes, straw bonnets and hats, tobacco &c; whips, mechanics' tools, wooden-ware; machine card, hand card, and letter presses; patent water-wheels, sashes, doors, blinds, fancy boxes, paper-hangings, window-blinds, musical instruments, marble monuments, japan and varnish, silver-plated ware, sieve and wire-work, reeds and harnesses, nuts and washers, umbrellas, trusses, copper and wood pumps, &c."

Even in Berkshire County, the last to be settled, there was substantial manufacturing. Adams boasted fourteen cotton and three woolen mills, two calico manufactories, and two furnaces; Cheshire had a cotton mill, Dalton two woolen mills, Hancock two woolen mills and Hinsdale one, Lee eleven paper mills, Pittsfield six woolen and two cotton mills, and two furnaces. Even Mount Washington, founded in

1799, with only 438 inhabitants, produced, in addition to hay, grain, fruit, vegetables, and honey, "Manufactures of iron casting, shovels, spades, forks, hoes, and lumber."

At this time when Massachusetts was energetically manufacturing everything under the sun, the highest perfection of performance in its wooden shipbuilding was being reached by one of its recently arrived residents from English Canada. Donald McKay, born in Shelburne County, Nova Scotia, in 1810, at the age of seventeen emigrated to New York, where he was apprenticed as a ship carpenter in the yard of Isaac Webb. Having mastered his trade, he eventually found his way to Newburyport, where in 1841 he formed a partnership with John Currier. Three years later he was induced by Enoch Train, owner of the Boston–Liverpool line of packet ships, to set up a shipyard in East Boston. For five years he built packets, but in 1850 he began building the great clippers that were the fastest and most dramatic of all sailing vessels. His *Flying Cloud,* launched on April 15, 1851, made the passage from New York around Cape Horn to San Francisco in less than ninety days, a record equaled only twice, once by the same ship. Spectacular clippers like this were fast but costly. Their day was brief, and after 1855 McKay turned to more economical designs. Steam was, in any case, about to put an end to sail, and the Civil War put a permanent crimp in the American merchant marine. McKay's last wooden ship, *Glory of the Seas,* was launched in 1869, the year that he closed his East Boston shipyard.

Symbolically, the closing of McKay's yard marks the end of a predominant concern with the sea that had begun in Massachusetts two and a quarter centuries before. Shipowners and merchants who had made fortunes in the China trade had long been investing them not only in the new manufacturing enterprises, but in railroads, mines, and the development of the rapidly expanding western frontier. The Michigan Central Railroad and the Chicago, Burlington, and Quincy Railroad, like the great Calumet and Hecla Mining Corporation, were controlled from Boston. In the first half of the nineteenth century, State Street in Boston was the link between the wharves and warehouses of the waterfront and the heart of the city. Later in the century, when the waterfront no longer greatly mattered,

it became the financial center of Boston. The name came to denote the place from which investors controlled the lines that led into many distant parts of the United States. Banking and investment, with the interplay that they implied with various forms of manufacturing and business, had become the principal occupation of Boston.

In the twentieth century, the business horizons contracted; while great sums continued to be invested outside of New England, fewer distant companies were controlled from Boston, for the amount of available capital of the city was no longer as significant in the national scene as it had once been. Nevertheless, Boston private trustees continued to show a skill in investment which caused them to be highly regarded in other parts of the country, and which eventually led to a wide development of Boston companies administering mutual investment trusts. Thus the investment of funds in a fiduciary capacity has become one of the most respected professional careers in twentieth-century Boston.

The Massachusetts textile industry passed into crisis in the 1920s, and with it the industrial cities on the Merrimack River created by Boston investment in the previous century. Company after company moved south, in search of cheaper labor supply, or failed, leaving vast empty mills behind. Some of those buildings have been demolished; others have been subdivided for the use of smaller businesses. Still others have been taken over by the huge Raytheon or a variety of smaller new industries. In many of the Boston suburbs—especially along the circumferential Route 128—a bewildering number of elegant new factories, often with cryptically unintelligible names, represent the extension of the scientific imagination of the Massachusetts Institute of Technology and of Harvard University into defense production.

Although ships and textiles have come and gone, learning has remained a staple industry of Massachusetts. The considerable wealth that has been accumulated over the past two centuries was in many instances devoted to the creation and maintenance of learned, cultural, and charitable institutions. The Puritan ethic discouraged ostentation and extravagance. The leisure that came from inherited property led less often to dissipation than to the quiet performance of some useful service. Ever since the eighteenth century, men engaged in the larger aspects of business in

Massachusetts have consorted harmoniously with those following the learned professions. When the Wednesday Evening Club was organized in Boston in 1777, it had but sixteen members, equally divided among clergymen, lawyers, physicians, and merchants. Later a class of "gentlemen at large" was added, eventually to be merged with the merchants to form the present inclusive fourth class of "Merchants, Manufacturers, and Gentlemen of Literature and Leisure."

Samuel Eliot Morison observed in *One Boy's Boston, 1887–1901* of the local pattern of life, "When a family had accumulated a certain fortune, instead of trying to build it up still further to become a Rockefeller or Carnegie or Huntington and then perhaps discharge its debt to society by some great foundation, it would step out of business or finance and try to accomplish something in literature, education, medical research, the arts, or public service. Generally one or two of the family continued in business, to look after the family securities and enable the creative brothers or cousins to carry on without the handicap of poverty. Of course there were families like that in other cities, but in Boston there were so many of them as to constitute a recognized way of life. One only has to think of the Prescott, Parkman, Shattuck, Cabot, Holmes, Lowell, Forbes, Peabody, Eliot, Saltonstall and Sargent families and what they have accomplished for the beauty and betterment of life, to see what I mean."

When John Adams instigated the creation of the American Academy of Arts and Sciences in Boston in 1780, the sixty-two incorporators included, with the clergy, learned professions, judges, and holders of high public office, a leavening of prosperous merchants and gentlemen of inherited property. The "end and design" of the Academy was "to cultivate every art and science which may tend to advance the interest, honor, dignity, and happiness of a free, independent, and virtuous people." Within the next half-century, as prosperity and leisure increased, a number of new institutions, both learned and philanthropic, were created in Massachusetts. In many cases fellows of the American Academy of Arts and Sciences were intimately involved. Although the academy can only claim to be the second oldest learned society in the United States, the Massachusetts Medical Society, founded in 1781, and the Massachusetts Historical Society,

organized in 1791, are the oldest in the country with a record of continuous operation.

The Boston Athenaeum, incorporated in 1807 by a group of Bostonians representing the typical mixture of professional men and China trade merchants, was (and is today) a proprietary institution, owned by shareholders but broadly conceived in the public interest. For some decades it was the only substantial library in Boston; in 1850 it was one of the five largest in the United States. During much of the nineteenth century the American Academy of Arts and Sciences lived under the Athenaeum's roof. In the 1820s an art gallery was added, which exhibited such examples of European paintings and sculpture as could be bought or borrowed, as well as the works of living American artists. It should be noted that the same group of people involved in the American Academy and the Boston Athenaeum had a considerable role in founding such charitable institutions as the Massachusetts General Hospital, incorporated in 1811, and the Provident Institution for Savings in the Town of Boston, founded in 1816, the first savings bank in the United States to receive by incorporation the protection and sanction of law.

Although Boston became a city in 1822, and was fast becoming a polyglot one through incoming tides of immigration, it retained well into the nineteenth century something of its earlier small-town character, where people of like minds knew each other, combining their activities with a disarming simplicity. For example, the Massachusetts Historical Society and the Provident Institution for Savings from 1833 to 1856 shared a building at 30 Tremont Street largely because the scholarly and beneficent James Savage was treasurer of both institutions. That banker-historian had a totally unanticipated effect upon scientific education in the United States, for in 1845 the Virginian geologist William Barton Rogers, who had come to New England in the summer to visit the White Mountains, met and married Savage's daughter Emma, whom he took back to Charlottesville. In 1853, however, Rogers resigned his professorship at the University of Virginia and returned to Boston with his wife, settling in with the Savages in Temple Place, across the street from the great China trade merchant, Thomas Handasyd Perkins, a benefactor of the Athenaeum and many other institutions. William Barton Rogers in 1861 achieved the incorporation of the Massachusetts Institute of Technology, of which he was the first president.

When the Boston Athenaeum was becoming overcrowded in the late 1860s, it joined with Harvard College and the Massachusetts Institute of Technology in incorporating in 1870 the Museum of Fine Arts. Although the new institution received the public grant of a plot of land in Copley Square, upon which its first building was constructed, its phenomenal growth over the next century was due entirely to the gifts of private individuals. In many instances Bostonians with property inherited from the sea or manufacturing devoted their lives to becoming scholarly collectors of works of art, which they gave to the Museum of Fine Arts.

When John Lowell, son of the textile pioneer Francis Cabot Lowell, died prematurely in 1836, his will created the Lowell Institute, which has ever since provided free public lectures in all branches of human knowledge. In recent years the Lowell Institute pioneered in educational television through its support of station WGBH-TV. The Boston Symphony Orchestra was created in 1881 through the singlehanded generosity of a State Street investment banker, Henry Lee Higginson, who supported it consistently until his death in 1919. The Isabella Stewart Gardner Museum, exhibiting a superb group of Italian paintings and other works of art collected by Mrs. John Lowell Gardner, has been open to the public since her death in 1924.

The spirit that created Harvard College as a "nursery of learning" in 1636 reproduced itself in many parts of Massachusetts among men and women of diverse origins. Far west in Berkshire County, the last part of the state to be settled, Williams College was chartered as early as 1793. Its foundation was due to a bequest for a free school from an early settler, Colonel Ephraim Williams, Jr., killed in 1755 during a battle at Lake George. In the Connecticut Valley, Amherst College was founded in 1821 to train men for the ministry. Nearby in South Hadley, with the help of eight thousand dollars raised by the town, Mary Lyon in 1837 opened Mount Holyoke, the oldest college for women in the country, while at Northampton another great college for women, Smith, was founded and endowed in 1871 by Miss Sophia Smith of Hatfield. Henry Fowle Durant, a Boston lawyer of strong evangelical principles, who had become a trustee of Mount Holyoke College in 1867, gave his house in Wellesley and his fortune to create another institution for the education of women, Wellesley College, chartered in 1870. Eliza Cabot Cary Agassiz, a granddaughter of Thomas Handasyd Perkins and wife of the Swiss-born Harvard scientist Louis Agassiz, created in 1879 the "Society for the Collegiate Instruction of Women" that ultimately became Radcliffe College, of which she was the first president. From being an "annex," in which separate instruction was given by members of the Harvard faculty, Radcliffe College is today an integral part of Harvard University.

Although less than forty miles west of Boston, Worcester has long had independent institutions of its own. The patriot newspaper publisher, Isaiah Thomas, who fled from Boston to Worcester on the night of April 18, 1775, with his press and type, retired from active business in 1802 with a decent fortune, which he devoted to learning. He published in 1810 *The History of Printing in America,* and in 1812 founded in Worcester the American Antiquarian Society, which has become a national scholarly library of American history. The oldest Catholic institution of the kind in New England, the College of the Holy Cross, was founded in Worcester by the Jesuit order in 1843. The Worcester Polytechnic Institute, a privately supported engineering school, was created in 1865, while Clark University, whose graduate schools were patterned on German models, dates from 1887. The Worcester Art Museum is another distinguished institution that has benefited from the generosity of the manufacturers of the city.

Around Boston an extraordinary number of educational institutions were created through the respect for learning and generosity of people of a variety of backgrounds. A Medford farmer and bricklayer, Charles Tufts, a devout Universalist, gave twenty acres of his farm for an institution that was incorporated in 1852 as Tufts College. In 1955 the name Tufts University was adopted in belated recognition of what the institution had been in fact for well over half a century. The establishment of Boston University in 1869 was chiefly due to three self-made Methodist laymen, with no more formal education than Charles Tufts: Lee Claflin, a Hopkinton tanner who expanded his business into making boots and shoes; Isaac Rich, a Wellfleet boy who came to Boston peddling fish; and Jacob Sleeper, a Maine man who had prospered in the manufacture of ready-made clothing. When an Irish-born Jesuit, the Reverend John McElroy, founded Boston College in 1863, one of his strong supporters was Andrew Carney, a partner in the clothing business with the Methodist Jacob Sleeper, and founder of the Carney Hospital in South Boston. Over the years Boston College has developed graduate schools that make it a university in fact, if not in name.

Another wholesale clothier, John Simmons, a native of Little Compton, Rhode Island, left trusts that caused the establishment in 1902 of Simmons College in Boston, a private, nonsectarian institution, which was, in the words of its first president, Henry Lefavour, "unique in that it was the first to stand in New England for a utilitarian education for girls, while aiming not to neglect any influence that may broaden the students' outlooks and deepen their lives."

Two other privately established Boston institutions have greatly broadened the educational possibilities for many young people who might not otherwise get to college. Northeastern University, founded in 1898, through its cooperative plan offers a possibility of alternating terms of study with work at an outside job. It is today the largest cooperative-plan university in the United States. Suffolk University, begun in 1906 on the north slope of Beacon Hill, is similarly an independent private institution, primarily designed for commuting students.

The establishment of Brandeis University in Waltham in 1948 sprang from the same motives that caused the Puritans to found Harvard, the Methodists Boston University, and the Jesuits Boston College, for it was due to "the desire of American Jewry to make a corporate contribution to higher education in the tradition of the great American secular institutions that have stemmed from denominational generosity." The nonsectarian character of Brandeis is emphasized by its provision of Jewish, Catholic, and Protestant chapels for its students.

With such a proliferation of privately founded colleges and universities, Massachusetts had nothing on the order of the great state universities, like Wisconsin, Illinois, and California, until the middle of the twentieth century. The creation of a state board of education in 1837, with Horace Mann as its first secretary, led to the establishment of publicly supported normal schools for the training of teachers at Framingham in 1839, at

Bridgewater in 1840, at Boston in 1852, at Salem in 1854, and at other points throughout the state later in the nineteenth century. A Massachusetts Agricultural College was created at Amherst in 1865 and a Massachusetts College of Art at Boston in 1873. It was, however, only after World War II that the legislature took steps toward the creation of a publicly supported state university. Since 1947 the cow barns at Amherst have been overshadowed by a huge University of Massachusetts; a sizable Boston campus began to be developed in 1965. The numerous normal schools have been enlarged and upgraded to the rank of state colleges which, with even newer community colleges, offer educational opportunities far and wide. These, with a myriad of Catholic and Protestant colleges, junior colleges, and professional and vocational schools too numerous to mention, have made education the greatest continuing industry of Massachusetts. What the first Puritans began in 1636 has been multiplied by their successors.

What Horace Mann was attempting in furthering popular education, led the statesman Edward Everett and his friend George Ticknor, historian of Spanish literature, to agitate for the creation of a public library in Boston. Between the Harvard College Library and the Boston Athenaeum —two of the five largest in the United States— Boston already had a larger number of books available than any other city in the country. Yet Everett in 1850 reasoned that a new library, supported by the city, "would put the finishing touch to that system of education that lies at the basis of the prosperity of Boston." Four years later the Boston Public Library opened. This was the first major instance in the United States of a tax-supported library, freely providing books to all classes of citizens; it set the pattern for the development of such institutions throughout the country.

The nineteenth century saw dramatic changes in the religious life of Massachusetts. At the time of the American Revolution, it was an exclusively Protestant corner of the world, with Puritan churches (governed on the congregational principle) and the Church of England accounting for almost all organized religious activity. The first permanent Catholic place of worship dated only from 1788; until the great wave of immigration the following century, there were few to attend it. Its fifth resident priest, Jean Louis

Anne Magdeleine Lefebvre de Cheverus—a gentle, learned, and untiring refugee from the French Revolution, who was created the first bishop of Boston in 1808—inspired the love and admiration of his neighbors of every faith. When in 1799 he undertook to build the Church (later Cathedral) of the Holy Cross in Franklin Street, Protestants swelled the subscription list. Bishop Cheverus was called back to France in 1823, where he died as cardinal archbishop of Bordeaux. In the decade that followed his departure, churches multiplied as thousands of Catholic arrived from Europe. In 1800 there was one Catholic church in Boston; in 1875, when the see was raised to the dignity of an archdiocese, there were twenty-eight. Since 1911 three successive archbishops of Boston have been elevated to the College of Cardinals soon after their appointments. Today nearly half the inhabitants of Massachusetts, and of the city of Boston, are Roman Catholics.

When Justin Winsor prepared *The Memorial History of Boston* on the occasion of the 250th anniversary of the arrival of the Massachusetts Bay Company, he included chapters on religious denominations, yet Jews were not mentioned, even in the index, for they were almost as invisible as they had been at the time of the 1790 census. A few from Germany were here in 1843 to organize the Congregation Ohabei Shalom, which built its first synagogue in 1851, but it was only after repressive Russian edicts in 1882 that eastern European Jews began to come here in great numbers. The tercentenary sequel to Winsor's *History* indicated that in 1930 there were some fifty Jewish congregations in Boston, with a Jewish population of 90,000 in Boston proper and 130,000 in greater Boston.

Today between the Catholic and Jewish populations, the Orthodox, and the unchurched, I suspect that the Protestants of Massachusetts would not exceed a quarter of the inhabitants. Moreover, there have been many divisions among them. By the end of the American Revolution, many Boston clergymen and their followers found the beliefs of liberal Unitarianism more congenial than those of the orthodox Calvinism that had dominated Puritan churches. The Anglican King's Chapel was, however, the first formally to embrace Unitarianism. It had been left without a clergyman in 1776 when its Loyalist rector left Boston with the British troops. During the Revolution, services were conducted by James Freeman, a recent graduate of Harvard, who in 1783 was chosen minister, even though not yet ordained. When Episcopal bishops were established in Connecticut and New York after the Revolution, they declined to ordain Freeman because of his forthright statement of disbelief in the doctrine of the trinity. Finally the wardens and vestry of King's Chapel, who preferred their minister to the bishops, reverted to the traditional New England Congregational practice and ordained him themselves. Thus, a century after its establishment, the first Anglican church in Boston became the first Unitarian church in the town.

It was, however, the first quarter of the nineteenth century before Unitarian doctrine produced permanent cleavages and splinter organizations. The breaking point came in 1805 when the liberal Reverend Henry Ware was appointed Hollis Professor of Divinity at Harvard. As Unitarian doctrine in that post represented the greatest possible threat to orthodox Calvinism, the Andover Theological Seminary was promptly founded to provide vigorous Calvinist opposition. A new church was established on Park Street in Boston in 1809 to provide enough fire and brimstone to counteract Unitarian hopefulness in the dignity and destiny of man.

The organization in 1825 by the Reverend William Ellery Channing of the American Unitarian Association transformed into a separate denomination what had previously been merely the liberal left wing of Congregationalism. Division ensued in most towns in Massachusetts. The First and Second Churches in Boston, now combined, are today Unitarian, while the Third (Old South) Church remained Congregational. In some Massachusetts towns the traditional Puritan meetinghouse remained in the hands of the orthodox, while the Unitarians built themselves a new church elsewhere; in others the situation was reversed. The orthodox, bent on holding the old faith against all comers, sometimes behaved with singleminded bigotry. Consequently they held themselves together against "foreigners," Catholics, or anyone who disagreed with them. That intolerance, which reached its climax with the Know-Nothing party in the 1850s, made the lot of recent arrivals in Massachusetts less than happy.

Even Unitarianism in the mold of Channing

proved too confining for Ralph Waldo Emerson, who, after three years as pastor of the Second Church in Boston, resigned in 1832 and moved from the Unitarian ministry into the literary expression of the philosophy of transcendentalism. Although transcendentalism throve best in Concord, or in other pure country air, the climate of Unitarian Boston and Harvard proved propitious for literary and historical endeavors, as well as for liberal highmindedness in social causes. Abolitionist sentiment ran high; there were few highminded efforts or impractical causes that did not have an airing in nineteenth-century Massachusetts. Then as now, many energetic doers of good seemed more eager to attack the social inequities of the distant South than those around the corner.

Nineteenth-century Massachusetts saw the creation not only of American Unitarianism but also of Christian Science. Mary Morse Baker Eddy (1821–1910), born in Bow, New Hampshire, published in 1875 the first edition of *Science and Health* while living in Lynn. The following year the Christian Scientists' Association was organized, and on August 23, 1879, the Church of Christ, Scientist was chartered. In the early 1880s Mrs. Eddy moved to Boston, conducting the Massachusetts Metaphysical College for the training of practitioners in her residence at 569 and 571 Columbus Avenue in the South End. She moved to 385 Commonwealth Avenue in 1887; within a few years construction was begun on Falmouth Street, off Huntington Avenue, of the Mother Church, dedicated on January 5, 1895. It seated just under a thousand persons. As it proved inadequate in size within a decade, a great domed Extension, seating 5,012 people, was begun in 1904; this, the largest church in Boston, was dedicated on June 10, 1906. Churches of Christ, Scientist, exist in all parts of the world, but the Mother Church in Boston is the equivalent of Rome or Mecca to devout believers. The birth and extension of that worldwide organization within the past century gives testimony to the continued strength of religious belief in Massachusetts, even though the latter-day forms would have startled the Puritan founders of the Massachusetts Bay.

The crowding that occurred from the astronomical increases in the population changed the face of much of Massachusetts. Each decennial census from 1810 to 1900 showed an increase of not less than 23.6 percent in the previous decade, while on five occasions the increase was more than 40 percent. The development of factories, not only in new cities like Lowell and Lawrence, but also in older towns that had once been agricultural, greatly altered the character of life. True, the factories offered work, however hard and uncongenial, to some of the newcomers. In Boston, where many of the incoming Irish families stayed, for want of knowing where else to go, hard labor for the men in the construction of buildings and railroads, or on the wharves, and domestic service for the women, offered the only means to sustain life. Rural starvation in Ireland had been exchanged for urban misery in Massachusetts. Employment in municipal service was a step upward; it eventually provided an entry into local politics, which proved to be the field in which the Irish most congenially and effectively established themselves. The culmination of this process was reached in 1960 when John Fitzgerald Kennedy, grandson of a man born in East Boston in 1858 whose parents had fled the potato famine a decade earlier, was elected president of the United States.

The evolutionary process by which John F. Kennedy arrived in the White House was the same as that by which older settlers of English origin, such as the Adamses, Cabots, Lodges, and Saltonstalls, had reached their place in American life. As the title of President Kennedy's book *A Nation of Immigrants* suggests, every mortal soul in the United States except the Indians, who may themselves have emigrated from Asia in the distant past, hails ultimately from somewhere else. Successive waves of immigrants from the British Isles and from the continents of Europe, Asia, and (involuntarily) Africa have been rolling into what is now the United States, and into Massachusetts, for close to four centuries. The British, having established the colonies whose revolt achieved American independence, provided our national language and for a couple of centuries ruled the roost. But men and women from elsewhere, as they get their feet under them, come to the fore. The means by which they do so is always the same: the acquisition of more than average education and property, preferably a combination of both. It is a matter of time, industry, and determination.

With the election of Hugh O'Brien in 1885, Boston had its first Irish mayor; the first Irish governor of Massachusetts, David Ignatius Walsh, was elected in 1914. Thirty-three years later, the first governor of Italian descent, Foster Furcolo, was elected. In 1965 his successor, the Republican John A. Volpe, defeated a Democratic candidate, Francis X. Bellotti; that was the first occasion on which both parties had put forward men of Italian descent. At times even old New Englanders like Leverett Saltonstall, Endicott Peabody, and Francis W. Sargent reached the governor's office; the present incumbent, Michael Dukakis, is the son of parents from Greece.

The Catholic bishops and archbishops of Boston have been a long-lived lot, for in the 153 years since Bishop Cheverus returned to France there have only been six. The first five were of English or Irish descent; the present incumbent, Humberto Cardinal Medeiros, is of Portuguese origin, of a family from Fall River.

Of the eight residents of Massachusetts who have sat upon the Supreme Court since 1789, two have been Jews: Louis D. Brandeis, in whose honor Brandeis University was named, associate justice 1916–1939, the son of parents from Prague, who first saw Massachusetts in 1875 when he came from his birthplace in Louisville, Kentucky, to enter the Harvard Law School; and Felix Frankfurter (1882–1965), born in Vienna, brought to the United States in 1894, who came to the Harvard Law School in the class of 1906, and was appointed to the court in 1939.

During the 1964 presidential election when President Johnson and Senator Edward M. Kennedy carried Massachusetts by a plurality of more than 1,000,000 votes, the spectacular Republican success of the day was the re-election of Edward W. Brooke as attorney general by a plurality of nearly 800,000. In view of that singularly personal tribute to a candidate of the Republican party on a day when his party's national ticket was being repudiated with extraordinary thoroughness, it is a small wonder that Brooke was sent to the United States Senate a couple of years later. Senator Brooke's career has been based upon ability rather than upon the color of his skin. So have those of two other notable black Bostonians: the Right Reverend John Melville Burgess, Episcopal bishop of Massachusetts, who retired at the end of 1975; and the late Julian

D. Steele, first commissioner of the Massachusetts Department of Community Affairs, who was, incidentally, a Harvard classmate (1929) of Robert C. Weaver, sometime Secretary of Housing and Urban Development, the first black member of a President's Cabinet.

Ralph Waldo Emerson as late as 1844 could call the United States "the country of the Future" and rhapsodize over "a heterogeneous population crowding on all ships from all corners of the globe to the great gates of North America," including Boston, "and quickly contributing their private thought to the public opinion, their toll to the treasury, and their vote to the election. It seems so easy for America to inspire and express the most expansive and humane spirit; new-born, free, healthful, strong, the land of the laborer, of the democrat, of the philanthropist, of the believer, of the saint, she should speak for the human race." This was fine rhetoric from transcendental Concord, a noble ideal, but the actuality was less happy. Even the simile that the white heat of the melting pot could refine and transmute whatever was poured into it, proved apocalyptically uncomfortable. Looking at twentieth-century Massachusetts, I am reminded rather of a mosaic in which a pattern is created by the subtle disposition of many tiny tesserae of different colors and shapes, each one of which adds to the variety and character of the whole. Delete any one of them and the effect is impaired.

More than a century ago, E. L. Godkin, editor of *The Nation,* who came to the United States from England in 1856, observed that "Boston is the one place in America where wealth and knowledge of how to use it are apt to coincide." There have been bleak moments, but when one looks at its institutions, Godkin's remark still has the ring of truth. The British philosopher Alfred North Whitehead, addressing the American Academy of Arts and Sciences in 1942, stated, "In so far as the world of learning today possesses a capital city, Boston with its neighboring institutions approximates to the position that Paris occupied in the Middle Ages." This is the most important thing to remember about Massachusetts.

WALTER MUIR WHITEHILL

A Pictorial History
NORMAN KOTKER

Massachusetts is said to mean "at the big hill," and indeed Great Blue Hill south of Boston is a prominent feature of its landscape. But if any natural feature is of prime importance to the state, it is the ocean that washes its miles of shoreline. That shoreline is a varied one, rich with peninsulas, islands, necks, salt marshes, coves, beaches, and the harbors which brought so much wealth to Massachusetts. The Bay State was born along the relatively low-lying shores of its great bays, low-lying except for a few bluffs or drumlins bordering the shore or rising from the marshes. These drumlins—low hills formed by the action of the great glacier that once passed over Massachusetts—are particularly common around Boston; Bunker Hill and Beacon Hill—with one side sloping and the other side, which faced the oncoming ice, steep —are two of the most notable. Along with the shoreline itself, the numerous small rivers that drain the region and the ponds left by the glacier are the most marked features of the eastern Massachusetts landscape. The photograph of glistening surf above (1) was taken on Cape Cod. The rocky beach and high oceanfront bluff to its right (2) are on Martha's Vineyard. The sand dune beach grass opposite (3) was also photographed on the Cape. At right (4) is a typical drumlin, rising in primeval isolation out of a marsh in the town of Essex on the North Shore.

The Land and the Sea

2

The Land and the Sea

The low, pond studded lands of eastern Massachusetts give way in the central part of the state to a well-wooded, hilly plateau, beginning about twenty-five miles west of Boston and reaching to the broad Connecticut River, New England's largest, which cuts across the state from north to south. A few miles west of the Connecticut, the mountains begin, varying in height and in name—the Berkshire Hills, the Hoosac Range, the Taconics, all of them known popularly as the Berkshires. In the northwest corner of the state they rise to just short of 3500 feet. It is a well-watered land, though a rocky one, and in many regions not an easy one to farm. The bare winter woods shown opposite (1) are at the eastern edge of the central Massachusetts plateau, in the town of Marlborough. At right is the marshy flood plain of the Sudbury River (2) which forms part of a river system that feeds the Merrimack and drains much of northeastern Massachusetts. The picturesque and narrow Housatonic (3) drains the opposite corner of the state, flowing through southwestern Massachusetts in the shadow of towering mountain ranges, among them Monument Mountain (4) just north of Great Barrington.

OVERLEAF: The bottom lands of the Deerfield River valley, like those along the Connecticut River into which the Deerfield flows, contain some of the state's most fertile farms.

1

Comparerden als Voor. Willem Bradfort ... oud 23. Jaers woon̄t tot Leyden, alwaer ... ende te hebben tot eewer, ... Dorothea Maijs oud 16. Jaers, ... woon̄t ... geassisteert met heŗ ... maijr. ...

Ende gaven aen dat se aen malkanderen verlooft ende niet trouwe verbonden waren, versoeken̄de haere drye Sondaeghse uytroepingen, omme naer de selve de voorsz trouwe te solenniseren, ende in alles te voltrekken, soo verre daer anders gheene wettighe verhinderinghe voor en valle. Ende naer dien sy bede waerheyd verklaerden dat se vrye persoonen waren, ende malkanderen in bloede ...

Waer door een Christelijk huwelijk mochte verhindert worden, niet en bestonden, zijn huy hare ghebode verwillight.

william Bradford   Dorothy May

2

Massachusetts's founders, the Pilgrims, embarked in 1620 on the *Mayflower* to set sail for America. They were fleeing, as one of them, William Bradford, wrote, "grim and grisly poverty" and a "strange and uncouth language." Bradford's own marriage certificate (1) was written in that "uncouth language," Dutch. In America the Pilgrims' landfall was at Provincetown. There in the raw November chill, Bradford, Edward Winslow (2), and all the other Pilgrim men signed a compact (3) aboard the *Mayflower,* establishing self-government. A few weeks later they sailed across Massachusetts Bay to Plymouth Harbor, shown opposite in a map (4) made by the French explorer Samuel de Champlain and published in 1613. At Plymouth Harbor, they came ashore, reportedly on Plymouth Rock (5), and on the slopes overlooking the harbor built their simple houses, some of which resembled a cottage in a sketch (6) found on one page of a seventeenth-century Bible. Supposedly the sketch and the accompanying notes were made by one of the Pilgrims.

3

In ye name of god Amen. We whose names are underwriten, the loyall subjects of our dread soueraigne Lord king James by ye grace of god, of great Britaine, franc, & Ireland king, defender of ye faith, &c.

Haueing undertaken, for ye glorie of god, and aduancemente of ye christian faith, and honour of our king & countrie, a voyage to plant ye first colonie in ye Northerne parts of Virginia. Doe by these presents solemnly & mutualy in ye presence of god, and one of another, couenant, & combine our selues togeather into a ciuill body politick, for ye better ordering, & preseruation & furtherance of ye ends aforesaid; and by vertue hearof to enacte, constitute, and frame shuch just & equall Lawes, ordinances, Acts, constitutions, & offices, from time to time, as shall be thought most meete & conuenient for ye generall good of ye Colonie: unto which we promise all due submission and obedience. In witnes wherof we haue hereunder subscribed our names at Cap-Codd ye 11 of Nouember, in ye year of ye raigne of our soueraigne Lord king James of England, franc, & Ireland ye eighteen, and of Scotland ye fiftie fourth. An: Dom .1620.|

William Bradford   Myles Standish

Willm Brewster   John Alden

George Soule Sen   ...

Francis Eaton   Edw Winslow

Isaac Allerton   Samuell Fuller

Peregrine White

John Cook   Resolued White

4

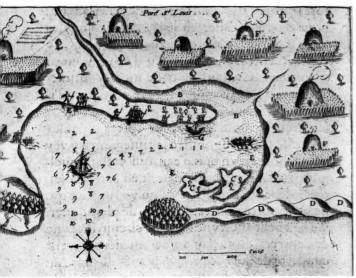

5

6

27

1

2

3

4

At Plymouth the Pilgrims began, as William Bradford wrote, to "fit up their houses and dwellings against winter." A reconstruction of the Pilgrims' village (1), near the original site, shows what the settlement soon looked like, with some houses roofed with thatch and others with wooden shingles. Each house was centered around an ample fireplace (2) and was sparsely furnished with hand-made tables and beds, and chairs such as the one shown here (3). Cooking was done in iron kettles and pans; the one at right (4) belonged to the Pilgrims' military leader, Myles Standish. The cradle below it (5) was used by Peregrine White, who was born on board the *Mayflower* while the Pilgrims were crossing the Atlantic. When he was only a few months old, his father died in the great epidemic that carried off fifty of the hundred or so Pilgrims soon after their landing at Plymouth. Peregrine's mother shortly remarried Edward Winslow, whose portrait appears on page 26.

5

Plymouth Plantation

Much of our knowledge of Plymouth comes from Governor William Bradford's history, *Of Plymouth Plantation* (1). During the hardship and hunger of the Pilgrims' first years, "God fed them out of the sea," Bradford wrote. By 1623 "God gave them plenty"—a "great store of wild turkeys" and valuable beaver and otter skins that could be sold profitably in England. Details from a Dutch map dating from around 1650 show a New England beaver (2), as well as all the territory belonging to Plymouth Colony (3). Another detail shows a turkey and rabbits (4), which along with deer provided a plentiful supply of meat. As the years went by and the colony became more secure, substantial structures were erected. A fine new meetinghouse (5) was built at Plymouth in 1683, and in 1653 John Alden constructed a solid, shingled, two-story house in Duxbury (6). Plymouth's early settlers, Bradford among them, are buried on a hill overlooking the town of Plymouth and Plymouth Harbor (7).

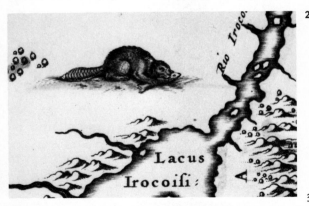

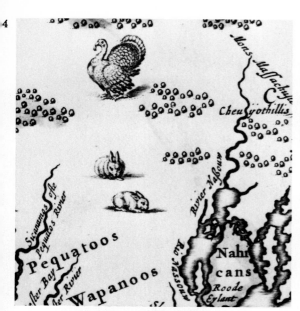

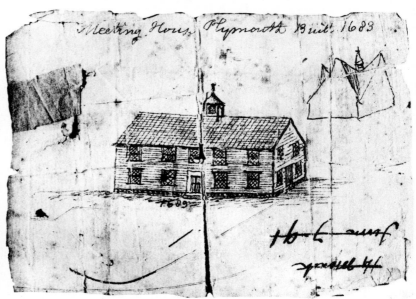

6

7

North of Plymouth

Some of the towns shown along the wooded shores of Massachusetts Bay in a 1616 English map (1) may be Indian settlements, despite their English names. The map was made by the English explorer John Smith, who named the region New England; its largest river, the Charles, he named after his patron, Prince Charles of England. Smith advised the English to colonize the region; soon fishermen, farmers, and fur traders began settling the country north of Plymouth, some of them Pilgrims who found life at Plymouth too constraining. Before Boston was founded in 1630 there were English outposts at Weymouth, Quincy, Charlestown, and Salem, and along the shores of Cape Ann. At first, the colonists constructed Indian-style wigwams, on a frame of saplings (2), which was then covered with straw (3). The exterior was covered with bark (4). Eventually wooden dwellings were built; the ones shown here (5) are reconstructions at Pioneer Village in Salem.

4

5

1

2

3

NEVV
ENGLANDS
PROSPECT.

A true, lively, and experimen-
tall defcription of that part of *America*,
commonly called NEVV ENGLAND:
difcovering the ftate of that Coun-
trie, both as it ftands to our new-come
Englifh Planters; and to thé old
Native Inhabitants.

Laying downe that which may both enrich the
knowledge of the mind-travelling Reader,
or benefit the future Voyager.

By WILLIAM WOOD.

Printed at *London* by *Tho. Cotes,* for *Iohn Bellamie,* and are to be fold
at his fhop, at the three Golden Lyons in *Corne-hill,* neere the
Royall Exchange. 1634.

Bearing the charter of the Massachusetts Bay Company (1), John Winthrop (2) set sail from England in the spring of 1630 at the head of a flotilla of ships carrying hundreds of Puritans fleeing from religious persecution. Their arrival to establish a new colony enormously swelled the English settlements in Massachusets. Soon the region of Boston was well populated and settlement extended westward, with Springfield, founded in 1635 by Thomas Pynchon (3). Before Winthrop's arrival, John Endecott (4) of Salem had served as governor of the region under the authority of the Massachusetts Bay Company. Winthrop's arrival moved the center of the colony's government from Salem to the new town of Boston. Endecott's chair (5) and sword (6) still survive. In the years after the Great Migration of 1630, a number of tracts were written to entice even more settlers to Massachusetts. *New Englands Prospect* (7), printed in London, dates from 1634.

The Puritans' Religion

"The Church hath no place left to fly into but the wilderness," John Winthrop had written in 1629 before the Great Migration. As soon as the Puritans arrived in their wilderness refuge, they set about building churches and looking to the care of their souls. The only surviving seventeenth-century church in New England is Hingham's Old Ship Church (1, 2), built in 1681. By 1638, there was a printing press in Cambridge, which published religious books, including a famous book of Psalms (3) translated by a committee headed by the Dorchester minister Richard Mather (4). For copies of the entire Bible, Puritans had to import books like the one shown here (5) from England. The silver Communion cup opposite (6) was donated to the First Church in Boston by John Winthrop. Reminders of the brevity of human life were present everywhere. The mortality rate was high and people often died young. The gravestone opposite (7) belongs to a Dorchester printer, John Foster, the man who made the portrait of Mather.

THE
VVHOLE
BOOKE OF PSALMES
Faithfully
TRANSLATED *into* ENGLISH
Metre.

Whereunto is prefixed a discourse de-
claring not only the lawfullnes, but also
the necessity of the heavenly Ordinance
of singing Scripture Psalmes in
the Churches of
God.

Coll. III.

*Let the word of God dwell plenteously in
you, in all wisdome, teaching and exhort-
ing one another in Psalmes, Himnes, and
spirituall Songs, singing to the Lord with
grace in your hearts.*

Iames v.

*If any be afflicted, let him pray, and if
any be merry let him sing psalmes.*

Imprinted
1640

Mr. Richard Mather.

THE
BIBLE,
THAT IS,
THE HOLY SCRIPTVRES
conteined in the Old and New
TESTAMENT.

7

6

Many of the houses built by the Puritans still survive in Massachusetts. The oldest is the Fairbanks House in Dedham (1), probably constructed in 1636. Others are Topsfield's Parson Capen House (2), built in 1683; the House of the Seven Gables in Salem (3), dating from around 1668 and probably the most widely known house in the Commonwealth; and the Browne House in Watertown, built around 1698 (4). A cradle, a high-backed chair, and a delicately carved chest, all dating from the seventeenth century, furnish a room reproducing a typical interior, the kitchen of the Parson Capen House (5). The Puritans' furniture was sturdy and often richly carved. The gateleg table (6) and elaborately decorated chair (7) come from Essex County. The paneled pine chest (8) was probably made in Massachusetts too.

1
2
3

At Home

6

7

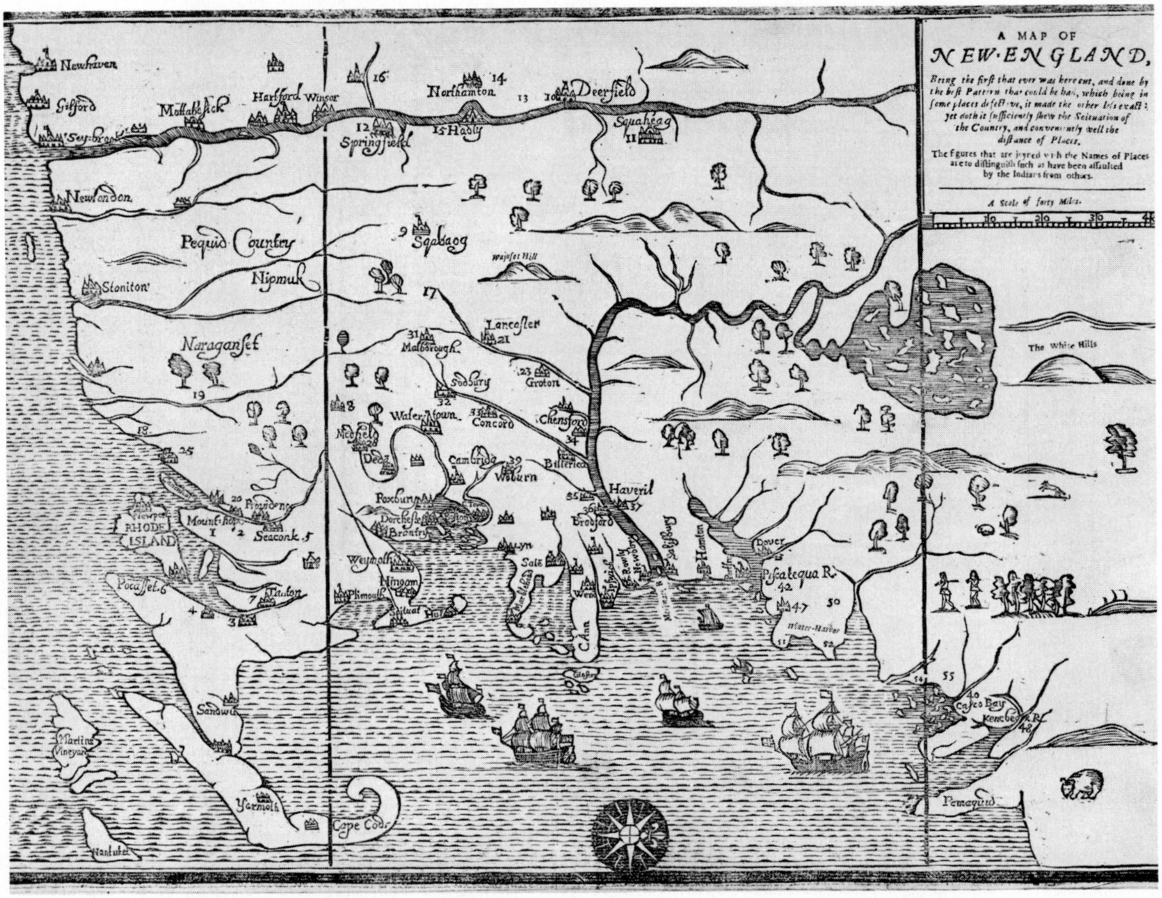

1

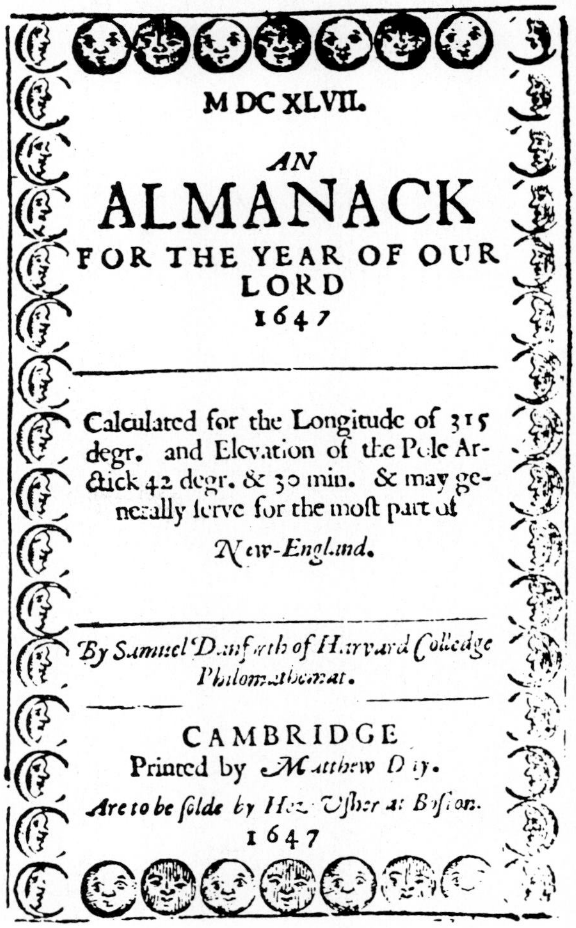

MDCXLVII.

AN
ALMANACK
FOR THE YEAR OF OUR LORD
1647

Calculated for the Longitude of 315 degr. and Elevation of the Pole Arctick 42 degr. & 30 min. & may generally serve for the most part of *New-England*.

By Samuel Danforth of Harvard Colledge Philomathemat.

CAMBRIDGE
Printed by *Matthew Day*.
Are to be solde by Hez: Usher at Boston.
1647

2

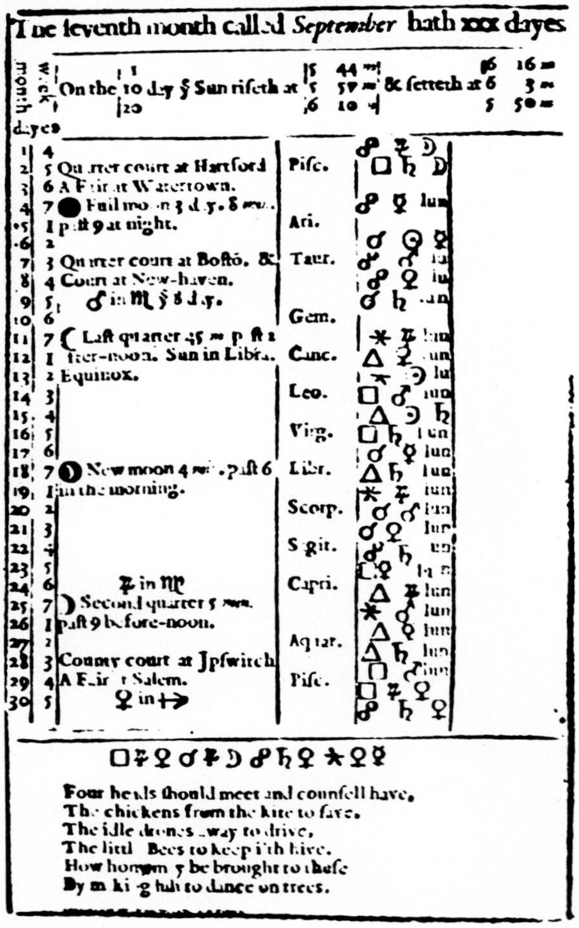

The seventh month called *September* hath xxx dayes.

On the 1 day the Sun riseth at 5 44 m. & setteth at 6 16 m.
On the 10 day the Sun riseth at 5 57 m. & setteth at 6 3 m.
On the 20 day the Sun riseth at 6 10 m. & setteth at 5 50 m.

month dayes	week dayes		
1	4		
2	5	Quarter court at Hartford	Pisc.
3	6	A Fair at Watertown.	
4	7	Full moon 3 day. 8 min.	
5	1	past 9 at night.	Ari.
6	2		
7	3	Quarter court at Bostō. &	Taur.
8	4	Court at New-haven.	
9	5	♂ in ♏ the 8 day.	
10	6		Gem.
11	7	Last quarter 45 m. past 2	
12	1	after-noon. Sun in Libra.	Canc.
13	2	Equinox.	
14	3		Leo.
15	4		
16	5		Virg.
17	6		
18	7	New moon 4 min. past 6	Libr.
19	1	in the morning.	
20	2		Scorp.
21	3		
22	4		Sagit.
23	5		
24	6	♃ in ♍	Capri.
25	7	Second quarter 5 min.	
26	1	past 9 before-noon.	
27	2		Aquar.
28	3	County court at Jpswitch	
29	4	A Fair at Salem.	Pisc.
30	5	♀ in ♐	

Four heads should meet and counsell have,
The chickens from the kite to save,
The idle drones away to drive,
The littl Bees to keep i'th hive.
How hony may be brought to these
By making him to dance on trees.

3

The Settlement of New England

Towne Marks agreed by yᵉ General Co'te for Horses, cx, x x x x x, ordered
to be set upon one of yᵉ nere q'r'ᵗ x x.

Charlestowne,	Braintree,	Hingham,
Cambridge,	Roxberry,	Hampton,
Concord,	Rowley,	Haverell,
Salem,	Redding,	Gloster,
Salsberry,	Wat'towne,	Meadford,
Sudberry,	Meymoth.	Manchest'
Strawberrybanke,	Woburne,	Andiver,
Dorchester,	Northam,	Bull,
dedham,	Linn,	Springfeild,
Do.er,	Ipswich,	x ashaway,
Boston,	Nuberry,	Exiter.

The flourishing new colony of Massachusetts Bay
soon sent out offshoots. A map of New England
(1) shows the numerous towns that had sprung
up by around 1670. A 1647 almanac (2) men-
tions court proceedings scheduled for Hartford,
New Haven, Boston, and Ipswich, and fairs to be
held at Watertown and Salem (3). Livestock had
been brought over in the Great Migration. Individual towns established easily recognizable brands
for horses and cattle, to make identification of
strays or stolen livestock easier. On the list above
(4), Strawberrybanke is the town later known as
Portsmouth in New Hampshire. Mills run by the
tides were built to grind the corn into flour; the
tidal mill shown here (5) was built at Hingham
in 1643. Forests were cut down with axes such as
these (6) and new lands laboriously brought under
cultivation. Town pounds were constructed to enclose stray cattle and sheep; the one at right (7)
was built in Westwood in 1700.

4

5

6

Workmen had at hand many of the raw materials needed for self-sufficiency. Charcoal was easily obtainable for blacksmiths and ironworkers; the seventeenth-century charcoal kiln above (1) is in the Pelham woods. The first ironworks in Massachusetts (2), at Saugus, exploited bog iron found in marshes along the Saugus River. By 1700, there were similar ironworks at Braintree, Concord, and Rowley, and in the Taunton region. Massachusetts's first printing press (3) had to use imported paper, though; no local paper mill opened until 1728. Saugus iron was used for what is probably the first iron pot cast in America (4), but in 1652, silver had to be brought in to mint shillings labeled with the name *Masathusets* (5). No doubt the Boston artist Thomas Smith had to import the tools of his trade, too; his self-portrait (6) is probably the first done in the English colonies.

43

5

6

Housework and frequent child-bearing made life difficult for Puritan women, unless they were prosperous like Rebecca Rawson of Boston (1) or young Margaret Gibbs (2), both of whom could afford to have a portrait painted in the year 1670. Below them are two other Puritans, Anne Pollard (3), and Mrs. Freake (4) with her daughter. Generally, women's work centered around the hearth (5), where meals were prepared. Much time was spent at the spinning wheel (6) or doing fine needlework, like the 1673 sampler at right (7). Rebecca Rawson's wealth did not save her from unhappiness. She married a dashing Englishman in 1679 and went back to England with him, only to learn that he was a bigamist. She spent thirteen poverty-stricken years in England and drowned on the way back to America. Anne Pollard, more happily, lived to be 105 in a house on Beacon Hill in Boston. As a child in 1630, she had been the first ashore when the Puritans landed in Boston.

Institutions

In their new land, the Puritans quickly established institutions similar to those they had left behind. Great attention was paid to military affairs. Governor John Leverett posed for his portrait in uniform (1), and a military company, now known as The Ancient and Honorable Artillery Company, was established and given a charter (2). The company's drill, beneath Beacon Hill, is shown in one corner of a portrait of its captain, John Savage (3). Below is the first flag the company used (4). A more important institution was Harvard College (5), which was founded in 1636. Charles Chauncy (6) was the college's second president. Increase Mather (7), an early graduate, became president of Harvard too, while continuing to serve that other great Massachusetts institution, the church.

3

1

2

48

3

Maſſachuſee PSALTER:

A S U H.

Uk-kuttoohomaongaſh

D A V I D

Weche

WUNNAUNCHEMOOKAONK

Ne anſukhogup JOHN,

Ut *Indiane* kah *Englifhe*
Nepatuhquonkaſh.

Ne woh ſogkompagunukhettit
Kakoketahteaekuppannegk, aketamunnat,
kah wohwohtamunat Wunnetuppantam-
we Wuſſukwhongaſh.

John ᴠ. 39.
Naſinneakontamook W'uſſukwhonkanaſh, newut-
che ut yeuſh kuttunnantamumwoo kuttahtom-
woo micheme pomantammooonk ; kah niſh-
naſhog wauwaonukqueniſh.

BOSTON, N. E.
Upprinthomunneau *B. Green*, kah *J. Printer*
wutche quhtiantamwe CHAPANUKKEG
wutche onchekehtouunnat wunnaunchem-
mookaonk ut *New-England*.&c. 1.7 0 9

English encroachment on the Indians' independence led to frequent conflicts; one shown here (1) is a detail from a 1675 map of New England. The English fervently tried to convert the Indians to Christianity. By 1651 John Eliot (2) had established a new town for "Praying Indians" at Natick, the first of fourteen such towns. Eliot translated the Bible and several religious books into the Indian language and compiled an Indian grammar. In 1709, a new Indian translation of the Psalms appeared (3, 4) in a dialect spoken by the Indians of Martha's Vineyard. In 1675, a fierce war broke out between the English and the Indians, led by a Wampanoag chief, Metacomet, who had been given the English name Philip. His mark appears at right (5). The English, under their commander, Josiah Winslow (6), were soon victorious. Nevertheless, Indian attacks still occurred occasionally; the Indian House in Deerfield (7) survived one in 1704.

4

5

THE

Massachuset PSALTER
.OR.

PSALMS of DAVID

With the ~~pure Byl~~

GOSPEL

According to JOHN,

In Columns of *Indian* and *English*.

BEING ~~Mayhew~~

An Introduction for Training up the Aboriginal Natives, in Reading and Understanding the ~~Understanding the~~ HOLY SCRIPTURES.

John ℣. 39.
Search the Scriptures, for in them ye think ye have eternal Life, and they are they which testifie of Me.

BOSTON, N. E.
Printed by *B. Green,* and *J. Printer,* for the Honourable COMPANY for the Propagation of the Gospel in *New-England, &c.*
1 7 0 9.

6

7

Witchcraft in Salem

In 1692, a number of girls and women in an outlying district of Salem began acting oddly. One ran across a room, crying, "Whish, whish," and attempted to fly; another, in church, called out, "Enough of that!" when the minister began to preach his sermon. The people of Salem imagined that witches were making them behave this way, and hundreds were arrested in an attempt to find out who the witches were. Belief in witchcraft was common. The Boston clergyman Cotton Mather, shown in a 1693 woodcut with a magic circle around him to protect him from the Devil (1), was considered an expert on the subject. "Tell mankind," he wrote, "that there are devils and witches." Mather was asked by the judges to write the official account of the Salem witchcraft trials. Two of those judges were Samuel Sewall of Boston (2) and William Stoughton (3), whose portrait shows him beside a building he donated to Harvard. "I have . . . set myself to countermine the whole plot of the Devil against New England," Mather wrote in his account of the trials. As a result of those trials, nineteen people were executed. At right (4) is the affidavit of one of the arrested, Mary Easty, who pleads with the judges not to "be guilty of innocent blood" in executing her. Below (5) is the house of seventy-one-year-old Rebecca Nurse, one of those hanged as a witch.

The Colony Grows

Massachusetts Bay Colony's shoreline, seen in a detail of a 1675 map (1), more than doubled in length after Plymouth Colony was annexed in 1691. The border between the two colonies had been at Marshfield, along the North River (2). Simon Bradstreet (3), husband of the poet Anne Bradstreet, was governor of Massachusetts at the time of the annexation; Bradstreet played an important role in Massachusetts affairs, helping establish a confederacy with the other New England colonies in 1643—the first American union. When New England, New York, and New Jersey were placed under the rule of a royal governor, Sir Edmund Andros, Bradstreet resisted the new governor's encroachments on local independence; and he was deeply involved when Bostonians rebelled against Andros. An address urging Andros's surrender was signed by Bradstreet and other Puritan notables (4). In western Massachusetts, the population increased despite Indian attacks. At Deerfield, the Frary House (5) dates from 1704.

At the *Town-House* in *Boston*, *April* 18. 1689.

SIR,

OUR Selves and many others the Inhabitants of this Town, and the Places adjacent, being surprized with the Peoples sudden taking of Arms; in the first motion whereof we were wholly ignorant, being driven by the present Accident, are necessitated to acquaint your Excellency, that for the quieting and securing of the People inhabiting in this Country from the imminent Dangers they many ways lie open and exposed to, and tendring your own Safety, We judge it necessary you forthwith surrender and deliver up the Government and Fortification to be preserved and disposed according to Order and Direction from the Crown of England, which suddenly is expected may arrive; promising all security from violence to your Self or any of your Gentleman or Souldiers in Person and Estate: Otherwise we are assured they will endeavour the taking of the Fortification by Storm, if any Opposition be made.

To Sir Edmond Andross Kt.

Waite Winthrop.   Elisha Cook.
Simon Bradstreet.   Isaac Addington.
William Stoughton.   John Nelson.
Samuel Shrimpton.   Adam Winthrop.
Bartholomew Gidney.   Peter Sergeant.
William Brown.   John Foster.
Thomas Danforth.   David Waterhouse.
John Richards.

FINIS.

4

5

The Metropolis

"Within a few years after the first settlement," Cotton Mather wrote in 1698, Boston "grew to be the metropolis of the whole English America." The town's growth was a result of its flourishing sea trade. To accommodate this trade, dozens of wharves lined the waterfront early in the eighteenth century, the greatest of them Long Wharf, which can be seen in the center of William Burgis's engraving of Boston (1). Purchasers of Burgis's engraving could keep their picture up to date as the Boston skyline changed; when new churches were built, Burgis provided engravings of their steeples (2) to be pasted on. A map of the Boston peninsula (3) made around the same time shows houses thickly clustered in the north end of town. At this time, there were some fifteen thousand inhabitants in Boston dwelling in about three thousand houses. All of the tidal mud flats surrounding the peninsula, shown by stippling on the map, were later filled in to provide more land for building on as the population grew.

2

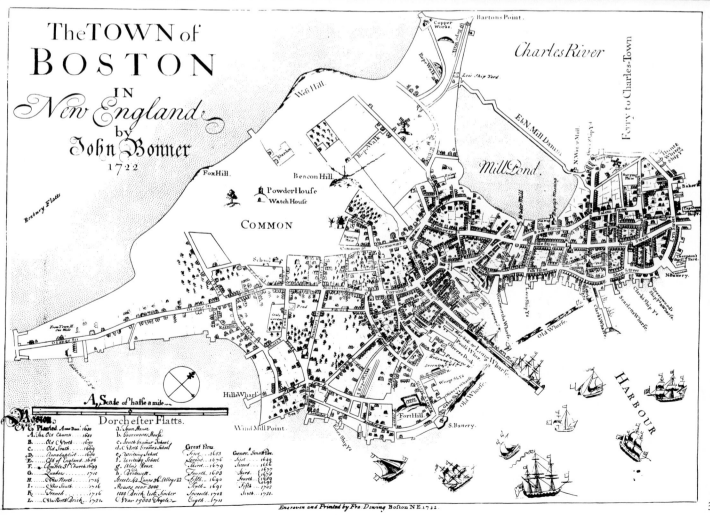

3

1

2

3

4

By the middle of the eighteenth century, Boston was an imposing town. Increasingly, buildings were made of brick rather than wood, which was vulnerable to fire. By 1722 about one-third of the houses were of brick, and fine brick public buildings could be seen throughout the town. Faneuil Hall (1) was constructed twenty years later, in 1742, to serve as a public meeting place and market. The picture shows it the way it appeared in 1789. The handsome brick Town House (2) was built in 1711 as a government center for both the town of Boston and the province of Massachusetts Bay. It also housed courts and a merchants' exchange. Today the building is known as the Old State House. Weathervanes, useful in a maritime society like Boston's, topped many of the public buildings. An Indian (3) stood atop Province House, where the governor lived. The grasshopper above (4) still indicates the wind direction at Faneuil Hall. The Anglican Christ Church (5) is the oldest surviving church in Boston, having been built in 1723.

5

1

2

58

3

4

As early as 1631, John Winthrop had a ship built alongside the Mystic River at Medford. With its rich supply of timber, New England quickly became an important shipbuilding center. Warships were constructed for the British Navy and merchant ships built for traders. Above is the *Bethel* of Boston (1); opposite, an armed sloop (2) sails by Boston Lighthouse, which was erected in 1716 for the benefit of ships calling at the town's busy port. Among the most prosperous traders in the Boston region was Isaac Royall of Medford, who lived in a beautiful mansion which is still standing (3). Royall is shown here with his family (4), posed around a table adorned with a carpet from the Near East. Shipbuilding and the manufacture of rum were the two most important industries in Medford. An advertisement (5) from a 1767 Boston newspaper lists some of the commodities that could be traded for locally produced rum, which was then shipped abroad.

5

Goods exchanged for New England rum.

Barbados Rum,
and Sugars by the Hogfhead or Barrel,
Bohea Tea,
Cotton Wool by the Bag,
New Flour,
Indigo.
☞ Dumb FISH.

Ruffia Duck,
Pitch, Tar,
and
Cordage.
Long & fhort Pipes.
Sole Leather.
Englifh Steel.
With,

A General Affortment of Englifh Goods and Hard Ware.

Many of the above Articles will be Exchang'd for New England Rum,

By **Samuel Allyne Otis,**

At Store No. 5, South-Side of the Town-Dock.

1

2

3

SINNERS
In the Hands of an
Angry GOD.
A SERMON

Preached at *Enfield*, *July* 8th 1741.

At a Time of great Awakenings ; and attended with
remarkable Impreſſions on many of the Hearers.

By *Jonathan Edwards*, A. M.

Paſtor of the Church of CHRIST in *Northampton*.

Amos ix 2, 3. *Though they dig into Hell, thence ſhall
mine Hand take them ; though they climb up to Heaven,
thence will I bring them down. And though they hide
themſelves in the Top of Carmel, I will ſearch and take
them out thence ; and though they be hid from my Sight
in the Bottom of the Sea, thence I will command the
Serpent, and he ſhall bite them.*

The Second Edition.

ſ T O N : Printed and Sold by S. KNEELAND
̊. GREEN in Queen-Street over againſt the
1 7 4 2.

4

Isaac Royall

A
TREATISE
Concerning
Religious Affections,
In Three PARTS ;

PART I. Concerning the Nature of the *Affections*,
and their Importance in *Religion*.

PART II. Shewing what are *no certain Signs* that *religious Affections* are *gracious*, or that they are *not*.

PART III. Shewing what *are diſtinguiſhing Signs* of
truly gracious and *holy Affections*.

By *Jonathan Edwards*, A. M.

And Paſtor of the *firſt* Church in *Northampton*.

Levit. ix. ult. and x. 1, 2. *And there came a Fire out from before the
Lord,----upon the Altar ; -----which when all the People ſaw, they
ſhouted and fell on their Faces. And Nadab and Abihu ----- offered
ſtrange Fire before the Lord, which he commanded them not : And there
went out a Fire from the Lord, and devoured them, and they died before
the Lord.*
Cant. ii. 12, 13. *The Flowers appear on the Earth, the Time of the
Singing of Birds is come, and the Voice of the Turtle is heard in our
Land ; the Fig-tree putteth forth her green Figs, and the Vines with the
tender Grape, give a good Smell. Ver. 15. Take us the Foxes, the
little Foxes, which ſpoil the Vines ; for our Vines have tender Grapes.*

B O S T O N :
Printed for S. KNEELAND and T. GREEN in *Queen-
ſtreet*, over againſt the Priſon. 1 7 4 6.

Country ministers like Silas Bigelow (1) of Paxton, whose tombstone shows him preaching, maintained the old Puritan traditions, but the influence of religion decreased in the eighteenth century. The age's most significant religious figure was Jonathan Edwards (2) of Northampton, whose famous sermon "Sinners in the Hands of an Angry God" (3) vividly describes the punishments awaiting the wicked. Edwards was the author of many theological works, among them "A Treatise Concerning Religious Affections" (4). Partly as a result of his preaching, a religious revival swept New England in the 1730s and '40s. Still, secular influence continued to grow. In 1740, around the time Harvard's Holden Chapel (5) was built, there were complaints that religious sentiment was lacking at the college. Religious tolerance increased, but anti-Catholic feeling remained. A 1755 broadside (6) proclaims that no Roman Catholic could enter the army.

By His EXCELLENCY

WILLIAM SHIRLEY, Efq;

Captain-General an. Governour in Chief in and over the Province of the Maffachufetts-Bay in New-England.

To John Beard Junet

SIR,

AS you have receiv'd Beating-Orders from Me to enlift Men into His Majefty's Service for the Expedition intended,

In the Management of that Truft, I give you the following Directions ;

1. You are to enlift no Perfon under the Age of eighteen Years, nor above Forty-five Years.
2. You are to enlift none but able-bodied effective Men, free from all bodily Ails, and of perfect Limbs.
3. You are to enlift no Roman-Catholick, nor any under five Feet two Inches high without their Shoes.
4. You are to affure fuch Perfons as fhall enlift, That they fhall enter into Pay
5. That they the Day of their Enliftment receive a good Blanket
6. That their Pay will be *Twenty-fix Shillings and eight Pence*, per Month, lawful Money, during their Service
7. That they fhall be exempt from all Impreffes for Three Years next after their Difcharge.

Artisans' Work

5

6

With increasing prosperity, local cabinetmakers and silversmiths were commissioned to make fine furniture and silver to adorn the new mansions being built. A chest of drawers (1) made in Boston around 1700 is painted to imitate Oriental lacquerware; it is an early example of the Oriental style which would become increasingly popular as the century progressed. The high chest of drawers with curved legs (2) beside it was made around 1730. Curved legs also appear on an armchair (3) in a Marblehead room dating from the same period. Many fine silversmiths worked in Boston. The tray (4), loving cup (5), plate shown in detail (6), and candlesticks (7) were all made by different artisans. The flowers and face decorating the plate are similar to motifs used in embroidery during the same period.

OVERLEAF: This paneled dining room from Fiskdale, near Sturbridge, dates from around 1740.

7

63

1

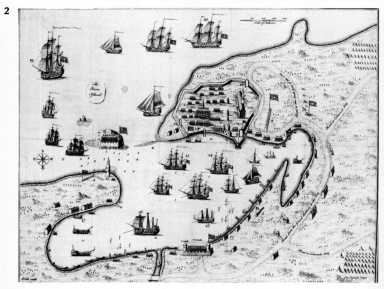

2

3

LT. GEN. SIR WM. PEPPERRELL, Bart.
The Victor of Louisbourg A.D. 1745.

4

THE PROVINCE OF MASSACHUSETS BAY IN NEW ENGLAND BY AN ORDER OF THE GREAT AND GENERAL COURT BEARING DATE FEBY 1ST 1759, CAUSED THIS MONUMENT TO BE ERECTED TO THE MEMORY OF GEORGE AUGUSTUS LORD VISCOUNT HOWE BRIGADIER GENERAL OF HIS MAJESTY'S FORCES IN AMERICA WHO WAS SLAIN JULY THE 6TH 1758, ON THE MARCH TO TICONDEROGA, IN THE 34TH YEAR OF HIS AGE: IN TESTIMONY OF THE SENSE THEY HAD OF HIS SERVICES AND MILITARY VIRTUES AND OF THE AFFECTION THEIR OFFICERS AND SOLDIERS BORE TO HIS COMMAND.

HE LIVED RESPECTED AND BELOVED: THE PUBLICK REGRETTED HIS LOSS, TO HIS FAMILY IT IS IRREPARABLE.

5

Rivalry between France and England in North America often led to war in the eighteenth century. In 1745, Governor Shirley of Massachusetts raised a force of 4,300 men to attack the French fortress of Louisburg (1) on Cape Breton Island, which dominated the North Atlantic and provided a base for raids on New England fishing boats. After a siege of forty-eight days, the fortress, surrounded by enemy ships and troops (2), surrendered. A detail from the view of the siege shows the ship (3) fitted out by Massachusetts to take part in the attack under the command of Sir William Pepperell (4). In the next decade, the war against the French continued along the western frontier. Massachusetts commissioned a memorial monument in Westminster Abbey in London for one of the victims of the struggle, the English general Lord Howe (5). Massachusetts's paper money (6) depreciated in value as a result of the expensive Louisburg expedition; England sent over hundreds of chests and barrels filled with hard money to stabilize the currency.

1

Harvard Hall.

3

"They don't admit of plays or music houses . . . ,"
an English traveler wrote in 1740, "but . . . they
don't seem to be dispirited or moped." Boston society was lively. A 1756 tapestry (1), depicting
a wedding party entering Boston's Old South
Church, shows a black slave and a coach—prerog-
atives of the rich. Two horsemen and a horse-
woman riding sidesaddle (2), and a coach and
four (3), rare in Massachusetts since few families
could afford one, appear in a view of Harvard
College. Part-singing (4), in which people sat
around a table singing Psalms or secular songs,
was one popular amusement; another was visiting
a pillory, such as the one in Charlestown (5),
where criminals were exposed to public shame.
"To encrease their sad disgrace, throw rotten eggs
into their face," bystanders were urged.

An Age of Elegance

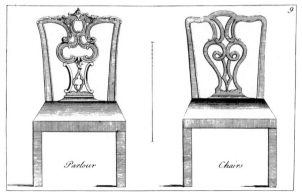

Parlour   Chairs

A few motifs, such as the pilasters and pediment seen on the facade of Major John Vassall's Cambridge mansion (1), appear again and again in the elegant designs of the mid-eighteenth century. The house, later occupied by Longfellow, was built with wealth derived from land speculation and the West Indian trade. In 1768, another rich merchant, Jeremiah Lee, built a house in Marblehead which boasted hand-painted wallpaper and a carved balustrade (2). Massachusetts furniture makers worked from English patterns. The fine Chippendale chair shown here (3) was based on a drawing in an English pattern book (4), but the American craftsman increased the chair's elegance by making curved legs. The tall secretary at left (5) is also characteristic of Massachusetts work.

Making a Living

6

7

Shipwrights in Medford, glassblowers at Germantown in Quincy, carters who bought firewood cheap in the countryside and sold it dear in Boston, hucksters who went about selling geese, housewives who sat spinning and weaving linen to sell at fourpence a yard—not all the inhabitants of colonial Massachusetts were farmers or fishermen, merchants or ministers. Buildings and artifacts surviving from the eighteenth century show a windmill at Eastham where a miller ground corn (1); the interior of another mill at Boxford (2); a shoemaker's shop (3), and a sawmill (4), also at Boxford; the handiwork of a woodcarver, a figure of Mercury (5); the bill of a ferry operator (6); a shop sign depicting a bull (7) which stood over a tanner's shop in Salem; a tavern at Swansea (8) where an innkeeper housed and fed travelers and served drinks to local inhabitants; and a jail at Nantucket (9) where a jailer locked up drunks and thieves.

8

9

1

Paul Revere is best known for his role as a patriot during the Revolution, of course, but he would be notable even if he had played no part in the struggle against the British. He was an extraordinarily versatile and gifted craftsman who made silver bowls, trays, and tea sets; brass andirons; gold thimbles; silver spurs for horsemen; false teeth; and even the Great Seal of Massachusetts. He also drew and engraved magazine illustrations and political cartoons; carved picture frames for the painter John Singleton Copley, who portrayed him (1) holding a teapot around 1768; and invented a process for rolling sheet copper, which gave birth to an important new industry. Above and at right are a teapot (2) and sugar bowl and creamer (3) made by Revere; below is a bowl made for a group of patriots, the Sons of Liberty (4). At lower right is Revere's 1768 advertisement for false teeth (5).

WHEREAS many Persons are so unfortunate as to lose their Fore-Teeth by Accident, and otherways, to their great Detriment, not only in Looks, but speaking both in Public and Private :— This is to inform all such, that they may have them re-placed with artificial Ones, that looks as well as the Natural, & answers the End of Speaking to all Intents, by *PAUL REVERE*, Goldsmith, near the Head of Dr. *Clarke's* Wharf, *Boston*.

THE
Royal *American* Magazine,

OR UNIVERSAL
Repository of *Instruction* and *Amusement*.

For JANUARY, 1774.

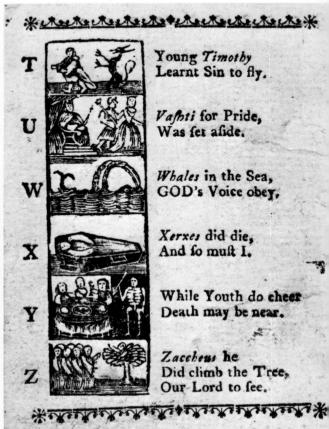

T — Young *Timothy*
Learnt Sin to fly.

U — *Vashti* for Pride,
Was set aside.

W — *Whales* in the Sea,
GOD's Voice obey.

X — *Xerxes* did die,
And so must I.

Y — While Youth do cheer
Death may be near.

Z — *Zaccheus* he
Did climb the Tree,
Our Lord to see.

5

6

In London, Harvard was called an "infant seminary," and even in America there were complaints that its library was inferior to Yale's; yet it was the center of Massachusetts's intellectual life in the eighteenth century. Paul Revere's engraving (1) shows the college around 1770 with Holden Chapel at far left. Most of the books published in Boston were religious works, although there were a number of magazines, like the *Royal American* (2), publishing new poetry. Printers and booksellers—like Andrew Barclay of Boston, whose bookbindery is shown here (3)—also sold schoolbooks such as the famous New England Primer (4), which had first appeared around 1690. Boston's most notable eighteenth-century intellectual was Benjamin Franklin (5), who worked in the city for a time on his brother's newspaper before moving to Philadelphia. Another eminent writer was the poet Phillis Wheatley (6). Born in Africa and kidnapped by slavecatchers, she was sold to the Wheatley family of Boston, who quickly recognized her talents and encouraged her writing.

1

2

Painting was esteemed "no more than any other useful trade . . . not as one of the most noble arts in the world," John Singleton Copley complained around 1760. The line between artist and craftsman was hazy, and many paintings done in Massachusetts were unsophisticated, like the Savage family portrait (1) by Edward Savage of Princeton. But there was a tradition of fine painting in Boston. Before 1750, Robert Feke portrayed Bostonians with the skill he devoted to his own self-portrait (2). Among Copley's notable portraits are those of Mr. and Mrs. Isaac Winslow (3), Governor and Mrs. Thomas Mifflin of Pennsylvania (4), Mrs. Thomas Boylston (5), and Mrs. John Winthrop (6).

Pages 80 and 81: In Copley's painting of his own family, the artist stands at back behind his father-in-law, Richard Clarke, one of the merchants whose tea was dumped into Boston Harbor.

3

4

5

6

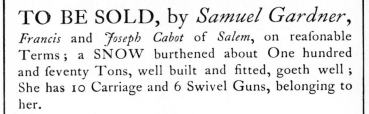

TO BE SOLD, by *Samuel Gardner*, *Francis* and *Joseph Cabot* of *Salem*, on reafonable Terms; a SNOW burthened about One hundred and feventy Tons, well built and fitted, goeth well; She has 10 Carriage and 6 Swivel Guns, belonging to her.

6

The merchant in his countinghouse (1) and the boy with his sea trunk, shipping out on an ocean voyage (2), were distinctive features of Salem as they were of Boston, for Salem, like Boston, was one of the major ports of the British Empire. An advertisement, opposite (3), offers for sale a snow or armed square-rigger. Around 1750, Salem was prosperous enough to afford an up-to-date fire engine (4) to protect buildings like those shown in a watercolor of one of its streets (5). The rest of the North Shore was well populated and derived much of its livelihood from the sea. The Samuel Gott house, above (6), was built in 1710 at Halibut Point, on the extreme tip of Cape Ann. The drawings of ships, below (7), come from a portfolio of sketches by a Marblehead seaman, Ashley Bowen, depicting ships that visited New England ports between 1739 and 1749.

7

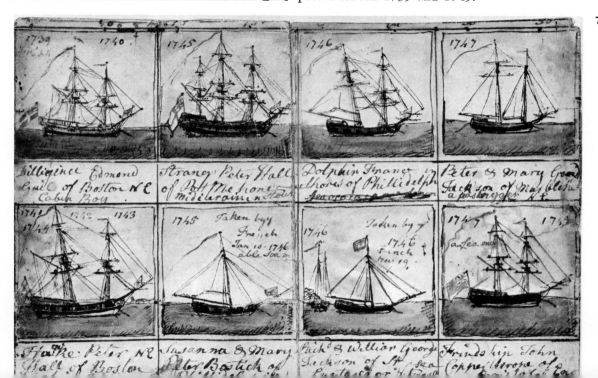

1

2

Receiv'd of William Cunningham in part of 150 Dollars which I lent him

1 SHILLING

254 P Dollars at the rate of 75 for one

£ s d
1 . 16
1 . 16
1 . 10
1 . 14
2 . 14
1 . 4
2 . 14
1 . 7
1 / 2
1 . 6
12
2 . 2
1 . 16
1 . 4
18
2 . 16 . 2
1 . 10
2 . 5
10
2 . 14
2 . 2

(Stamped Paper)

1 SHILLING

3

Glorious News.

BOSTON, Friday 11 o'Clock, 16th *May* 1766.
THIS Inftant arrived here the Brig Harrifon, belonging
to *John Hancock*, Efq; Captain *Shubael Coffin*, in 6
Weeks and 2 Days from LONDON, with important
News, as follows.

From the LONDON GAZETTE.

Weftminfter, March 18th, 1766.

THIS day his Majefty came to the Houfe of Peers, and being in his royal
robes feated on the throne with the ufual folemnity, Sir Francis Moli-
neux, Gentleman Ufher of the Black Rod, was fent with a Meffage
from his Majefty to the Houfe of Commons, commanding their atten-
dance in the Houfe of Peers. The Commons being come thither accordingly,
his Majefty was pleafed to give his royal affent to
An ACT to REPEAL an Act made in the laft Seffion of Parliament, in-
tituled, an Act for granting and applying certain Stamp-Duties and other Duties
in the Britifh Colonies and Plantations in America, towards further defraying
the expences of defending, protecting and fecuring the fame, and for amending
fuch parts of the feveral Acts of Parliament relating to the trade and revenues
of the faid Colonies and Plantations, as direct the manner of determining and
recovering the penalties and forfeitures therein mentioned.
Alfo ten public bills, and feventeen private ones.

Yefterday there was a meeting of the principal Merchants concerned in the
American trade, at the King's Arms tavern in Cornhill, to confider of an Ad-
drefs to his Majefty on the beneficial Repeal of the late Stamp-Act.
Yefterday morning about eleven o'clock a great number of North American
Merchants went in their coaches from the King's Arms tavern in Cornhill to the
Houfe of Peers, to pay their duty to his Majefty, and to exprefs their fatisfac-
tion at his figning the Bill for Repealing the American Stamp-Act, there was
upwards of fifty coaches in the proceffion.
Laft night the faid gentleman difpatched an exprefs for Falmouth, with fifteen copies of the Act for repealing the Stamp-Act, to be forwarded immediately for New York.
Orders are given for feveral merchantmen in the river to proceed to fea immediately on their refpective voyages to North America, fome of whom have
been cleared out fince the firft of November laft.
Yefterday meffengers were difpatched to Birmingham, Sheffield, Manchefter,
and all the great manufacturing towns in England, with an account of the final
decifion of an auguft affembly relating to the Stamp-Act.

After the French and Indian War, the British gar-
risoned ten thousand men in America and the
West Indies to guard against attacks by the French
and Indians. To support them and pay off an immense war debt, they tightened customs collection
in the colonies and imposed new taxes. A Stamp
Act was passed, requiring that all legal and commercial documents bear tax stamps such as the
one shown here (1). Fierce opposition developed,
and attempts were made to boycott British goods.
Still, many merchants purchased stamps for business documents (2). The hateful act was repealed
in 1766 (3). A contemporary cartoon about the
Stamp Act crisis shows Americans tilting with a
British demon (4). When the act was repealed,
a commemorative obelisk was erected in Boston;
an engraving (5) by Paul Revere shows views of
its four sides.

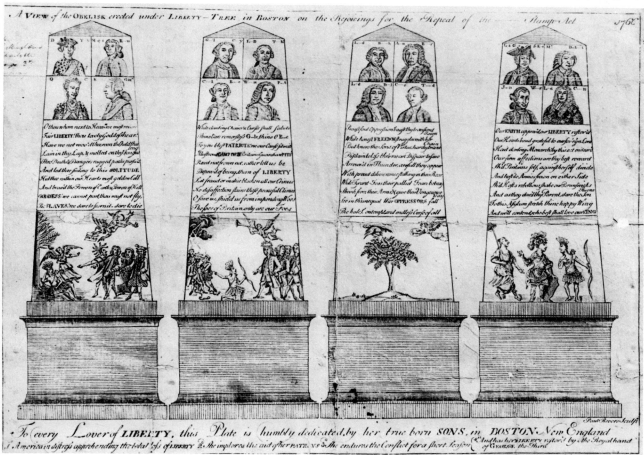

A VIEW OF PART OF THE TOWN OF BOSTON IN NEW

As American resistance to the payment of English taxes stiffened, the British sent troops to Boston to impose their will in 1768. An engraving by Paul Revere shows the troops debarking on Long Wharf. With bayonets fixed to their rifles, the British marched through the streets of Boston to the sound of drums and camped on the Common and in Faneuil Hall.

The Boston Massacre

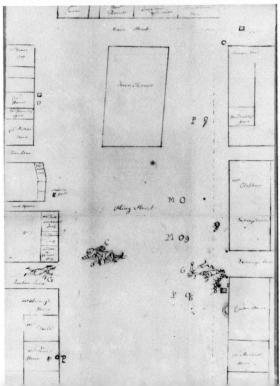

There were numerous quarrels between the young men and boys of Boston and the British troops encamped on the Common beneath John Hancock's great mansion (1). On March 5, 1770, gangs of Bostonians began roving the streets taunting British soldiers; they converged on the open space near the Town House (now the Old State House) where the main British guard post was. "There's the soldier who knocked me down," a boy in the crowd shouted, pointing at a British guard. "Kill him! Knock him down!" other people cried. The British opened fire and, as a result, three of the Bostonians were killed on the spot and several others seriously wounded. The British were brought to trial for manslaughter and defended by John Adams. A diagram (2) sketched by Paul Revere was used at the trial to show the scene of the action. Paul Revere's famous engraving (3) shows the British troops firing. A dog is in the foreground because it was said that after the shooting dogs licked blood off the streets.

BUTCHER'S HALL

CUSTOM HOUSE

Engrav'd Printed & Sold by PAUL REVERE BOSTON

3

89

1

2

When England imposed a tax on tea without American consent, Americans began a boycott. The British lowered the tax and optimistically sent ships laden with tea to Boston, New York, Philadelphia, and Charleston. Bostonians tried to force the ships' return to England; when that failed, a band of local men, disguised as Indians, boarded the ships and dumped tea into the harbor (1). The British countered by closing the port of Boston, setting up Marblehead as a rival port of entry, and removing the colony's capital to Salem. The Chinese tea chest above (2) is supposedly part of the shipment thrown overboard. A British caricature (3) shows Bostonians emptying tea into the harbor while others force unwanted tea down the throat of a tarred-and-feathered tax collector. Another British cartoon (4) shows the Bostonians in a cage, hanging from a Liberty Tree after the closing of their port. The royal governor who executed British orders was Thomas Hutchinson; an American caricature shows him being speared while a demon holds up a list of his crimes (5).

3

4

5

1

2

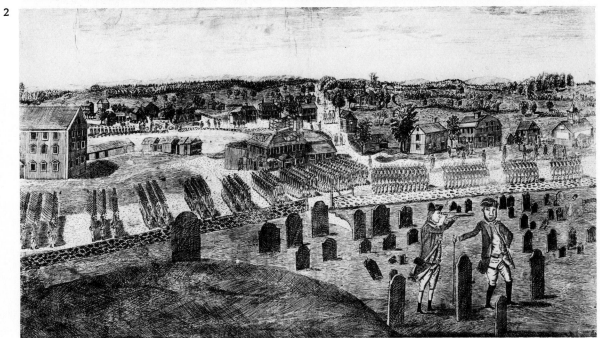

3

Lexington and Concord

4

As British control over Boston tightened, representatives of every Massachusetts town met to establish an alternate government and an army with war supplies stored at Concord. On April 18, 1775, the British marched to Concord to seize the supplies, unaware that they were being sent to Worcester for safety. To the surprise of the British, the Americans fought back. Contemporary engravings of the next day's battle show the British firing at the Lexington militia (1); British troops entering Concord while their commanders, standing in a cemetery, survey the landscape (2); and the battle at Concord's North Bridge (3). The Bedford militia, one of many Massachusetts contingents, carried the flag above (4). A broadside (5) lists the names and towns of the Americans killed and wounded that day.

5

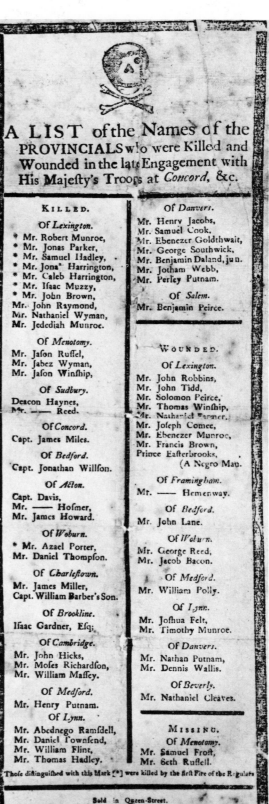

A LIST of the Names of the PROVINCIALS who were Killed and Wounded in the late Engagement with His Majesty's Troops at *Concord*, &c.

KILLED.

Of Lexington.

* Mr. Robert Munroe,
* Mr. Jonas Parker,
* Mr. Samuel Hadley,
* Mr. Jonaⁿ Harrington,
* Mr. Caleb Harrington,
* Mr. Isaac Muzzy,
* Mr. John Brown,
Mr. John Raymond,
Mr. Nathaniel Wyman,
Mr. Jedediah Munroe.

Of Menotomy.

Mr. Jason Ruffel,
Mr. Jabez Wyman,
Mr. Jason Winship,

Of Sudbury.

Deacon Haynes,
Mr. —— Reed.

Of Concord.

Capt. James Miles,

Of Bedford.

Capt. Jonathan Willson.

Of Acton.

Capt. Davis,
Mr. —— Hofmer,
Mr. James Howard.

Of Woburn.

* Mr. Azael Porter,
Mr. Daniel Thompson.

Of Charlestown.

Mr. James Miller,
Capt. William Barber's Son.

Of Brookline.

Isaac Gardner, Esq;

Of Cambridge.

Mr. John Hicks,
Mr. Moses Richardson,
Mr. William Maffey.

Of Medford.

Mr. Henry Putnam.

Of Lynn.

Mr. Abednego Ramfdell,
Mr. Daniel Townsend,
Mr. William Flint,
Mr. Thomas Hadley.

Of Danvers.

Mr. Henry Jacobs,
Mr. Samuel Cook,
Mr. Ebenezer Goldthwait,
Mr. George Southwick,
Mr. Benjamin Daland, jun.
Mr. Jotham Webb,
Mr. Perley Putnam.

Of Salem.

Mr. Benjamin Peirce.

WOUNDED.

Of Lexington.

Mr. John Robbins,
Mr. John Tidd,
Mr. Solomon Peirce,
Mr. Thomas Winship,
Mr. Nathaniel Farmer,
Mr. Joseph Comee,
Mr. Ebenezer Munroe,
Mr. Francis Brown,
Prince Easterbrooks,
    (A Negro Man.

Of Framingham.

Mr. —— Hemenway.

Of Bedford.

Mr. John Lane.

Of Woburn.

Mr. George Reed,
Mr. Jacob Bacon.

Of Medford.

Mr. William Polly.

Of Lynn.

Mr. Joshua Felt,
Mr. Timothy Munroe.

Of Danvers.

Mr. Nathan Putnam,
Mr. Dennis Wallis.

Of Beverly.

Mr. Nathaniel Cleaves.

MISSING.

Of Menotomy.

Mr. Samuel Frost,
Mr. Seth Ruffell.

Those distinguished with this Mark [*] were killed by the first Fire of the Regulars

Sold in Queen-Street.

The Siege of Boston

After Lexington and Concord, some thirteen thousand British troops, surrounded by an American army in Charlestown, Brighton, and Roxbury, were bottled up in the Boston peninsula for almost a year—except for one attempted breakout at Bunker Hill. To keep the Americans from fortifying Dorchester Heights, the present South Boston, the British burned every shelter on it (1). The Heights' strategic position, dominating Boston from across the harbor, can be seen in a 1776 sketch (2) made by a British officer on Beacon Hill and showing the town, the harbor, and the Heights. In 1775 George Washington, depicted on a medal (3) commissioned by the Continental Congress to commemorate the siege, had taken command of the American troops at Cambridge. By March 1776 his men had fortified Dorchester Heights with cannons captured at Ticonderoga. When the British saw the fortifications, they knew they were beaten; in June 1776 they boarded their fleet, visible at upper right in a contemporary view of Boston (4), and evacuated the city.

3

4

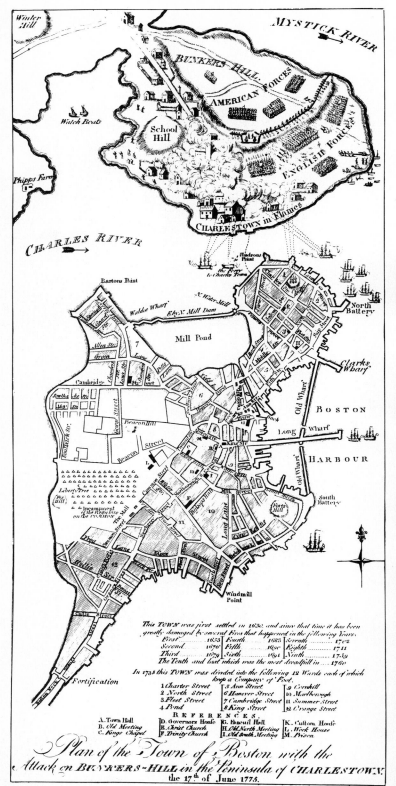

1

Plan of the Town of Boston with the Attack on BUNKERS-HILL in the Peninsula of CHARLESTOWN. the 17th of June 1775.

2

PROSPECT HILL.	BUNKER's HILL.
I. Seven Dollars a Month.	I. Three Pence a Day.
II. Fresh Provisions, and in Plenty.	II. Rotten Salt Pork.
III. Health.	III. The Scurvy.
IV. Freedom, Ease, Affluence and a good Farm.	IV. Slavery, Beggary and Want.

When the Americans occupied the Charlestown hills opposite Boston, the British sailed across to attack (1). They were met with resistance so fierce that almost half the British force of 2,300 was slaughtered. After the battle, the Americans withdrew to nearby Prospect Hill and distributed handbills to the British camp comparing the state of the two armies (2). A contemporary sketch (3) shows the battle and the burning of Charlestown. Other depictions of the battle include an engraving (4) published soon after the battle and an imaginative primitive painting (5).

OVERLEAF: John Trumbull's memorable painting shows the battle of Bunker Hill. In the foreground, the Boston patriot Joseph Warren lies mortally wounded.

5

BOSTON

CHARLES TOWN

1

2

GREAT
ENCOURAGEMENT
FOR
SEAMEN.

ALL GENTLEMEN SEAMEN and able-bodied LANDSMEN who have a Mind to distinguish themselves in the GLORIOUS CAUSE of their COUNTRY, and make their Fortunes, an Opportunity now offers on board the Ship RANGER, of Twenty Guns, (for FRANCE) now laying in PORTSMOUTH, in the State of NEW-HAMPSHIRE, commanded by JOHN PAUL JONES Esq; let them repair to the Ship's Rendezvous in PORTSMOUTH, or at the Sign of Commodore MANLEY, in SALEM, where they will be kindly entertained, and receive the greatest Encouragement.---The Ship RANGER, in the Opinion of every Person who has seen her is looked upon to be one of the best Cruizers in AMERICA.---She will be always able to Fight her Guns under a most excellent Cover ; and no Vessel yet built was ever calculated for sailing faster, and making good Weather.

Any GENTLEMEN VOLUNTEERS who have a Mind to take an agreable Voyage in this pleasant Season of the Year, may, by entering on board the above Ship RANGER, meet with every Civility they can possibly expect, and for a further Encouragement depend on the first Opportunity being embraced to reward each one agreable to his Merit.

All reasonable Travelling Expences will be allowed, and the Advance-Money be paid on their Appearance on Board.

In CONGRESS, MARCH 29, 1777.

RESOLVED,

THAT the MARINE COMMITTEE be authorised to advance to every able Seaman, that enters into the CONTINENTAL SERVICE, any Sum not exceeding FORTY DOLLARS, and to every ordinary Seaman or Landsman, any Sum not exceeding TWENTY DOLLARS, to be deducted from their future Prize-Money.

By Order of CONGRESS,

JOHN-HANCOCK, PRESIDENT.

DANVERS: Printed by E. RUSSELL, at the House late the Bell-Tavern.

3

The British left Massachusetts after the siege of Boston was lifted, but involvement in the war did not slacken. Privateers sailed into Boston and Salem with captured British cargoes. In 1778 a French fleet anchored off Nantasket for repairs (1) after a battle with the British. Massachusetts men and naval resources played a significant role in the new American Navy. The seamen to whom John Hancock's enlistment broadside (2) was directed had served on local merchant ships. On land Massachusetts soldiers served throughout the war. Judah Alden (3), born in Duxbury, was sketched at Valley Forge by Washington's aide, Tadeusz Kosciusko. Deborah Sampson (4), a young girl from Canton, dressed in men's clothing and joined the army. William Glysson (5) of Dudley served the army as a doctor. At home people were prepared for another British invasion. Below is a powder house (6) at Attleboro used for military stores.

4

6

The Revolutionaries

3

"If necessary, fight and even die," John Hancock harangued a Boston crowd in March 1774 on the anniversary of the Boston Massacre. "Blood cries to you from the ground," Joseph Warren called out in another anniversary speech; ". . . scorn to be slaves!" Hancock was a prominent merchant, Warren a well-known doctor. Many of their fellow patriots were also well-connected and prosperous leaders of society; fortunately, their desire for liberty coincided with Massachusetts's mercantile interests. After the Revolution, John Hancock, shown here with his wife, Dorothy (1), became governor of Massachusetts; John Adams (2) became president; his distant cousin Samuel Adams (3) succeeded Hancock as governor. Joseph Warren (4) never held high office; he was killed at the battle of Bunker Hill. Paul Revere's 1774 cartoon (5), based on an earlier design by Benjamin Franklin, shows the American colonies as a snake confronting a devilish griffin representing Britain.

4

JOIN OR DIE

5

Although centered around Boston's busy cobbled streets (1, 2), Massachusetts reached north, in the Maine district, as far as Canada. Past the hills and fields of Worcester County (3), the Commonwealth stretched to the Mississippi, theoretically. Western lands, claimed under the original charter, were ceded to the nation only in 1785. When the new country's president, George Washington, visited Boston, a triumphal arch (4) was erected in his honor. The Massachusetts cent, opposite (5), was issued in 1787, five years before a national mint was authorized. At the time, money of any kind was scarce. In 1786 western Massachusetts farmers, unable to pay taxes, rebelled against the Commonwealth. The uprising, led by Daniel Shays, convinced many Americans of the value of a strong central government. The silver bowl shown here (6) was presented to the militia general who suppressed Shays's Rebellion.

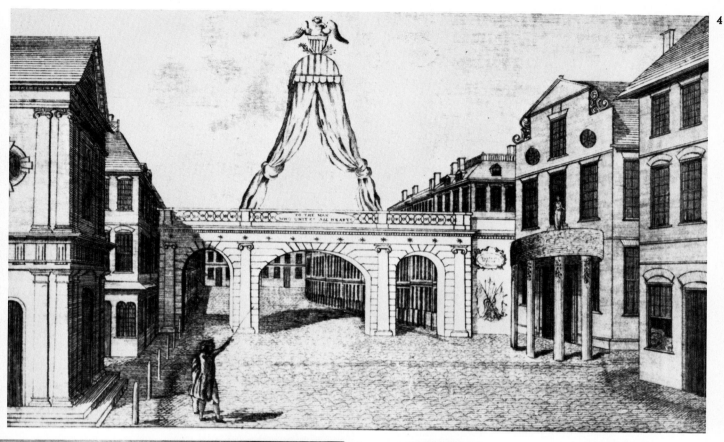

4

5

6

105

Dreadful Riot on Negro Hill!

" O ! read wid tentions de melancoly tale, and e send you yelling to you bed !"

" To Arms ! to Arms ! was sounded Pompey's cry,
" To Arms ! to Arms !" PHILLIS' and KATE's reply !

A Copy of an intercepted *Letter* from Phillis to her Sister in the Country, describing the late R iot on Negro-Hill.

4

Although the population was overwhelmingly made up of descendants of the Puritans, there was a smattering of French and Italians, Irish and Jews, Indians and blacks in Massachusetts. One black, Captain Paul Cuffe or Cuffee (1), was a prosperous shipowner in Dartmouth. Another, Elizabeth Freeman (2) of Boston, was a freed slave. Occasionally there were race riots in Boston. An anti-black broadside (3) dating from 1816 purports to describe one, which took place in the city's black district, Negro Hill, the back of Beacon Hill. There was a tiny colony of Jews in Boston; for one of them, Moses Michael Hays, Paul Revere made a silver cup (4) which could be used in religious ceremonies. Advertisements from a 1794 Boston newspaper show that Irish immigrants were arriving (5) and setting up businesses (6). Occasionally an Italian name could be found (7), but English names still dominated the columns (8).

THE Traverser was tried at bar on an indictment for seducing artificers to go to Boston, in North-America, and after a trial of three hours acquitted without going into defence:

He was tried upon a second indictment for a similar offence; but the lawyers for the prosecution declined any further proceedings, he was of course acquitted.

When Mr. Cox was acquitted of the second indictment, Lord Chief Justice Clonmel, addressing himself to Mr. Cox, said, "whatever satisfaction I have in seeing an individual fairly and honorably acquitted of an offence in its nature highly mischievous to the nation; I cannot but feel some pain in reflecting, that a man to whose talents the public have borne such ample testimony, and which they have so fully encouraged and rewarded, should even give a pretence for such a prosecution. The evils which would arise, if the practice of spiriting away artificers was not strongly resisted by law would be infinite, and would in a short time leave his country poor indeed!—I shall however say no more upon the subject; but I trust the little I have said will make you, Mr. Cox, careful in future how you give even a pretence to any description of men to charge you again with this offence against the laws of a country which has fostered

6

Pot and Pearl-Ashes.

GAD KELLEY, on Spear's Wharf, wishes to purchase a quantity of POT and PEARL ASHES, for which cash and the highest price will be given. He keeps constantly for sale, a general assortment West-India GOODS and GROCERIES.   July 19.

7

Ten Dollars Reward.

WHEREAS Emanuel Dollar, alias Smith, an Italian, left his Lodgings, at Bartholomew Broaders, in Fore-street, Boston, on Friday last, without previous notice, and carried off as follows—Two Animals, named Mococo's, male and female; a Mongoose; a book of Natural History, and divers other things, the property of the said Bartholomew Broaders;—this is to give notice, that that should he offer any of them for sale, or should he seen with them in possession, the reward abovementioned shall be given to any person, (either on application to the Printer of this paper, or to the abovesaid Broaders) who will apprehend the said Emanuel Dollar, alias Smith, so that he may be brought to punishment. Said Emanuel Dollar is about five feet eight inches high, dark hair, black eyes, speaks very indifferent English, but Spanish, Italian, &c. very fluently. Had on when he went off, a green short jacket, and striped trowsers. The animals abovementioned, are very remarkable, are about the size of a small Fox, of a beautiful grey colour, have exceeding long tails, with thirteen natural black rings round them, are very fond of each other, and have faces very much resembling those of lambs. The Mongoose is rather larger, of a dark colour, and has very red eyes.   July 16.

8

RUNAWAY from the Subscriber on the 2d inst. an apprentice Boy, fifteen years old, by the name of CALEB GILL WHITEMAN—had on when he went away, large Beaver Hat, Fustian jacket and striped trowsers. All persons are forbid harbouring, trusting, or masters of vessels carrying off said boy—two pence reward and necessary charges paid to any person who shall return him to   JAMES KIMBALL.

Bradford, July 4, 1794.

Charles Bulfinch

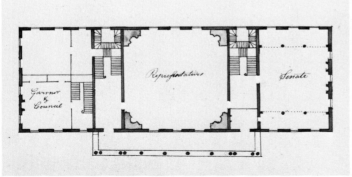

A young man with what he described as "a taste for architecture" was to change the face of Boston. Charles Bulfinch (1) started out as an amateur, advising friends who were building houses. As his talents were recognized, he was given commissions, most notably for the State House (2), which at its completion in 1797 was the nation's finest public building. At left is Bulfinch's drawing of the State House's front elevation and plan (3). As Boston grew, Bulfinch designed the elegant houses of Tontine Crescent (4, 5) and Colonnade Row, laid out streets on Beacon Hill, and designed an incredible number of public and private buildings. Although many have been destroyed, some Bulfinch buildings survive, among them St. Stephen's Church on Hanover Street, University Hall at Harvard (6), the original building of the Massachusetts General Hospital, and several mansions on Beacon Hill.

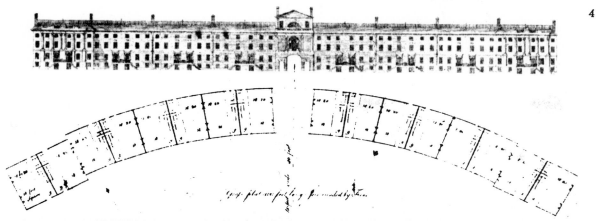

4

5

6

109

1

THE
FARMER's ALMANACK.

[No. II.]

Calculated on a new and improved Plan;
FOR THE YEAR OF OUR LORD
1794:

Being the Second after Leap Year, *and Eighteenth
of the* Independence of America.

Fitted to the town of BOSTON, but will serve for any of the
adjoining States.

Containing, besides the large number of *Aftron-
omical Calculations* and *Farmer's Calendar* for every month
in the year, as great a variety as are to be found in any other
Almanack,

Of New, Uf ful and Entertaining Matter.

BY ROBERT B. THOMAS.

" The various ord'nances of the sky
 Witness the great ARCHITECT on high ;
 Summer and winter, autumn and the spring,
 For him, by turns, their attestation bring."

PRINTED AT THE Apollo Prefs, IN BOSTON.
By BELKNAP and HALL : Sold by them, at No. 8, Dock
Square, *Bofton* ; by the Author, and M. Smith, *Sterling* ;
and by the principal Booksellers in Town and Country.
Price 40s. per groce, 4s. per dozen, 6d. fingle.

2

3

5

4

Except for along the seacoast, Massachusetts was an agricultural land, and most of its inhabitants were farmers. In 1792 Robert Bailey Thomas of Sterling began to print the *Farmer's Almanack* (1), which is still being published. A native of Plymouth and former banker, Elkanah Watson (2) settled in Pittsfield and became interested in improving agriculture and in breeding Merino sheep. The popular response to his exhibition of sheep on the town green in Pittsfield (3) eventually inspired him to form the Berkshire Agricultural Society, which inaugurated the practice of running regular county fairs. Merino sheep appear on a medal (4) presented by the Massachusetts Society for Promoting Agriculture to the Connecticut man who had first imported them from Spain. The farm wagon above (5), dating from the second half of the eighteenth century, comes from Tyngsborough; below is a depiction of haying time at the Worcester County farm of Moses Gill (6).

6

On the Road

BOSTON,
Plymouth & Sandwich
MAIL STAGE,

CONTINUES TO RUN AS FOLLOWS:

LEAVES Boston every Tuesday, Thursday, and Saturday mornings at 5 o'clock, breakfast at Leonard's, Scituate; dine at Bradford's, Plymouth; and arrive in Sandwich the same evening. Leaves Sandwich every Monday, Wednesday and Friday mornings; breakfast at Bradford's, Plymouth; dine at Leonard's, Scituate, and arrive in Boston the same evening.

Passing through Dorchester, Quincy, Wyemouth, Hingham, Scituate, Hanover, Pembroke, Duxbury, Kingston, Plymouth to Sandwich. *Fare,* from Boston to Scituate, 1 doll. 25 cts. From Boston to Plymouth, 2 dolls. 50 cts. From Boston to Sandwich, 3 dolls. 63 cts.

N. B. Extra Carriages can be obtained of the proprietor's, at Boston and Plymouth, at short notice.— STAGE BOOKS kept at Boyden's Market-square, Boston, and at Fessenden's, Plymouth.

LEONARD & WOODWARD.

BOSTON, *November 24, 1810.*

Eleven years after Paul Revere was ferried over to Cambridge to spread word that the British were coming, a bridge was built across the Charles (1). More than 1,500 feet long, it had a draw to let boats through and walkways along either side. It is shown on a commemorative silver tankard (2). Roads improved throughout the Commonwealth. An arched bridge (3) crossed the Merrimack and in 1818 a modern covered bridge with lattice-framed walls (4) was built over the Nashua River. Over the years, numerous milestones (5, 6) were set by roadsides to indicate distances, and stage-coach routes were established between towns. The Boston, Plymouth, and Sandwich stage (7) made three round trips a week; one-way fare was $3.63, but that included two meals en route. A corporation to build a turnpike from Boston to Worcester was formed in 1806. This view of the turnpike, with a tollgate and a gatekeeper's cottage (8), is from the corporation's stock certificates.

1

2

3

To the wharves of Salem's merchants, like that of the Crowninshield family (1), came ivory and gold, tea and silks, iron, and even an elephant which was landed on this wharf in 1796 and sold for $10,000. Salem ships like the *Fame,* shown being launched in 1802 (2), traveled all across the globe. George Crowninshield (3) was a leading Salem sea captain and merchant; he retired young, but devoted the remainder of his life to yachting, building a famous oceangoing yacht, *Cleopatra's Barge.* In the streets of Salem shipchandlers' shops (4) were common. Nathaniel Bowditch was an apprentice at one of them. The young Bowditch became an astronomer and mathematician. His famous book *The New American Practical Navigator* (5) went through numerous editions. Bowditch wrote his book because he found that the book on navigation which was then in common use contained thousands of errors.

4

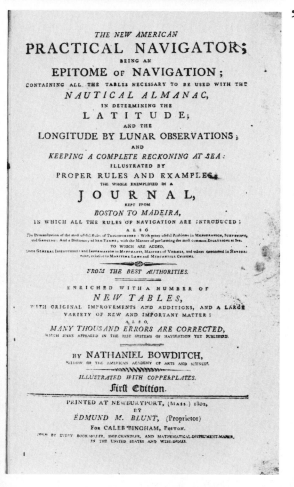

5

THE NEW AMERICAN
PRACTICAL NAVIGATOR;
BEING AN
EPITOME OF NAVIGATION;
CONTAINING ALL THE TABLES NECESSARY TO BE USED WITH THE
NAUTICAL ALMANAC,
IN DETERMINING THE
LATITUDE;
AND THE
LONGITUDE BY LUNAR OBSERVATIONS;
AND
KEEPING A COMPLETE RECKONING AT SEA:
ILLUSTRATED BY
PROPER RULES AND EXAMPLES
THE WHOLE EXEMPLIFIED IN A
JOURNAL,
KEPT FROM
BOSTON TO MADEIRA,
IN WHICH ALL THE RULES OF NAVIGATION ARE INTRODUCED:
ALSO
The Demonstration of the most useful Rules of TRIGONOMETRY: With many useful Problems in MENSURATION, SURVEYING, and GAUGING: And a Dictionary of SEA-TERMS; with the Manner of performing the most common EVOLUTIONS at Sea.
TO WHICH ARE ADDED,
Some GENERAL INSTRUCTIONS and INFORMATION to MERCHANTS, MASTERS of VESSELS, and others concerned in NAVIGATION, relative to MARITIME LAWS and MERCANTILE CUSTOMS.

FROM THE BEST AUTHORITIES.

ENRICHED WITH A NUMBER OF
NEW TABLES,
WITH ORIGINAL IMPROVEMENTS AND ADDITIONS, AND A LARGE
VARIETY OF NEW AND IMPORTANT MATTER:
ALSO,
MANY THOUSAND ERRORS ARE CORRECTED,
WHICH HAVE APPEARED IN THE BEST SYSTEMS OF NAVIGATION YET PUBLISHED.

BY NATHANIEL BOWDITCH,
FELLOW OF THE AMERICAN ACADEMY OF ARTS AND SCIENCES.

ILLUSTRATED WITH COPPERPLATES.
First Edition.

PRINTED AT NEWBURYPORT, (MASS.) 1802,
BY
EDMUND M. BLUNT, (Proprietor)
FOR CALEB BINGHAM, BOSTON.
SOLD BY EVERY BOOK-SELLER, SHIP-CHANDLER, AND MATHEMATICAL-INSTRUMENT-MAKER IN THE UNITED STATES AND WEST-INDIES.

The Derbys of Salem

Enriched by the American Revolution, Elias Hasket Derby (1) became Salem's most prominent merchant. His wealth increased greatly during the wars that followed the French Revolution, as neutral American carriers played an important role in European trade, despite hazards such as that encountered by Derby's *Mount Vernon* (2), which is seen here escaping an attacking French fleet. The membership certificate in the Salem Marine Society (3) showed a picture of Derby's Wharf. One of the ships that docked there was Derby's famous *Grand Turk* (4), which was engaged in the China trade. In Salem Derby built a mansion, "a most superb house," one contemporary commented. He also constructed a small summer house (5) in Peabody. The Salem mansion was one of several houses the Derby family built in the town. A room (6) from one of them is now on display in a Philadelphia museum.

SHIP GRAND TURK

AT CANTON 1786

4

6

Salem Common

An 1808 painting shows militiamen marching on Salem Common while crowds line the edge of the parade ground. Outside the fence around the Common, vendors have set up booths to sell snacks to the spectators.

1

2

Samuel McIntire's Work

3

4

5

Salem's distinguished classical style reached its peak in the work of Samuel McIntire. In 1782, while still in his early twenties, McIntire constructed a splendid house for the East India merchant Jerathmeel Pierce (1). This and McIntire's other houses, including the Gardner House (2), with its delicate portico, helped make Salem a treasure trove of American architecture. "In sculpture he had no rival in New England," one contemporary wrote of McIntire. He carved mantelpieces, decorative capitals, cornucopias, baskets of fruit, and bunches of grapes to adorn his houses. He made figureheads such as the one shown above (3) for the ships of Salem merchants and in 1798 carved a famous bust of John Winthrop (4). A few examples of McIntire's furniture survive, including the sofa above (5), adorned with a design showing a basket of fruit.

1812

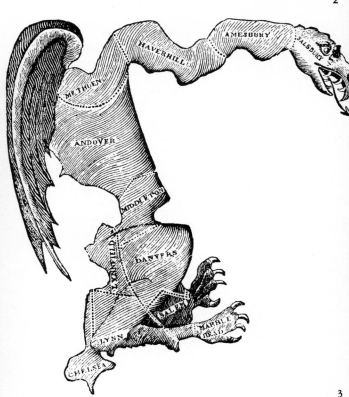

4

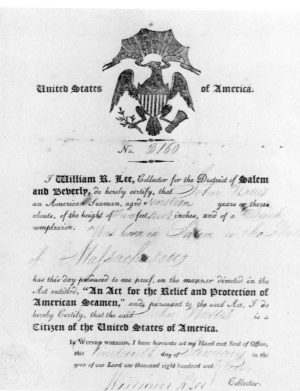

A Marblehead merchant who started out trading dried codfish to the West Indies, Elbridge Gerry (1) had a distinguished career in Massachusetts politics. As governor in 1812, he redistricted Essex County so his supporters could dominate a separate voting district, a district as oddly shaped as a salamander (2). A "gerrymander," someone called it, and a new word entered the language. During the war with England, which erupted that year, privateers, like the *America* out of Salem (3), seized British vessels; some 450 sailed out of Massachusetts ports. One cause of the war was the seizure of American seamen to serve on British ships. To avoid impressment, John Wallis of Salem carried papers (4) proving his citizenship. Threatened by the British Navy, Nantucket (5) was forced to declare its ships neutral in the war. Economic pressure made New England oppose the war. A contemporary cartoon (6), satirizing the situation, shows Rhode Island, Connecticut, and Massachusetts, jumping into the English king's arms.

5

6

123

The Adams Family

One of Massachusetts's most notable contributions to the nation was the Adams family of Quincy. John Adams (1), the founder of the dynasty, shown here alongside his wife Abigail (2), was president from 1797 to 1801. After leaving the presidency he retired to his farm in Quincy and survived to the age of ninety; the portrait bust shown here was made from a life mask taken in 1825, a year before his death. Adams lived to see his son John Quincy Adams (3), shown here alongside his wife (4), elected president too. After leaving the White House in 1829, John Quincy Adams, like his father, retired to the family house (5); but he was soon elected to Congress. Unhampered by party lines, Adams became a fierce opponent of slavery and the foremost spokesman for individual liberty. He was buried alongside his father in a stone memorial temple in Quincy (6), after dying of a stroke which occurred when he was rising to speak in Congress (7).

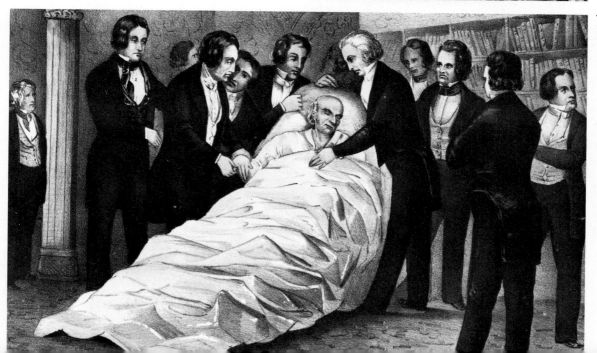

1

2

3

4

Soon after the Revolution, Massachusetts ships found their way to China, carrying silver, furs, and ginseng root to exchange for tea, porcelain, and silk. Great fortunes were built up in the China trade. A number of the Salem mercantile houses and individual ships whose flags appear here (1) were involved in it. Massachusetts ships, among them the *Levant* and the *Milo* of Boston (2), crowded the approaches to the Chinese port of Canton. At Canton were the trading houses of American merchants; opposite is the residence and trading house of one, Augustine Heard of Ipswich (3). Until 1842, Canton was the only port at which foreign traders could live; their houses are shown at left (4) on a lacquer tray made around 1825 for the American market. The Chinese customs clearance certificate (5) is for the *Astrea* of Salem, owned by Elias Hasket Derby. Below is a porcelain plate (6) made to order for Derby in China.

An Age of Churchbuilding

A new white-spired church, its entrance adorned with columns or pilasters, had been erected in almost every Massachusetts town by about 1830, usually to accommodate a growing population or a congregation that had broken away from its old church because of doctrinal differences. Shown here are the First Parish Church of Wayland (1), a building in Carlisle that serves both as a church and as a town hall (2), a church in Sandwich modeled on the work of the great English architect Christopher Wren (3), a columned structure that is used today as the Pelham Town Hall (4), and the Congregational Church in Oldtown, near Attleboro (5).

5

The Industrial Revolution

In 1812 Samuel Slater, who had made the first effective textile machinery in America, founded the town of Webster (1) and built a cotton mill there. There had been industry in Massachusetts before—including a glassworks at Chelmsford which provided dwellings for its workers (2)—but Slater's mill was the harbinger of the state's industrialization. In 1813 Francis Cabot Lowell (3) established a cotton factory at Waltham; later it was moved northward to a new town, named Lowell, on the Merrimack. A good portion of the mill's profits were donated by Francis Lowell's son John (4) to found the Lowell Institute in Boston. Soon Lowell was a thriving city (5), attracting mill-workers (6) from farms and villages. When two Boston textile importers, Abbott Lawrence (7) and his brother Amos (8), eventually decided to manufacture goods at home, another factory town utilizing the Merrimack's water power was established; it was named Lawrence.

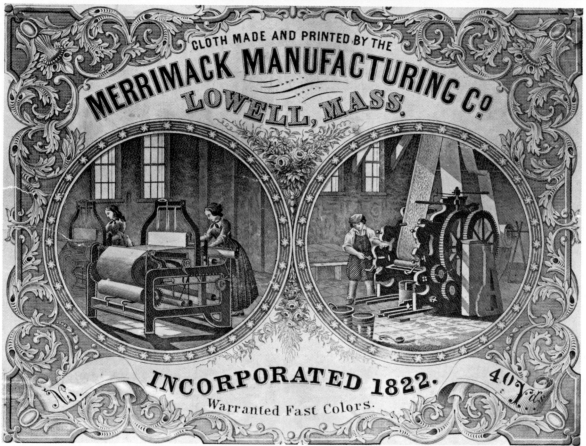

Manufacturing Towns

In the early years of the Industrial Revolution Massachusetts's factories were not devoted solely to making textiles. There was a federal arsenal at Springfield manufacturing armaments, and shipyards along the coast and along the North River in Pembroke and Hanover made the vessels for which the state was famous. Shoes were produced in Lynn, Brockton, and Bridgewater. Machinery for use in textile mills was manufactured in Worcester and other towns. There were tanneries in Danvers and Peabody, and paper was manufactured along the Connecticut River. In Canton, seen at right in a painting by Joseph Hidley, the chimneys of an iron works sent smoke into the air above the town's hotel and neatly planted fields.

1

2

3

The Granite Railway

One of the great engineering feats of American history was the construction of the country's first railway to carry granite four miles from a quarry in Quincy to the Neponset River, where it could be shipped to Charlestown for use in the Bunker Hill Monument. Down a slope (1), the stone was transported in horse-drawn railroad cars (2) running on wooden wheels (3) to a wharf (4) at the edge of the river. From there it was shipped by boat across Boston Harbor to Charlestown, where the monument commemorating the famous, if misnamed, battle was rising atop Breed's Hill (5). The monument was finally completed in 1842. An 1850 engraving (6) shows it surrounded by an iron fence and towering over the fine brick town houses that were constructed around the square in which it stood. It was the architect of the monument, Solomon Willard, who discovered the existence of veins of suitable granite in Quincy and devised machines to cut building stone to measure within the quarry itself.

6

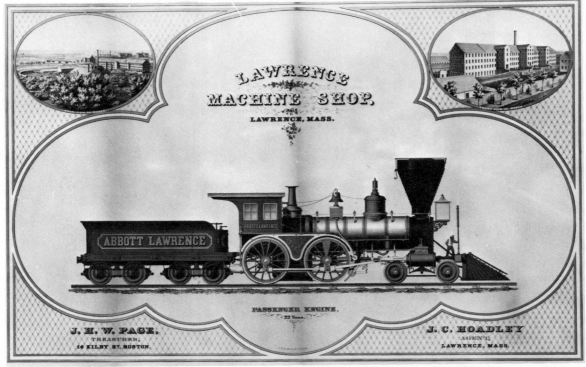

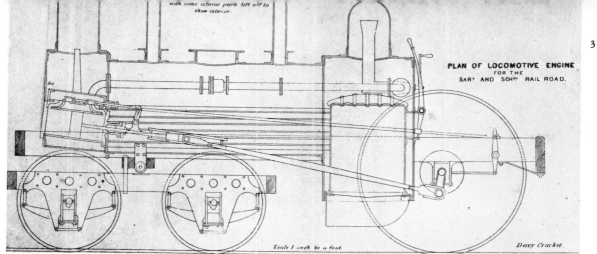

PLAN OF LOCOMOTIVE ENGINE
FOR THE
SAR? AND SCH? RAIL ROAD.

Scale 1 inch to a foot.

Davy Crocket.

Construction of the first steam railroad in New England between Boston and Lowell began in 1831. By 1835 the first train (1) ran over the line, pulled by an English-made locomotive. Soon locomotives were being manufactured in Massachusetts at Lawrence (2). A lithography firm in Boston published a print of the American locomotive *Davy Crockett* (3) to show people how the remarkable new engine worked. The first significant American canal used for transporting manufactured goods was opened by 1803 between the Mystic and the Merrimack. Alongside the canal in Wilmington stood a lock keeper's house (4). Another canal, shown on an 1831 map (5), was planned to run between the Boston area and Narragansett Bay. The growth of railroads soon made the construction of new canals unprofitable, however.

5

The City of Boston

A lithograph, published shortly after Boston out-grew town government and became a city in 1822, shows the busy waterfront. In the foreground is the toll bridge opened in 1805 to connect Boston with the newly annexed district of Dorchester Heights, now renamed South Boston. South Boston's annexation began a process that was to go on until the present boundaries of the city were fixed in 1912.

1

2

3

Municipal Life

As hills have been lowered and wetlands filled in, Boston has changed shape more than any other American city. The top of Beacon Hill was leveled (1) around 1810. The city's second mayor, Josiah Quincy (2), filled in waterfront land near Faneuil Hall, and there built a public market which is still called by his name. To help control the city's frequent fires, Quincy also reorganized the fire department; the fire shown here occurred in 1832 (3). In the 1820s Boston had, for a population of more than fifty thousand, twenty-four constables, dressed, like the man shown here (4), in civilian clothes. In times of civil disturbance, as during the anti-Catholic riots of 1834, the governor could call out the militia; one militia group was the National Lancers, shown receiving their company standard from the governor on Boston Common (5). Municipal services were often primitive; an 1839 engraving shows a street-cleaning sprinkler (6) in front of the Old State House.

Modern Living

Although the 1820s were a time of moderniza-
tion in Boston, with gas street lights introduced
and steamboats appearing in Boston Harbor, customers in William Ladd's pleasant restaurant (1)
still had to share tables and sit on stools rather
than chairs. The first American restaurant with

separate tables for individual diners was in Boston's Tremont House (2), opened in 1829. The
innovative Tremont House also provided locks
for bedroom doors and—a wonder in its time—
indoor plumbing. In the elegantly furnished
houses of the rich, easy chairs had not yet made
an appearance. At social occasions, such as the
tea party shown here (3), guests usually sat in
straight-backed chairs arranged along the walls.

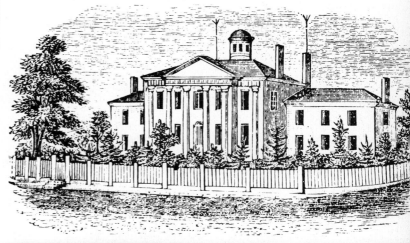

The Center of Civilization

"Boston . . . was appointed in the destiny of nations to lead the civilization of North America," Ralph Waldo Emerson wrote. While Emerson was still a student at Harvard, Boston's intellectual groups, such as the literary Wednesday Evening Club (1), gathered regularly for conversation. In 1815 the influential *North-American Review* (2) began publication in the city, and in Worcester a few years later the American Antiquarian Society, devoted to studying the American past, moved into an impressive new building (3). Nathaniel Bowditch (4), a scholar with a growing international reputation, moved to Boston in 1823, and Edward Everett (5) began teaching Greek at Harvard, where he influenced a generation of writers. The visual arts flourished too. The young Samuel F. B. Morse, the son of a Charlestown minister, was allowed to paint after his father had been assured that painting was not immoral. The artist portrayed his family posed around a globe (6).

Religious Change

By 1800 the old religion had lost much of its hold over intellectual leaders. Puritan severities and Puritan doctrine were often rejected, and many congregations split. One New Bedford church was actually cut in two, with one half moved to accommodate the quarreling parties (1). The leader of the new thought was William Ellery Channing (2); in 1819 he laid down the tenets of the faith that had newly evolved out of Congregationalism and gave it a name: Unitarianism. The previous year, in a famous court case, the Unitarians of Dedham received title to the town church, forcing the orthodox Congregationalists to build another; a pencil drawing (3), published here for the first time, shows the two churches (the Unitarian church is at the left). By 1836 eighty-one Massachusetts churches had become Unitarian and many new Unitarian churches had been constructed; the one opposite is in East Boston (4). The movement led to a change in the state constitution; citizens no longer had to pay taxes to support the Congregational churches. Numerous other religions flourished. Among them was that of the Shakers, whose settlement in the town of Harvard was depicted by a member (5).

4

5

Granite from Medway

Slate Roof

white Post and sent Road

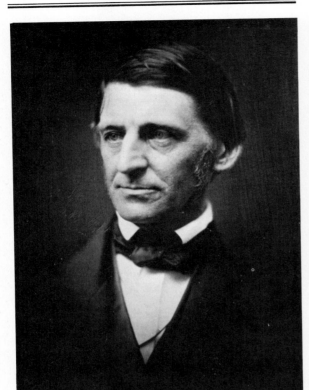

4

In the 1830s and '40s Concord was the capital of American literature. Under the leadership of Ralph Waldo Emerson (1), an immensely productive literary circle flourished, with Henry David Thoreau (2) one of its most notable members. Emerson purchased some land on the shores of Walden Pond (3) not far from his house; he often went there and walked in the woods to be in touch with nature. In 1845 Thoreau built a cabin (4) on Emerson's land, and he spent two years living there. The book that resulted from his stay, *Walden,* has become one of the classics of American literature. Another member of the circle, the philosopher Bronson Alcott (5), was a zealous advocate of the plain living and high thinking that the Concord writers so fervently admired; at his house (6) Alcott prepared lectures which the intellectuals of Boston, Cambridge, and Concord attended.

The Flowering of New England

1

2

3

The novelist Nathaniel Hawthorne (1) became a friend and neighbor of Emerson's in Concord. Another friend was Margaret Fuller (2), a noted lecturer and feminist. In 1841 a group of intellectuals, including Hawthorne, established a utopian communal settlement in West Roxbury, Brook Farm, named for a brook on the property (3). Hawthorne's college friend Henry Wadsworth Longfellow (4) lived nearby in Cambridge, teaching at Harvard. One of the few noted Massachusetts writers not in Emerson's orbit was John Greenleaf Whittier of Amesbury (5). The poet Oliver Wendell Holmes was a member of the circle; he is shown with Emerson in Boston's Public Garden (6). In 1858 Emerson and other Boston intellectuals visited the Adirondacks and camped there to commune with nature (7).

Doing Good

3

166	CITY OF BOSTON.

Boylston Medical—N. P. Rice, Sec.
British Charitable—Geo. Greig, Sec.
British Colonial Society, 78 State
Bromfield Lyceum, J. H. Brown, Cor. Sec.
Cape Cod Association—11½ Trem. r.
Charitable Orthopedic Association, J. P. Healey, Sec'y
City Missionary Soc'y—A. L. Stone, Sec'y, 96 Washington st.
Collegiate and Theological Education Society—19 Cornhill
Doctrinal Tract and Book Society, 156 Washington
E. B. Lib. Assoc.— J. B. Drew, Sec.
Emigrant Society.—Thos. Barrett, Agent, 4 Congress square
Fatherless and Widow's Soc.—Mrs. William Reynolds, Treasurer
Female Medical Education Society and N. E. Medical College,—Sam'l Gregory, M. D. Sec. 15 Cornhil
Female Samaritan Society—Mrs. J. P. Lakeman. Sec.
Fragment—Miss M. C. Smith, Sec.
Franklin Typog.—Thos. J. Lillie, Treasurer.
Handel & Haydn—J. L. Fairbanks, Secretary
Howard Benevolent— M. Grant Pres't; Artemas Simonds, Sec'y
Humane Society of Mass.— Rev. S. K. Lothrop, Cor. Sec'y
Irish Charitable—P. Harkins, Sec.
Ladies' Am. Home Ed.—10 Albany
Ladies' Soc. for Promotion of Educ. at West, Miss Sarah Tuttle, Sec.
Latin School Association—N. B. Shurtleff, Sec.
Mass. Charitable Fire Soc.—27 State, W. P. Gregg, Cor. Sec'y
Mass. Charitable Mechanic Association—Savir gs Bank Building.
Mass. College of Pharmacy—H.W. Lincoln, Secretary
Mass. Char.—Dan'l Henchman, Sec.
Mass. Colonization—Joy's Building
Mass. Gen. Hosp.—Blossom, c. Allen
Mass. Historical—Savings B. Build.
Mass. Home Miss.—28 Cornhill
Mass. Medical Society—H. I. Bowditch, Sec.
Mass. Sabbath School—13 Cornhill
Mass. Horticultural—School st.
Mass. Anti-Slavery—21 Cornhill
Mass. Institution for Idiots — First street, Mount Washington, S. B.
Mass. Bible—15 Cornhill
Mass. Charitable Eye and Ear Infirmary—Charles street
Mass. Temperance—Moses Grant, Treasurer and Secretary
Mattapan Library Association—B. Capen, Sec.
Mattapan Literary Asso., S. Boston
Mech'nic's Institute—Dan'lWarren, Secretary
Medical Assoc.—Francis Minot, Sec.

Mechanic Apprentices' Library—Phillips place
Mercantile Lib. Assoc.—Bromfield
Merchant Tailors' Association—A. H. Powers, Sec.
MountWashingtonLyceum—South Boston
Musical Fund—J.N. Pierce, Sec.
Musical Education—H. L. Keyes, Secretary
Needle Woman's Friend Society—Washington st. cor. of Temple av.
New England Historic-Genealogical Society,—5 Tremont
Non-Resistance Society — H. C. Wright, Cor. Sec'y
Odd Fellows—21 School st.
Parent Washington T. A. Society—Washington Hall, Bromfield st.
Perkins Institution and Mass. Asylum for Blind—M. Wash. House, S. B., Office, 21 Bromfield
Peace Society [American]—Wm. C. Brown, Rec. Sec'y, 21 Cornhill
Penitent Female Refuge—Rutland street, near Shawmut avenue
Phonographic Reporting Association—Henry M. Parkhurst, Sec.
Printers' Union—H. H. Boardman, Cor. Secretary
Prison Discipline—L. Dwight, Sec.
Scots Charitable—J. Patterson, Sec.
Seaman's Friend — Rev. G. W. Bourne, Cor. Secretary
Society for Prevention of Pauperism—F. R. Woodward, Sec'y, 16 Franklin [Sec.
Society Cincinnati—Thos. Jackson, Soc. Civil Engineers—S. Nott, Sec.
Society for Medical Improvement—Wm. W. Morland, Sec'y
Society for Medical Observation—460 Washington
Society for Promoting Christian Knowledge. Piety and Charity—Rev. F. A. Whitney, Sec.
Society for Relief of Aged and Destitute Clergymen — Rev. J. H. Clinch, Secretary
Society for Propagating the Gospel among the Indians and others in North America—Rev. S. X. Lothrop, Secretary
Suffolk District Medical Society—J. B. Alley, Sec'y
Sons of Temperance—E. B. Dearborn, Grand Scribe, 46 Wash.
St. Vincent de Paul's Female Orphan Asylum—40 Purchase st.
Trustees of DonationsforEducation in Liberia—Joy's building
Young Men's T. A. Society—H.L. Richardson, Cor. Secretary
Young Men's Benevolent Society—Geo. A. Brown, Sec.
Widows and Orphans of Episcopal Clergymen (Relief Society)—Rev. A. I. Baury, Treasurer

Reformers abounded in Massachusetts. The Puritan tradition brought to life societies to aid widows, orphans, the blind, the poor, seamen, the aged, and those ignorant of the benefits of religion. Many leading reformers were women. Dorothea Lynde Dix (1), a Boston schoolteacher, worked to aid the insane by reforming the conditions of their treatment. In 1837 Mary Lyon (2) founded the first women's college in America, Mount Holyoke Seminary, at South Hadley. A page from the 1854 *Boston Almanac* (3) lists some of the city's numerous charitable organizations. The emblem of one of the societies on the list, the Young Men's Total Abstinence Society, appears opposite (4). A model poorhouse was built on Deer Island in Boston Harbor in 1849. A few years later a reformatory was built there, too. Engravings from 1856 show the dining room of the reformatory (5), the hospital for indigent women (6), and the nursery for poor children (7).

4

5

6

7

1

2

4

422   PLAIN TRIGONOMETRY.

To take the height of an Object standing on a Hill, which is inacceſſible.

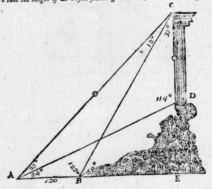

AT two Stations, as at A and B, take the angles, *viz.* CAE and CBE, which the Top of the Object makes with an horizontal line, and that, which the bottom of the object makes with the firſt Station, at A, *viz.* DAE, then take DAE from CAE, and the remainder is CAD.

Note, when an angle is expreſſed by three letters, the middle one ſhews the angle. Now, ſuppoſe the Stationary diſtance AB 120, the angle ACB 12°, and Angle CBA 122°, then by Problem 1ſt, of oblique Trigonometry, we have two angles and a Side oppoſite to one of them given, to find the ſide AC. Therefore,

		Cs. Ar.
As S. of ACB	12°,00′	0,58213
Is to S. of CBA	122 ,00′	9,92842
So is Stationary diſtance	120	2,07918
To Side AC	489,5	2,68973

Note, I ſubtracted 122° from 180°, and worked with the remainder, and in the following, 114° from 180°. Now, having found AC 489,5, ſuppoſe the angle CDA 114°, and the angle CAD 22, and we have two angles and a Side oppoſite to one of them, as before, to find the perpendicular height of the object CD, Therefore,
A

3

Education

"It shall be the duty of legislatures and magistrates . . . to cherish . . . public schools," the Massachusetts constitution proclaims, and schooling was widespread, though sometimes cursory. In small schoolhouses like the oak-shaded building at Brighton (1), or the one-room West Part School at Pittsfield (2), as in private seminaries like Worcester's Oread Institute for Girls (3), "wisdom and knowledge, as well as virtue" were supposed to be taught. One teaching tool was Nicholas Pike's famous *Arithmetic,* first printed in Newburyport in 1788 and often reprinted (4). Despite high ideals, the school year was short. Around 1810, one boy in Franklin attended school only eight or ten weeks each year. That boy, Horace Mann (5), grew up to reform public schools in the state and the nation, founding teacher-training schools, establishing a minimum school year, and improving teaching methods. Below is a Boston private school (6), photographed around the time Mann's reforms were taking root.

6

Colleges

As it had since the seventeenth century, Harvard (1) dominated formal higher education in Massachusetts. Farm boys walked miles just to gaze at the college in Cambridge; they were less interested in such diversions as the class day ceremonies (2) or the football match between freshmen and top-hatted sophomores (3) than they were in seeing wonders like the new astronomical observatory (4) on a hill north of the campus. Respect for learning spread throughout New England. In almost every town and city there were public lectures on chemistry or botany, history or philosophy. These lectures were attended by almost every class of the population. The cause of universal education was advanced by the founding of Mount Holyoke (5) as a seminary for educating women. Williams College (6) in northwestern Massachusetts was an intellectual center for the entire Berkshire region.

156

4

5

6

1

2

Western Massachusetts

3

4

While eastern Massachusetts grew, the western counties remained sparsely settled. Industry was almost nonexistent except along the Connecticut River, and even there, there were vast rural stretches, as can be seen in Thomas Cole's 1846 painting of the Oxbow of the Connecticut River near Northampton (1). South of that Oxbow were several industrial towns, with Springfield (2) the largest. In 1850 the city manufactured cotton sheeting, axles, textile machinery, tools, engines, and paper, along with muskets and other armaments. Although Springfield was busy, its Court Square (3) was still relatively tranquil. Northampton (4) and Pittsfield were small, essentially rural towns. A pencil drawing by John W. Barber (5) shows two of Pittsfield's four churches.

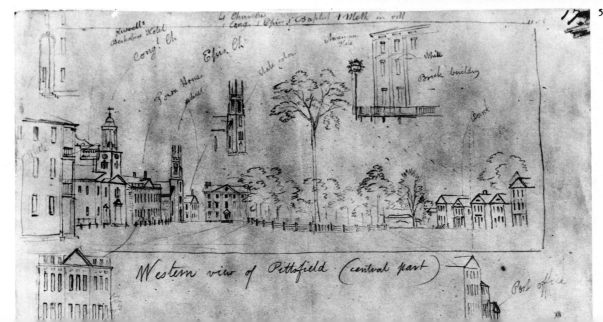

5

Western view of Pittsfield (central part)

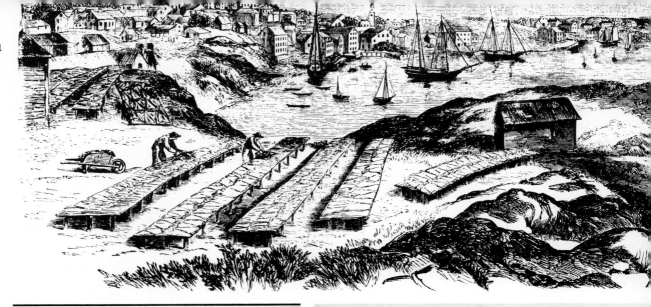

All along Massachusetts's varied coastline, port towns carried on a flourishing commerce and sent out fleets of ships to catch fish. At Marblehead, codfish for export dried on racks overlooking Marblehead Harbor (1). Newburyport (2), near the mouth of the Merrimack, was a shipbuilding center and trading port, important enough to have its harbor mapped by the government (3). In 1826 the beach at Provincetown (4) was lined with windmills; they were used to pump ocean water into large vats where it would eventually evaporate. The salt that remained was used to cure the fish the town's fishermen caught. Nantucket, with its columned Atheneum (5) at the center of town and its streets lined with substantial houses (6), developed into one of the state's most important maritime centers after the Revolution, surpassed only by Boston and Salem. By 1842 there were ninety ships sailing out of the island port.

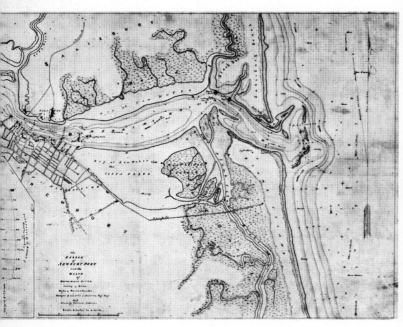

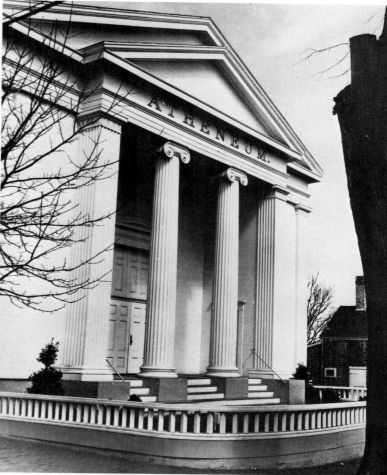

Immigration

X George W Gahan	25		Fayall
X Henry Haner	20	white	Herkemer NY Jerc.
X Henry Grant	18		West Brook me Wil
X Joseph Broadrick	18		Aroostick No 2. 5th Ra
Xd David Smith	21		Philadelphia
X J Warren Stedman	25		Boston
X Thomas Johnson	22		Norwich NY
X Enoch Read	24		Warren Oh
X Joseph Luce	20		Fayall
X Wilson Barnard	25		Elizabeth City NJ
X George Eliot	23		N York
X John Adams	21		Cape de Verds
X Richard J Green	21		Rochester
X John Wright	18		Haybridge It
X Ephraim Walcot	35		Stow Ill
X Charles Wc Green	19		New York
X William Marden	38	Col	Philadelphia
X Herman Melville	21		New York ←
Daniel Mc White	35		Scotland

Immigrants came to Massachusetts from within the United States as well as from abroad. The crew list of the New Bedford whaling ship *Acushnet* in 1840 (1) lists men from Vermont, Maine, and Connecticut, and at the bottom a New Yorker, Herman Melville, who was later to write *Moby Dick.* Fugitive slaves came to Boston, most notable among them Frederick Douglass (2). On Beacon Hill, the African Meeting House (3), built in 1806, was the most important community center for blacks throughout the state. The Jews of Boston built a synagogue (4) in 1851; the congregation, incorporated about a decade earlier, was called Ohabei Shalom, which means "Lovers of Peace." Peace was the lot of the Jews in Boston, but not of Catholics. Anti-Catholic hostility is evident in the placard reading "No Foreign Police" (5) carried by a group of strikers in Lynn in 1860. The foreign police were, of course, Irish immigrants.

Massachusetts was changed significantly by the great migration that followed the potato famine in Ireland in the 1840s. Thousands of poor Irish peasants left their cottages (1) and took ship for America at the port of Cork (2). At their destination they were often greeted, like the Irish family shown above arriving at Constitution Wharf in Boston in 1857 (3), by relatives who had preceded them to America. By 1857, about half the population of Boston was Catholic, and most of those Catholics were Irish. New churches were built; below is the Church of St. Peter and St. Paul (4) in South Boston, constructed because the Catholic population outgrew the old Chapel of St. Augustine (5), built in 1819.

The Catholic Church

Boston's few Catholics did not have a regular resident priest until 1788. With the arrival of French priests, notably the Reverend Jean de Cheverus (1), later bishop of Boston, a church (2) was built, designed by Bulfinch. By around 1830 there were more than ten thousand Catholics in Boston and Charlestown alone. Endemic anti-Catholic feeling burst into the open in 1834 when a mob burned the Ursuline Convent in Charlestown (3); twenty years later the convent was still in ruins (4). With the great increase in Irish population a new Catholic newspaper, the *Boston Pilot* (5), was founded. In 1844 Catholicism gained great strength in the state with the conversion of Orestes Brownson (6), a former Unitarian minister and an influential friend of Emerson.

BOSTON  PILOT.

Be just, and fear not—let all the ends thou aim'st at, be thy God's, thy Country's, and Truth's.

$2,50 In Advance.　　　　BOSTON, MAY 25, 1844.　　　　Volume VII-----No. 21.

THE BOSTON PILOT,

IS PRINTED AND PUBLISHED BY THE PROPRIETORS,

DONAHOE & ROHAN.

On every Saturday morning, at No. 1 Spring Lane, near Washington street, Boston, Mass. where all orders and communications in all matters of expense must be addressed.

TERMS —$2.50 in advance, or $3.00 if not paid within three months from the time of subscribing.

$1.50 for six months. Four months $1.

Any of our present subscribers procuring a new one, and making payment at our office, or to any of our agents, will be entitled to receive for $4.00 each send separately.

In order to comply with the above terms, the whole must be paid in advance.

Any Post master may enclose money in a letter to the Publisher of a newspaper to which he is a subscriber or a third person to frank a letter, if written by himself.

Particular Notice. In future, no letter except from Agents will be taken out of the Post Office, unless the Postage is paid. Our Agents will bear this in mind, and mark the initials of their name on the outside cover of the letter.

Our Jubilee.

Having had some share in freighting the last British steam ship, which left these shores to travel over the unnumbered leagues of the glorious sea, the *corps editorial* of the *Pilot* assembled on the evening of the day, with the contributors, to whom we are so deeply indebted, with many prominent friends of the cause, to celebrate that epoch in American Agitation. The place of meeting was the venerable apartment in which the first club of friends to Repeal ever assembled on this continent, from whose social compact the Boston Repeal Association afterwards emerged into existence. A fine painting of one of our ancestors, mounted on his milk white steed, in the act so minutely described by the legend, of walking the azure waters of Killarney's fairy lake, hung

That emblem once heard through Byzantium, such notes
As those you now utter, from Moslman throats,
And as it fell prostrate from the domes of the East
A spirit of light bore it off to the West.

Mahomet then trampled it, He trod it sore
And the facot to-day as the Pagan of yore,
But Isreal with more and the Russian bath risd
The Crescent of Ottoma deep in the sea.

Beware oh, beware ye faithless and sold,
I'm nice into bondage and senseless of Christ;
Forsooth your painted fetters the cross of Christ;
But nah such a crime for men can stand aloof.

Are ye mad in your reason? what have ye both at done—
'Tis as long Cross which Count as to glory of on,
'Twas that Cross who by your Fotery feed aspired to his breast
When his soul plumed its flight to the home of the blest.

Bless have not your nations be-fold destroyed; they
Come I take up one-o more the cast garment of say.
It would be to upbraid you, or the wrong and disgrace
You have bought on the fair fame they left to their race.

Shout, louder and louder, and do it as if you can
The abhorrence of God and adoration of man,
Nor stay your great labor—but finish the work
Which to you was resigned by few Pagan and Turk.

A go down with the Cross. I ascend am of love
Be seen the red City of Rudolove,
Give to Bigots your cheers and Religion a grave
In the hand of the free and this home of the brave.

There was silence painful and prolonged, and then the memory of the Revolutionary Fathers was drunk in solemn silence.

"I fear much," said the elder Mr. Redshanks, "that the disgrace of this odious event will be laid upon the whole land, which does not, in truth, deserve it. Those who have really had an American ancestry—who have read their country's history—who desire to add each one honorable leaf to its continuation in the 20th century—abhor and abjure such deeds."

"We will want another Bolivar, if these things go on," said M'Manus to the Colonel.

The Riots.

THOUGHTS FOR THE PEOPLE.

All was quiet in our city yesterday. It was a strange thing, however, to see the Military promenading our streets on the Sabbath, but still stranger to feel that their presence was necessary to the maintenance of the public peace! Into all the churches, as the chiming bells pealed out their solemn tones, poured crowd after crowd to give thanks, perhaps, to the Deity for their safety. Into all the churches, we should have said, *excepting*—the Roman Catholic. They stood desolate, silent and untenanted. In obedience to the orders of the Bishop they were not opened for public worship. The solitary tread of the sentinel, or the clank of the musket, was the only sound that disturbed their solitary repose.

And this was a Sabbath picture of the "City of Brotherly Love!" This was a picture of the "Quaker city! Could William Penn have risen from his grave and looked at such a scene; could he have gazed on the bristling bayonets that offended the quiet eye in almost every direction; could he have been told that this pomp and panoply of war were necessary to secure the liberty of religious opinion; that here, on this very spot where he had planted the Christian banners, which he had made the asylum of the persecuted for opinion's sake, and had peculiarly consecrated to Religious Freedom; could he have been told that here all this exhibition of military force was required simply to enable men to exercise one of the inalienable privileges of humanity, to worship God according to the dictates of their own consciences, what that great and good man would have said we leave the reader to imagine. He could not have credited the evidence of his senses. He could not have believed his descendants so monstrously degenerated. He

forsooth, where is it? If you are an Atheist, and deny a God, it is well. If you are a Hebrew and deny our Saviour, it is also well. If you are a Musselman and adore Mahomet, it is equally well. The unmolested possession of your opinion is guaranteed to you in Philadelphia. But if you are a brother Christian, differing with us in Biblical interpretations, fly for your life, abandon your home, forsake your altars—we, descendants of Wm. Penn, have but the faggot and the musket for such terrible unbelievers. Our presses shall call you unfitted to share in the blessings of freedom, and our people in the name of the Bible and the American Flag, shall drive you forth by the flame and the sword, lest your presence should contaminate their righteousness!

Alas! this is a contemplation for a Sabbath in Philadelphia. Who feels not ashamed that it is true? Who would not give world's to wipe off this foul blot from the disgraced name of our city, occasioned by a few misled and maniacal leaders? Who knows not that the fiery stain will stick to our people, as did the poisoned shirt to Nessus, hugging to its death their social reputation? And all this, too, at a moment when, after so much trial, Pennsylvania has shaken off the obloquy consequent upon her financial embarrassments. Having taken so much pains to stand erect before the world in her honesty, to be again made the pointed at of nations, the contemned of every liberal and enlightened spirit!—*Philadelphia Spirit of the Times.*

FORBEARANCE. The Philadelphia Catholic Herald says:—

"What we can say fearlessly and sincerely is, that Catholics, as a body, desire to live in friendship with their fellow-citizens, and utterly abhor lawless violence. This feeling is no doubt common to all good

1

JOURNAL

OF

DOCTOR JEREMIAH SMIPLETON's

TOUR TO OHIO.

I have been · *I am going to Ohio*

CONTAINING
An account of the numerous difficulties, Hair-breadth
Escapes, Mortifications and Privations, which the
Doctor and his family experienced on their
Journey from Maine, to the 'Land of Pro-
mise,' and during a residence of three years
in that highly extolled country.

BY H. TRUMBULL.

Nulli Fides Frontis.

BOSTON--PRINTED BY S. SEWALL.

Emigration

Like other Americans, Massachusetts people moved west in the nineteenth century in search of better land. Around 1800, thousands of New Englanders migrated to Ohio; the tract at left (1) is an attempt to stem the tide. Sometimes emigration was for political reasons; at lower left is the stock certificate of the New England Emigrant Aid Company (2), which helped populate Kansas with people opposed to slavery. Land agents (3) examined titles to new lands; ships (4) carried emigrants around Cape Horn to the gold fields of California. Europeans landed in Boston and then traveled west; opposite (5), Swedish immigrants proceed along Tremont Street in 1852. Many Massachusetts emigrants made important contributions to their new homes. The poet William Cullen Bryant (6), of Cummington, and the painter and inventor Samuel F. B. Morse (7), of Charlestown, became prominent New Yorkers.

2

New England Emigrant Aid Company.

No. 152

Boston, *April 14th* 1855

This is to Certify, That *Edw E. Hale Worcester Ms*
is Proprietor of *One* Shares, of the par value of twenty
dollars each, in the Capital Stock of the New England Emigrant
Aid Company, transferable on the books of said Company, on the
surrender of this Certificate.

John M. S. Williams V. President.

Thomas H. Webb, Secretary.

3

W. B. YOUNG & CO.,
WESTERN LAND AGENTS,
34 Union Building, 40 State Street,
BOSTON, MASS.

Titles examined.   Taxes paid for non-residents in the West.

Investments made for parties by loan, or by purchase of Western City property, town lots, improved or unimproved farms, for a commission, or on joint account.
Land Warrants procured for widows or minor children of persons who were in any war with the United States since 1775. Land Warrants also bought, sold or located.
Persons interested by *heirship* or otherwise, in *old Patent Titles or Tax Titles,* whose interest may be doubtful, can have their rights looked after by application to us.

We act as Agents for purchase of Land at Government Land Sales.

Colonists, or persons about to go West in search of farms, or other Western property, will find it to their interest to call on or write to us before starting.
All business in our line promptly and carefully attended to, and letters answered fully without delay.

W. B. YOUNG & CO., Western Land Agents,
34 UNION BUILDING, 40 STATE STREET, BOSTON, MASS.

FOR
CALIFORNIA!
Mutual Protection
Trading & Mining Co.

Having purchased the splendid, Coppered and very fast Sailing
Barque EMMA ISIDORA,
Will leave about the 15th of February. This vessel will be fitted in the very best manner and is one of the fastest sailing vessels that goes from this port.

Each member pays 300 dollars and is entitled to an equal proportion of all profits made by the company either at mining or trading, and holds an equal share of all the property belonging to the company. Experienced men well acquainted with the coast and climate are already engaged as officers of the Company. A rare chance is offered to any wishing a safe investment, good home and Large profits.
This Company is limited to 60 and any wishing to improve this opportunity must make immediate application.
An Experienced Physician will go with the company.
For Freight or Passage apply to 23 State Street, corner of Devonshire, where the list of Passengers may be seen.

JAMES H. PRINCE, Agent,
23 State Street, corner of Devonshire St., Boston.

For further Particulars, see the Constitution.   Propeller Power Presses,
142 Washington St., Boston.

169

1

2

3

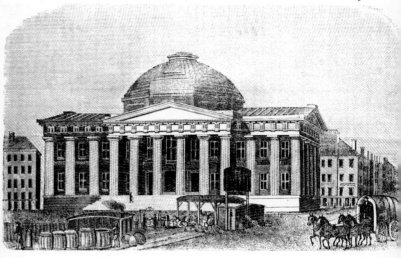

4

5

By 1856, when the photograph above (1) was taken from the State House, looking north toward the Bunker Hill Monument at upper left and the Charlestown Navy Yard at top center, the entire area of the Boston peninsula was covered with buildings. The city now had a reliable water supply. Previously water had been pumped in from Jamaica Pond through hollow pine logs. To replace the logs, pipes were laid to Long Pond in Natick; when the new water line was opened in 1848 and a jet of water rose above Boston Common (2), a great celebration was held. Newly important Long Pond became known once again by its Indian name, Lake Cochituate; Long Pond, it was felt, was too ordinary a name. New buildings reflected Boston's wealth; among them were the Custom House (3) and the Suffolk Bank (4). The rest of the state was suspicious of the city's growth. An 1840 cartoon shows Boston as a monster devouring other towns (5).

Tremont Street

1

2

A walk along Tremont Street in 1853, when this "Grand Panoramic View" was made, would take the stroller past some of Boston's finest buildings. The engravings on these and the next two pages show both sides of the street from its beginning to

Boston Common. At top, reading from left to right and heading north, are Boston Common and the State House; the Park Street Church; the Old Granary Burying Ground with its Egyptian-style gateway; and part of the city's finest hotel, the Tremont House. At bottom, reading from left to right and heading south from the beginning of Tremont Street, is the grocery store of S. S. Pierce; a theater called the Boston Museum; Kings Chapel; and, at right, Tremont Temple, a Baptist church.

Tremont Street

Proceeding up Tremont Street away from the Common, the traveler would see (top, left to right) the columned entrance to the Tremont House and then two of the city's lesser hotels, the Albion and

174

the Pavilion. At far right is a music store under the proprietorship of George P. Reed. At bottom at far left is another establishment devoted to music, Johnson's piano-forte salesrooms. A few doors down the street heading south is the imposing building of the popular magazine *Gleason's Pictorial*. At far right, facing Boston Common, is a row of dwelling houses.

The Streets of Boston

A series of engravings, published in 1858, shows some of the most important business streets of Boston. Above is Milk Street (1), looking up toward Washington Street; at left the other direction can be seen, looking down toward the harbor (2). Summer Street is at lower left (3), and Washington Street, the city's central thoroughfare, is directly below (4). At top opposite is Pearl Street (5); the gap between the buildings in the distance marks the waterfront. Quincy Market (6) was opened in 1826 because Faneuil Hall Market was overcrowded. The American House (7), on Hanover Street, was one of the city's major hotels.

178

The Port of Boston

Although the great fortunes now came from manufacturing rather than from trade, Boston remained a busy port in the nineteenth century. Around 1830 the packet *Morning Star* was depicted in full sail passing Boston Light (1). Clipper ships built in East Boston were among the fastest ships in the world. The *Flying Cloud* (2), built in 1851, reached San Francisco ninety days after leaving New York. Another notable East Boston-made ship was the *Sovereign of the Seas* (3). The East Boston shipyard was under the direction of Donald McKay (4), an immigrant from Nova Scotia famous for his shipbuilding skill. Across the harbor from McKay's East Boston yard were the Charlestown Navy Yard and Boston's numerous piers, the streets around them crowded with shops of maritime interest such as George Townsend's, which according to an advertisement (5) specialized in repairing ships' bottoms and raising sunken vessels.

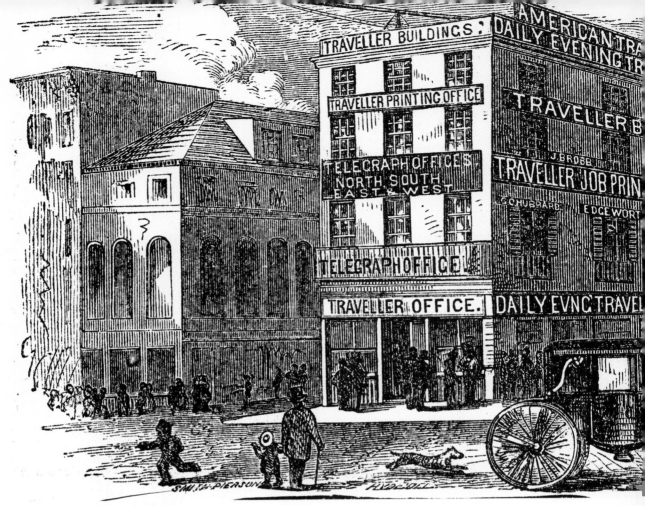

1

2

3

The Publishing Industry

Publishing was one of Boston's major industries, far more important in its impact than can be measured by its dollar value, $5.5 million in 1855. In that year the state had twenty-two daily newspapers, including the *Boston Traveller,* whose State Street building is shown here (1). In the days before photographic reproduction, numerous wood-engravers, like John Andrew, whose advertisement appears opposite (2), were kept busy preparing illustrations. Many periodicals had their home in Boston, including the *Lady's Almanac* (3) and *Ballou's Pictorial,* all of whose issues showed, rather inaccurately, Boston Harbor and Beacon Hill (5). In 1858 the city contained more than eighty booksellers, among them James French and Company (4). Income publishers earned from the work of local authors—Longfellow and Lowell, Emerson, Whittier, and Holmes—was supplemented by money from the sale of less literary works. Above is an illustration from one such book, the 1845 *Child's Pictorial History of the Bible,* showing St. Peter denying Christ (6).

City Diversions

1

2

Before the Civil War, small-town pleasures were still available to Bostonians. When the ice was good, crowds came out to skate on Jamaica Pond (1). On winter days there were sleigh rides on Boston Neck (2). Proper Bostonians, though, preferred to go sleighing on the Brighton road, a more fashionable resort. The most fashionable Bostonians gathered for parties (3), beginning at nine or ten in the evening, a time, one visitor commented, "calculated . . . to draw a line between those who can afford to turn night into day and those who can not."

3

Simple Pleasures

A class day dance at Cambridge (1), a clam chowder party in Lynn (2), a Fourth of July picnic at Weymouth (3)—there were many occasions for festivity. Harvard's class day dance began outdoors, after a class parade and a formal oration; then the dancers moved indoors to Harvard Hall, where they had to keep a sharp eye out to avoid colliding with the supporting columns that kept the old building steady. The clambake at Lynn was arranged in 1860 to keep up the spirits of shoe workers during a bitter strike. At the Weymouth picnic gentlemen wore vests and top hats and their ladies wore shawls and bonnets despite the summer heat.

1

"Young ladies," Mrs. John Farrar, the wife of a Harvard professor, advised readers in *The Young Lady's Friend,* an etiquette book published around 1830, "should not take up all their thoughts with love and marriage." Nevertheless, then as now, love and marriage took up a lot of thought. Around the time Mrs. Farrar's book was published, a sailor aboard a New Bedford whaling vessel carved out of whalebone a picture of what was on his mind: proposing marriage to a buxom girl (1). After marriage came families—usually as large although not necessarily as prosperous as the Hollingsworth family of Milton (2). Like their descendants today, women were expected to run sizable households efficiently. Abigail Adams, they were reminded in an 1844 book of advice to mothers, "the admiration of European courts, . . . knew how to make butter and cheese as well as any woman in Weymouth."

2

A Small Town

Life in and near the small and typical town of South Reading was recorded in the tranquil years before the Civil War by a local resident named Franklin Poole, a house painter who turned his talents to art. Poole depicted the Lynnfield Hotel (1) on the nearby Newburyport Turnpike in South Lynnfield; the doors of the hotel's stable are large enough to accommodate stagecoaches. Around 1845, he painted a view of South Reading (2) after a railroad was built through the town; the sign across the road said, "Beware the Engine." A picture of South Reading Common (3) shows the town's hay scale at right, the school behind it, and, beneath the oak tree, a small outdoor privy. At top is the Baptist church (4). Below it is shown the large factory of the Wakefield Rattan Company (5), built around 1860 to produce rattan furniture. In 1868 the town changed its name to Wakefield in honor of Cyrus Wakefield, the factory's builder.

Two Maritime Cities

1

2

A Salem housewife hangs out the wash in her back yard (1), delivery wagons rattle over the dirt streets (2), and smoke comes out of the factory chimneys. Salem in 1853 was past the days of its maritime glory, but it was still the third largest city in the state, exceeded in size only by Lowell and Boston. Although it did not have the extensive manufacturing works of some of the other cities, it was the metropolis of the North Shore. New Bedford (3), shown in a lithograph dating from around 1858, had almost the same population as Salem—some twenty thousand. New Bedford had one sizable cotton mill, but it drew most of its wealth from the sea, from the whale fisheries that made the city their home.

3

1

2

Whaling was one of the great industries of Massachusetts, and New Bedford (1) was its center. By 1857 the town had 330 whaling vessels, more than half the American total, far outdistancing Nantucket, Edgartown, and the other whaling ports. Before setting out on a long voyage, New Bedford's whalers prayed in The Seamen's Bethel (2). A navigator with his sextant (3) hung as a shop sign over a New Bedford street, and the figurehead of the Indian queen Awashonks (4) stood at the bow of a New Bedford whaling ship. Millions of dollars were brought into the town by the whaling industry. Log books, such as this one from the bark *Mary and Susan* (5), recorded the number of whales caught and the number of barrels of whale oil that each one produced. The whale oil would be sold for use in lamps or for making spermaceti candles.

3

4

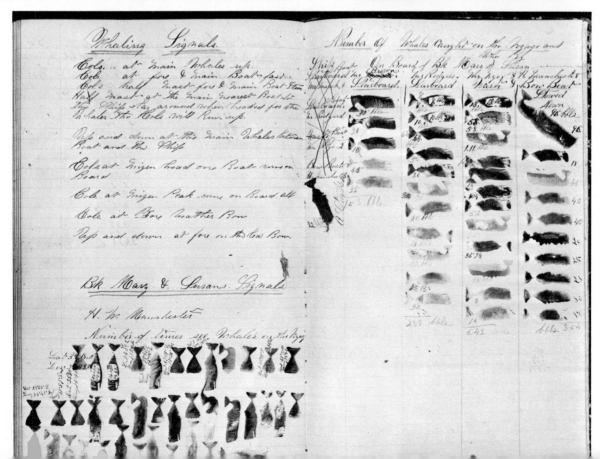

5

193

The Death of the Whale

Whaling was dirty and difficult work, and the whalemen, whose fleets (1) sailed to distant seas, led lives of extraordinary hardship. Even if the seas were calm, taking the whaleboat over the side and then rowing out to harpoon a whale (2) was risky work. A whale thrashing about could swamp his attackers or even crush both the whaleboat and its occupants in his jaws (3). Once a whale was successfully harpooned, it had to be hauled alongside and made fast to the whaling ship. Seamen, clambering over its slippery and heaving corpse, cut the blubber into strips and then into thick pieces that were suitable for boiling down into oil. Boiling the blubber was hot, stinking, grimy work. The whale oil then had to be strained into barrels and stowed below. The whaler's life has often been romanticized; actually it was a terrible existence, full of danger and hard labor.

2

3

Agriculture

As the towns' population grew, farmers began to find a substantial market for their produce. *The New England Farmer* (1), a Boston magazine, gave farmers hints on, among other things, proper storage of crops so that they could be sold when prices were high. New farm implements increased productivity; an 1841 advertisement for modern plows (2) shows a plowing contest at Worcester, presumably won by the plow in the foreground, the subject of the advertisement. Fairs were frequent and elaborate. At the National Horse Exhibition (3), held in Springfield in 1853, horses from twenty states were shown. Horses from Vermont and New Jersey won the competition for fancy matched pairs (4). From all over New England, cattle, hogs, and sheep were driven to the livestock market at Brighton (5). There they were sold to butchers for slaughtering. One such butcher was young Gustavus Swift of Cape Cod, who came up to Brighton each week, bought a steer, killed it, and then peddled the meat; Swift founded the great Chicago meat-packing concern that bears his name.

5

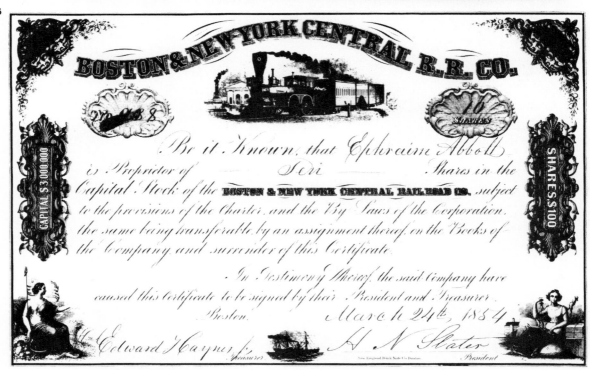

The Era of Railroads

Within a few decades after the establishment of the state's first railroad, train tracks reached from Cape Cod to the Berkshires and beyond. Numerous lines converged on Boston. At left, a train of the Providence Line crosses the marshy lands of the Back Bay in 1844 (1). Below it is an express train on the Boston and Albany route (2), which was of great economic significance since it linked the industrial towns of Massachusetts with the West. At lower left is a stock certificate for the Boston and New York Central Railroad (3), which followed the same route. Local railroad lines tied all of New England more closely together. The Lynn railroad station (4) was one of the stops along the Eastern Line, which went along the North Shore. A detail from an 1853 map of Boston (5) shows some of the tracks that linked Boston with the North.

4

5

1   2

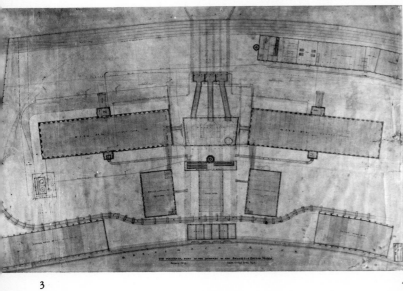

3   4

By the middle of the nineteenth century, Massachusetts produced about one-third of the country's textiles. Lowell, with its thirty-five cotton mills (1), including the impressive Boott Mills (2), was the state's leading industrial center after Boston. It was soon to be rivaled by the newer town of Lawrence, which obtained water power by building a stone dam across the Merrimack in 1847. At lower left are the floor plans of part of the immense Atlantic Cotton Mills at Lawrence (3). Below is a view of the dam's construction (4). Textile plants were built throughout the state. In 1855, Taunton had five cotton mills, Newburyport six, Holyoke three, and Chicopee eleven. There were also numerous plants for making textile machinery and finishing plants, like the Waltham Bleachery, whose boiling room is shown at right (5). When the Pemberton Mills at Lawrence burned and collapsed in January 1860 (6), about one hundred textile workers were killed.

1

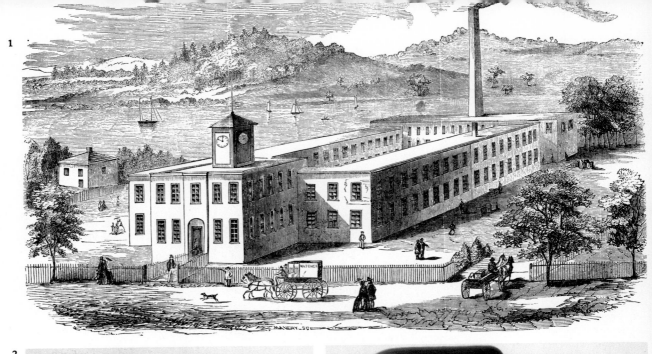

2

4

Manufacturing

With its watch factory (1) overlooking the Charles, Waltham was famous for inexpensive watches, the first to be mass-produced; opposite is one of the first made in the town (2). Elias Howe, an apprentice to a Boston watchmaker, invented a sewing machine (3) in 1845. Soon a number of firms were manufacturing sewing machines, most of them infringing on Howe's patent. In 1856, by the time this view of the sales room of Hunt & Webster's sewing machine factory in Boston was engraved (4), Howe was receiving proper royalties from his invention. Almost everywhere that there was water power, as at Turner Falls (5), manufacturing plants sprang up. Ingenuity added value even to raw materials. Ways were found to cut Quincy granite into very large pieces, like the 105-ton piece of granite at right (6), destined to be shipped to New Orleans and made into a column for a new custom house.

Stone quarried at
Quincy Mass. for a
Column in Doric Style — contract
with the New Custom House n New Orleans
34.7 x 8.8 x 8.8

J.h.Whea
Oct. 18.

Industrial Might

The census of 1850 reported that Massachusetts, with less than one-twentieth of the nation's population, contributed one-seventh of the wealth gained from industry. The most important industry in the state was the manufacture of boots and shoes, with Lynn, the greatest center, turning out more than nine million pairs a year. In 1860 there was a great shoe workers' strike in Lynn. Women workers paraded (1); a rally was held in Central Square (2) in front of the railroad crossing; and the workrooms (3), many of them in small two-story wooden structures that resembled houses, were all but deserted. Heavy industry played a large part in the economy. An ambrotype dating from around 1860 shows workmen inside a railroad shop in South Framingham (4). The Lazell, Perkins and Company Iron Works at Bridgewater (5), with its twenty-eight buildings, rolling mills, forges, iron and brass foundry, and machine shops, was the largest ironworks in New England.

1 2

3

204

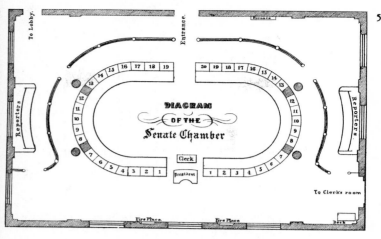

During the decades before the Civil War, Massachusetts politics, like those of the nation itself, were dominated by the brilliant lawyer Daniel Webster (1), who served as senator and secretary of state. A painting depicting his famous Senate speech defending the Union against the voices urging the secession of southern states now hangs in Faneuil Hall (2). Webster's only equal as an orator in Massachusetts was Edward Everett (3), who, like Webster, served both as senator and as secretary of state. Everett was so much in demand as an orator that when Lincoln delivered the Gettysburg Address, it was he, not the president, who was featured as the main speaker of the day. At left below, Everett is shown addressing the New York state assembly (4). A diagram above shows the floor plan of the Massachusetts senate chamber (5). The oval lithograph below (6) portrays the members of the state senate in 1856.

Abolition

Investors, and textile merchants and workers throughout the state, wanted to maintain good relations with the cotton producers of the South, but a small band of abolitionists, led by William Lloyd Garrison (1), battled unceasingly against slavery. In 1831 Garrison, a native of Newburyport and a printer by trade, established a newspaper, *The Liberator* (2), to give voice to his views. One of his most important allies was Wendell Phillips, whose father had been mayor of Boston; Phillips is shown speaking before an antislavery meeting on Boston Common (3). Gradually antislavery sentiment increased in Massachusetts; rallies were held (4) to fight against the admission of more slave states into the Union; and a vehement spokesman against slavery, Charles Sumner (5), entered the Senate in 1851. Feeling against the abolitionists was still so strong, though, that a few years before the Civil War, an antislavery meeting in Boston ended in a riot (6).

RALLY

SPIRITS OF '76!

ALL CITIZENS OF

LEOMINSTER,

without distinction of party, who disapprove of the

"Nebraska Iniquity,"

are requested to meet at the

TOWN HALL,

Monday Evening, July 10th,

AT 7 O'CLOCK,

to choose delegates to meet in a

Mass Convention,

at Worcester, the 20th inst., to teach the "South" we have a "North," and will maintain our CON-STITUTIONAL RIGHTS.

CALEB C. FIELD, LEONARD BURRAGE,
MERRITT WOOD.

Leominster, July 8, 1854.

The Civil War

Massachusetts, whose strong abolitionist movement had helped bring on the Civil War, played an important role once the war began. The state militia, seen parading near Concord in 1859 (1), quickly joined what Governor John A. Andrew called "the great and necessary struggle." Massachusetts volunteers heading south were greeted with cheers along the way; the reception shown below took place at Jersey City (2). But at Baltimore one regiment was attacked by a mob of southern sympathizers who killed four men and wounded thirty-six (3). After the excitement of the war's beginning had worn off, recruiting offices (4) had to be set up to attract men into the army and bounties had to be given for enlistment. Manufacturers and suppliers in the state, like the Rubber Clothing Company (5), provided war materiel. Often this was shoddy. One local manufacturer put paper soles on soldiers' shoes.

1776 LIBERTY   1861 UNION

MASSACHUSETTS VOLUNTEERS

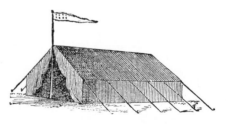

Fighting the War

In Haverhill, a newspaper editor who sympathized with the South was tarred and feathered by a mob (1). There were riots against the draft in Boston. But most people worked on behalf of the northern cause. The Boston artist Winslow Homer, whose work provides a vivid picture of the Civil War, traveled out to Watertown to sketch workers filling cartridges at the town's arsenal (2). Within the state, far from the battlefields, life was peaceful; this tranquil painting of Salem Common (3) was done in the year of Gettysburg. Massachusetts contributed more than soldiers to the cause. Governor John A. Andrew (4) was a stalwart advocate of black rights and a decisive and effective war governor. Clara Barton (5), born in Oxford and later the founder of the American Red Cross, worked tirelessly to aid soldiers in the field and, after the war, oversaw a program to search for missing soldiers.

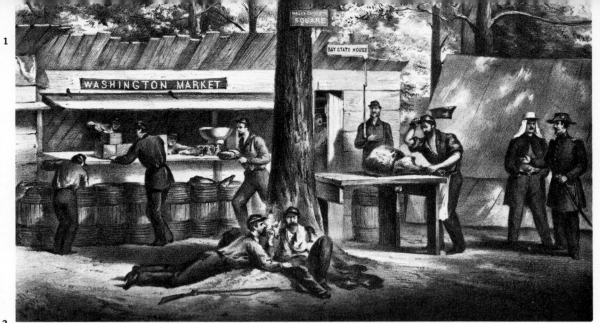

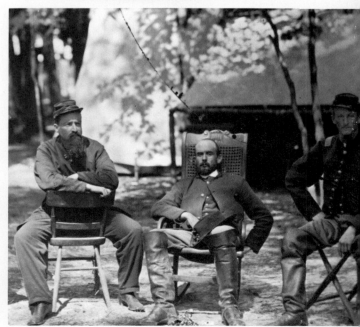

214

The Grand Army

Soldiers were supposed to be well supplied with decent clothing and wholesome food from a well-stocked commissary, like that of the Sixth Massachusetts Regiment (1). Yet there were often serious shortages. The First Massachusetts Regiment, shown charging the enemy (2), had ragged uniforms even before they went into battle. Nevertheless Massachusetts men fought zealously and suffered relatively high losses. Among their officers—and casualties—were Colonel Paul Revere (3), a descendant of the patriot, who was killed at Gettysburg, and Colonel Robert Gould Shaw (4), the commander of one of the state's two black infantry regiments. Charles Francis Adams, Jr., John Adams's great-grandson, is seen opposite at center, along with other cavalry officers (5). At right is General Ben Butler (6), a controversial, high-living politician from Lowell who later became governor. Casualties were particularly severe in infantry regiments. One was Captain Christopher Hastings of Berlin, whose military funeral took place in September 1863 (7).

HE WHO DIES SERVING HIS COUNTRY IN DEFENCE OF UNION AND LIBERTY LEAVES A GLORIOUS AND AN HONORED NAME.

ALL HONOR TO

OUR BRAVE DEAD

FUNERAL OF CAPTAIN C.S. HASTINGS. OF BERLIN SEPT 15TH 1863.

Around 1869, when the young Ohio writer William Dean Howells returned from a literary pilgrimage to Boston, he called on a friend. "I was beginning to speak of the famous poets I knew," Howells later wrote, when his friend stopped him. "He ran . . . and waved a wild arm of invitation to the neighbors. . . . 'Come over here,' he shouted. 'He's telling about Holmes, and Longfellow and Lowell and Whittier!' . . . Dim forms began to follow him up to his verandah. 'Now go on,' he called to me, when we were all seated. . . ." Massachusetts writers were revered throughout the country. Photographs show: the bearded Longfellow with Senator Charles Sumner (1); Howells himself, who settled in Boston (2); Whittier (3); Louisa May Alcott (4); Edward Everett Hale with Oliver Wendell Holmes, at right (5); the almost unknown Amherst poet Emily Dickinson (6); and a composite picture showing, left to right: Whittier, Holmes, Emerson, Motley, Bronson Alcott, Hawthorne, Lowell, Agassiz, and Longfellow (7).

The Landscape

1

2   3

218

The marshes, the hills, the rivers, the coastline, all fascinated Americans in an age when cities were beginning to expand. The nature worship of Thoreau and Emerson found an echo in the work of painters who depicted the varied scenery of Massachusetts in the closely detailed style that they and their patrons found so appealing in the second half of the nineteenth century. The Newburyport marshes (1) along the Merrimack were painted by Martin J. Heade; similar marshes beside the Mystic in Medford (2) were painted by George Loring Brown. The Neponset River with the Blue Hills in the distance (3) was painted by Benjamin Smith Rotch. Thomas Doughty, who taught art for some years in Boston, depicted the lighthouse at Nantasket Beach (4). The popular landscape artist John Frederick Kensett painted a scenic waterfall in the Taconic Mountains in Massachusetts's southwest corner (5).

5

Working People

In 1875 there were some 266,000 people employed in manufacturing in Massachusetts. The great majority of these were millhands laboring in the factories of North Adams (1), Brockton, Taunton, Lowell, and the other mill towns. In 1868 Winslow Homer depicted a throng of such millworkers leaving the Washington Mills in Lawrence at "bell time" (2). During the post–Civil War period, immigration changed the character of the work force from primarily Yankee to Irish, German, and French Canadian. The work was tedious and the hours long, but laborers could still turn out for a baseball game, as the employees of a company in Readville are shown doing in an 1869 pencil drawing (3). That same year, a broadside (4) was circulated in Fall River in the form of a petition to President Ulysses S. Grant, urging him to back national legislation establishing a shorter work week for cotton and woolen goods workers. The petition demanded a fifty-five-hour work week, ten hours on weekdays and five on Saturdays.

A FACTORY OPERATIVE'S
APPEAL,

To the President of the United States.

Respectfully dedicated to all our Fellow Operatives engaged in the manufacture of Cotton and Woolen Goods throughout the Union.

BY WILLIAM FORSTER,

OF FALL RIVER, MASS.

To thee, O Grant, who art our Nation's pride, laying mercenary thoughts aside, we wish to honor thee, and therefore pray, God give thee tuition to recommend the conditions to our Constitution, guaranteeing to every citizen throughout our land, Freedom's fundamental institution.* Ope one night each week for six months in the year where they may meet and generate,† And preserve all pure, free government throughout our Union; making of it one vast communion; a brotherhood of man.‡ We pray for thee and them.

And, O Grant the Oath of Allegiance, needs amending. For if the citizen must be bound to fight and bleed, it is but just he should be bound to perform his political duties conscientiously, for the interests of the whole people, and especially the producing classes, as in themselves alone are elements that constitute the nation, therefore worthy the first consideration of all legislative bodies Local, State, or National; being the source whence all the wealth and power, and greatness is derived, direct or indirect. God make them wise, ere the propitious moment flies. We pray for thee and them.

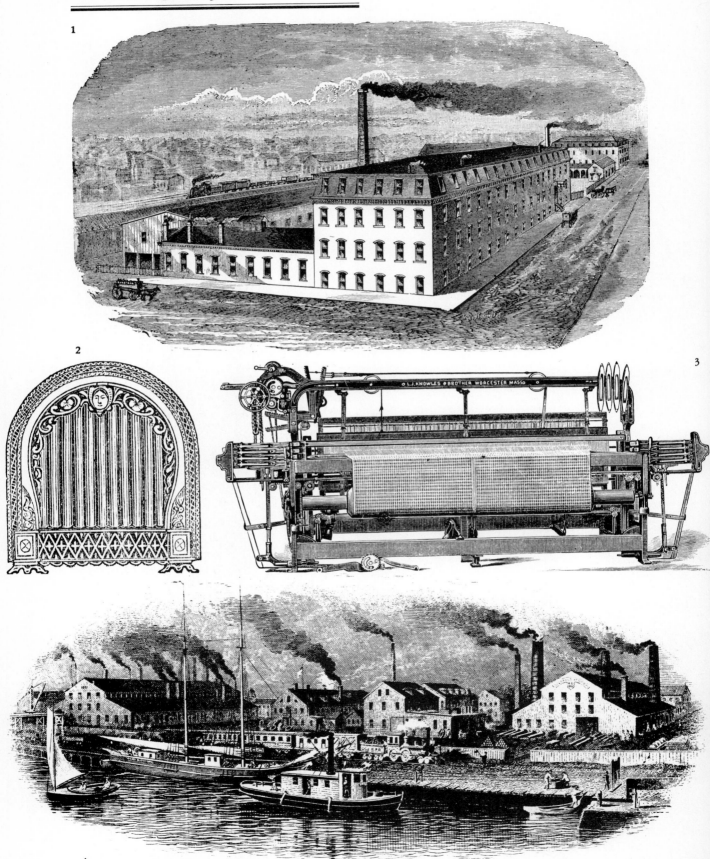

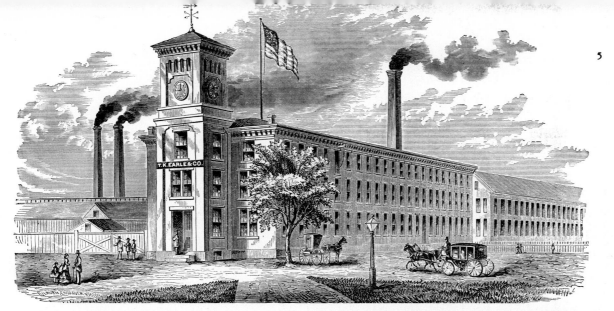

The Richardson Manufacturing Company of Worcester made farm machinery (1); S. E. Chubbuck and Son of Roxbury manufactured ornate steam heaters (2). Looms for "almost every kind of textile goods, whether of cotton, wool, or silk," were made by L. J. Knowles and Brother of Worcester (3), and immense steamship boilers were made at the South Boston Iron Works (4). Manufacturing burgeoned in the years after the Civil War. Boston and Worcester had the most diversified industries, but throughout the state there were hundreds of mills making everything from anchors to zinc. The textile industry played a predominant role. The T. K. Earle Company (5) of Worcester manufactured textile machinery. In 1876 Lawrence's Pacific Mills produced cloth commemorating the centennial of American independence (6). The Nonotuck Silk Company had offices in Boston and other American cities, and a factory in the town of Florence near Northampton (7).

Expanding Railroads

1

WHITTEMORE

WALD

2

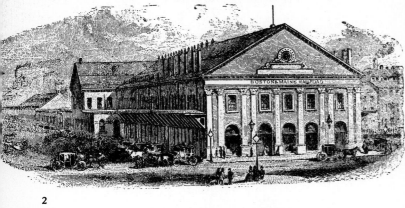

3

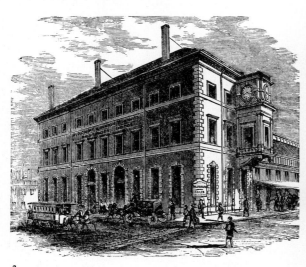

Worcester, with its impressive Union Station (1), was the focus of several railroads; but Boston was New England's major transportation center. From the Boston and Maine Depot (2) vacationers left for Maine and the White Mountains. Travelers to Cape Cod departed from the Old Colony Railroad terminal (3). Both lines served major industrial centers along the way. In 1851 a celebration (4) marked the extension of rail service to Canada and the Great Lakes, which, it was hoped, would bring great prosperity to Boston. The route to the West was improved by the construction of the Hoosac Tunnel (5) near North Adams. After the Civil War, the most comfortable route to New York was by way of the famous boats of the Fall River Line, such as the *Bristol* (6), run by the Old Colony Railroad.

1

2

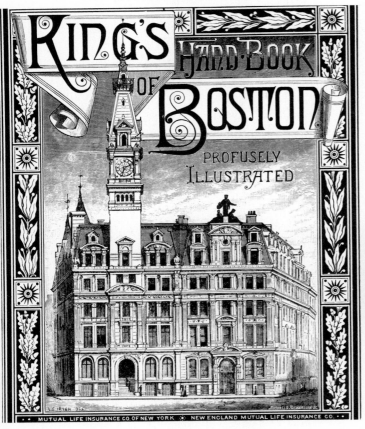

3

4

At first Boston's wealth came from trade and land speculation. Later it came from manufacturing. But the greatest wealth came from money itself, in the banks and insurance companies that proliferated as the nineteenth century advanced. This money, carefully invested, made Boston enormously rich. The Maverick National Bank (1) was one of the numerous banks clustered in downtown Boston. Nearby were the fine new buildings of Equitable Life (2) and the neighboring Mutual Life and New England Mutual (3). Boston business leaders moved easily between the worlds of finance and public service. Typical was Charles Francis Adams (4), the president of both the Union Pacific Railroad and the Massachusetts Historical Society. Financiers congregated at the Merchants' Exchange (5, 6), where they could check stock prices and confer with each other.

6

1

2

3

Down on the Farm

Although Massachusetts was highly industrialized, thousands of flourishing farms remained. Farmers followed their traditional tasks, among them corn husking in autumn; the group shown at left (1) is in a Nantucket field. Massachusetts Agricultural College at Amherst (2), now the University of Massachusetts, was a leading center of agricultural education. Dairy products and fruit crops were mainstays of the state's agriculture. The Chenery stables at Belmont (3) housed Holstein cattle, the first ever imported to America. Even out-of-state farmers bought plants and fertilizer from the advertisements of the Boston dealer George Davenport (4). The cranberry crop was important, as it still is, on Cape Cod and in Plymouth County. An 1875 engraving (5) shows sunbonneted girls picking and sorting cranberries in a Cape Cod bog.

Casks of whale oil could still be seen lined up on the wharves of New Bedford in 1868 when this photograph was taken (1), but the market for whale oil was disappearing, and gas lights (2) increasingly came to be used for household lighting. Fishing continued to be an important industry, however. An 1874 engraving (3) shows fish spread out on racks at Marblehead to be dried. Gloucester was even more important than Marblehead as a fishing port. Winslow Homer's picture of shipbuilding at Gloucester Harbor (4) appeared in *Harper's Weekly* in 1873. The artist Fitzhugh Lane was born in Gloucester and spent most of his life there. His serene view of Gloucester Harbor (5) now hangs in the Boston Museum of Fine Arts.

231

MACULLAR, WILLIAMS & PARKER

The Boston Fire

The great fire of 1872 burned down 776 buildings in the city of Boston and destroyed an entire district between Washington Street and the harbor (1). Guards, shown at the bottom of the picture at upper left, had to be called out to protect ruined stores from looters. Fire engines (2) came from all over the city and suburbs. Part of a stereoscopic view (3) shows the spot where the fire started at the corner of Summer and Kingston streets. Only a few months before, the city had proudly celebrated its second great Peace Jubilee; a ticket for the Jubilee (4) shows an enthroned figure representing music and peace. One factor contributing to the spread of the fire was the age of the water mains in the burned district. After the fire, modern mains were laid down carrying water from a new reservoir at Chestnut Hill, one of a chain of reservoirs around Boston. The various waterworks are shown in an illustration (5) dating from around 1878.

4

5

1

2

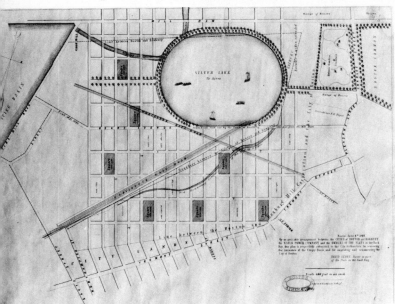

Boston's Public Garden (1), visible from the steeple of the Arlington Street Church, had been set aside in 1824 on the edge of the muddy and often smelly Back Bay where the Charles's tidal waters rose and fell twice each day. There were many plans for draining and filling "inodorous" Back Bay. The plan shown at left (2) dates from 1849. Work finally got under way in 1858. With the aid of a newly invented digging machine called a steam shovel manufactured in South Boston, gravel for land fill was excavated in Needham (3) and transported to its destination along railroad lines that conveniently crossed the Back Bay. Soon handsome brick and stone houses were being built along Commonwealth Avenue (4) and other Back Bay streets. By the end of the century, the Back Bay was completely built up (5).

3

4

5

1

2

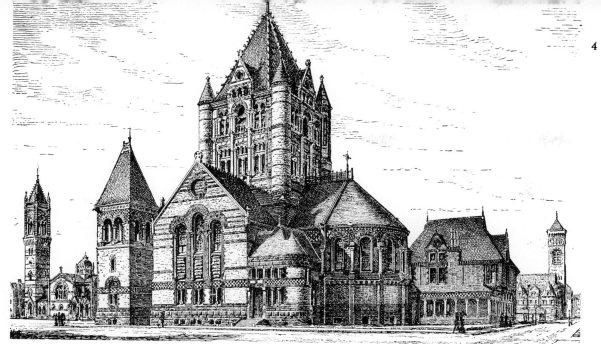

4

5

6

"Without exaggeration, it can be said that no city in the country presents a finer or more substantial class of buildings," a guidebook to Boston proclaimed in 1878. Engravings from the book show some of the structures of which Bostonians were so proud. The Post Office and Subtreasury Building (1) and the City Hall (2) were both built in the popular French Renaissance style. Two splendid new churches adorned Copley Square: the New Old South Church (3) and the monumental Trinity Church (4), designed by a great architect, H. H. Richardson, and led by a great preacher, Phillips Brooks. The Museum of Fine Arts (5) also overlooked the square, although not as grandly as in the illustration; portions of the building shown topped by towers were planned but never built. Within the museum, the Lawrence Room (6) displayed old paneling, armor, and furniture.

1

PROFESSOR BELL'S LECTURE AND DEMONSTRATION IN LYCEUM HALL, SALEM, MASS.

DIRECT
Intermittent

REVERSED
Intermittent

Pulsatory

Pulsatory

Undulatory

Undulatory

Undulations made by the Telephone

SPEAKING THROUGH A MAN'S BODY.

BLACKBOARD EXHIBITED AT THE SALEM LECTURE.

PROFESSOR BELL TEACHING A DEAF MUTE TO SPEAK.

A SCENE AT PROFESSOR BELL'S EXPERIMENTING ROOM, NO. 5 EXETER STREET, BOSTON.

The Telephone

With a pioneering institute established in Northampton to teach the deaf to speak and a public school for the deaf in Boston opened in 1869, Massachusetts led the nation in work with people unable to hear. One of the state's foremost teachers of the deaf, Alexander Graham Bell, experimented with electrical hearing aids and, out of his experiments, invented the telephone. In March 1876, the first telephone message was transmitted in Bell's workrooms in Boston and a few months later, at a demonstration in Salem, a telephone call was made all the way to Boston (1). The garret on Court Street, Boston, where Bell did his work is above (2), along with the first telephone (3) and the switchboard (4) used in the first telephone exchange, opened in Boston in May 1877. Within a few years switchboards became much more elaborate, as can be seen from the one at right (5), which was photographed in Worcester in 1896.

The Bicycle

Under the hands—and feet—of an ordinary person, the bicycle, a revolutionary new invention, could outdistance a horse. A Boston-born manufacturer, Albert A. Pope, saw the potential popularity of bicycles and began manufacturing them (1). In Boston he maintained a practice room (2), where even the most timid could be taught to ride. Pope promoted interest in bicycling by sponsoring races, including a four-day world championship bicycle race in Boston in 1879. The beginning of the race is shown at left (3). At right, the League of American Wheelmen, a bicycling group, parades along Columbus Avenue, Boston, in 1881 (4). At a bicycle tournament which took place at Hampden Park in Springfield two years later, an ingenious tricycle for the entire family was displayed (5).

1

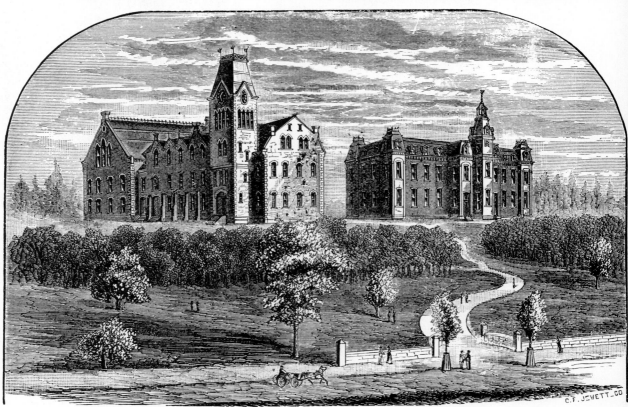

2

3

5

4

6

The second half of the nineteenth century witnessed the expansion of established colleges and the founding of new ones. In 1865 Holy Cross (1) was granted the power to confer "such degrees as are conferred by any college in the Commonwealth except medical degrees." Nearby, the Worcester County Free Institute of Industrial Science (2) opened its doors in 1868; it is now known as Worcester Polytechnic Institute. More attention began to be paid to the education of women. Mount Holyoke had been in operation since 1837; a zoology laboratory there is shown above (3). Wellesley (4) was founded in 1875 and Smith in 1871. Boston College was established in 1860, Boston University in 1869, and in 1866, M.I.T. moved to a new home in the Back Bay (5). At Amherst (6) many new buildings were constructed, including a Gothic-style chapel—Stearns Chapel, seen at left—and massive Walker Hall at right.

1

2

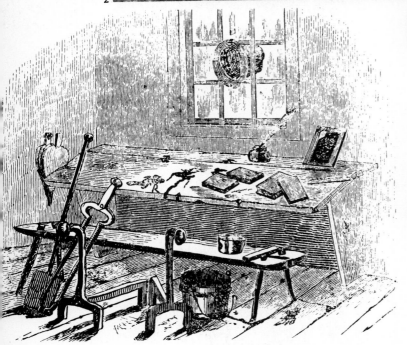

3

HOLBROOK SCHOOL APPARATUS.

G. B. GLADWIN.

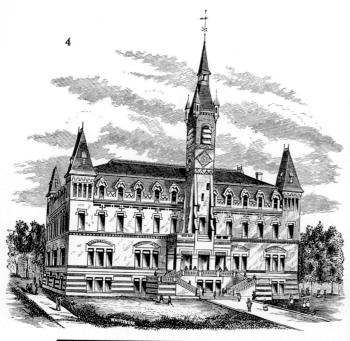

One-room schoolhouses survived in rural regions. Opposite, children pose in front of one at Province-town (1). But as the nineteenth century progressed, there was increasing emphasis on improving old schools and building new ones. A book published in Worcester in 1861 shows the equipment of an old-fashioned school (2) and of an up-to-date school, well supplied with apparatus for teaching science (3). In 1870 Worcester built a high school with room for five hundred pupils (4). New schools were constructed to accommodate children unwilling, for social or religious reasons, to attend the public schools. At right is the chapel of Groton School (5), a boarding school for the sons of the rich. Below is a parochial school (6) built by parishioners of Brighton's St. Columb-kille's Church.

A New Harvard

1

2

3

4

Under the leadership of Charles W. Eliot (1), who became its president in 1869, Harvard changed from a provincial seat of learning to one of the world's major centers of scholarship. A graduate school was established, the law and medical schools were improved, and the divinity school came to stress original scholarship rather than the training of ministers. New buildings were constructed in and around Harvard Yard (2). Notable among them was Memorial Hall, just north of the Yard; it contained a dining room (3) and Sanders' Theater (4) where concerts and important lectures were given. In 1886 Harvard celebrated its two hundred and fiftieth anniversary. A contemporary magazine illustration (5) shows two dignitaries entering Harvard Yard for the celebration: Governor George D. Robinson of Massachusetts and President Grover Cleveland, who is acknowledging cheers by doffing his hat.

5

Literature and Learning

1

man and politician in New York State.

22. Dr. John I. Brown, the oldest apothecary in Boston, died aged 92. He carried on the business on Washington street, about 70 years.

28. Mr. Gladstone, in the British House of Commons, stated that the cost of the war in Egypt was estimated at £3,500,000.

28. Dr. Oliver Wendell Holmes, who had been a professor in Harvard Medical School for many years delivered his farewell lecture.

29. Rev. Jacob M. Manning, D.D., pastor of the Old South Church, Boston, for about twenty-five years, died at Portland, Me., aged 59.

30. National and State Thanksgiving was observed in the usual manner.

was elected mayor of Boston. Also a majority of democratic city councilmen.

14. George W. Simmons, the founder of Oak Hall Clothing Store died aged 70.

14. The 8th annual gathering of the Veteran Odd Fellows Association of Massachusetts, was held at Odd Fellows Hall, Boston.

14. The annual re-union of the Boston Wesleyan University Club was held at Hotel Vendome.

14. The annual meeting of the Civil Service Reform Association of Boston, was held to-day.

15. A fire at Toledo, Ohio, caused a loss of $500,000.

17. John G. Whittier, the poet, completed the 75th year of his age.

18. Henry James, Sr., philosopher and author, died at Cambridge, aged 71.

3

Although Massachusetts was no longer the center of the nation's intellectual life after the Civil War, both literature and learning continued to flourish. In November 1882, as the contemporary chronicle at upper left shows (1), both Holmes and Whittier were still active; that same month the philosopher Henry James, Sr., died in Cambridge. The historian Henry Adams (2) and the philosopher William James (3) were notable Harvard professors in the 1870s. The Boston Public Library, whose reading room is below (4), had become the nation's second largest library by the 1880s. A new Museum of Natural History (5) was constructed in the Back Bay, and in Cambridge the scientific community could boast of two famous biologists, Louis Agassiz (6) and the botanist Asa Gray (7).

4

7

1

2

With its book and newspaper publishers, its dozens of printers, and dealers in printers' ink, type, and printing machinery, Boston was, after the Civil War, a major center of the printing industry, which still plays an important part in the Massachusetts economy. The lithographer Louis Prang did not have far to go to find models for his instructional lithograph (1) showing how printers work, selecting type and making plates ready for letterpress printing. The center of Boston's literary world was the Old Corner Bookstore on Washington Street (2), an early eighteenth-century house which had been a bookstore since 1828. Nearby was the publishing and bookselling firm Little, Brown, & Company (3) which traced its ancestry back to a bookstore established in 1784. The Riverside Press in Cambridge (4) was one of the most important printing establishments in the nation.

Printing and Selling Books

3

4

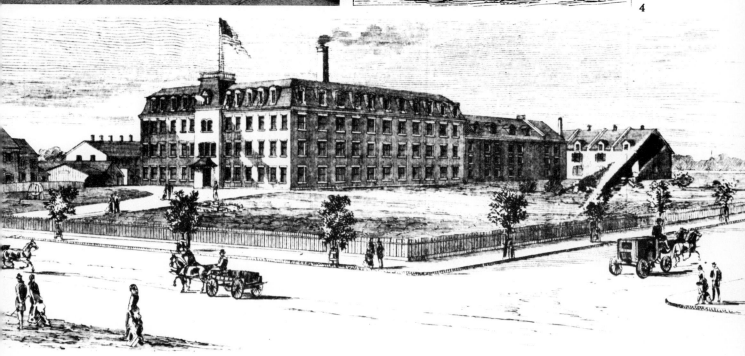

1

2

4

5

As Massachusetts's importance in American life diminished, its reputation swelled. Artists and writers, celebrating its past, established a glorious image of the state's history that came to pervade American thinking. Generations of schoolchildren learned about the midnight ride of Paul Revere and looked up to see, on the classroom wall, a copy of George F. Boughton's 1867 painting, *Pilgrims Going to Church* (1). Oliver Wendell Holmes's famous poem, *Old Ironsides,* inspired children throughout the nation to contribute their pennies to preserve the U.S.S. *Constitution* (2). For the centennial of the battle of Lexington and Concord, the young, unknown sculptor Daniel Chester French made a statue that came to symbolize the American soldier, the Minute Man (4), commemorating the embattled farmers who, Emerson wrote, "fired the shot heard round the world." Massachusetts, abetted by the rest of the nation, had begun its impassioned and sometimes obsessive love affair with its own past. As part of that phenomenon, the New England Historic–Genealogical Society purchased a substantial building (3) for its headquarters in 1870, and in 1897 a memorial (5) commemorating the famous Civil War soldier Robert Gould Shaw was dedicated on Boston Common. A year later, Faneuil Hall, whose interior is shown at right (6), was reconstructed for posterity, with iron, steel, and stone replacing inflammable wood.

6

1

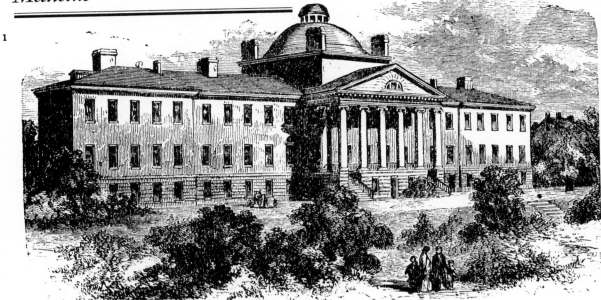

2

3

4

5

Inoculation against smallpox had been introduced to Boston quite early, and during the Revolution there was a course of medical study in which students worked on soldiers' corpses. But it was the incorporation of the Massachusetts General Hospital (1) in 1811 that would seal Boston's renown as a medical center. By 1880, the city's other medical institutions which had evolved around the hospital included the Charitable Eye and Ear Infirmary (2), the City Hospital (3), Boston University School of Medicine (4), Harvard Medical School (5), and the Children's Hospital (6). Ether had been introduced to Boston in 1846, and the distinguished Boston dentist Dr. J. R. Dillingham (who was the editor of a trade journal called, appropriately enough, *The Dental Mirror*) promised painless treatment through its use (7).

6

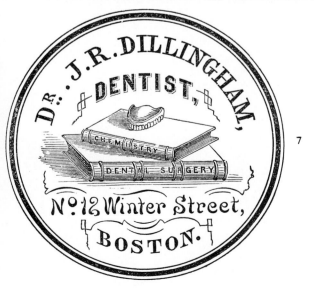

7

Dr. J. R. DILLINGHAM, DENTIST,
CHEMISTRY
DENTAL SURGERY
No. 12 Winter Street,
BOSTON.

1

2

3

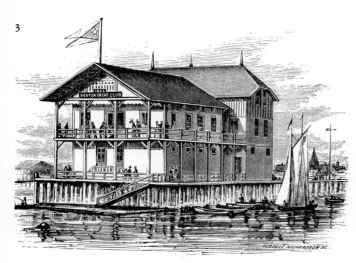

4

Although young ladies were supposed to suppress their animal energies in the nineteenth century, Mount Holyoke College girls (1) attended calisthenics classes where they worked out with dumbbells and rings. At Lake Quinsigamond, the Worcester Natural History Society established a summer camp in 1885 (2) at which boys could learn to build canoes, birdwatch, go on nature walks, and hear lectures on "the breeding habits of birds" and "hygiene of the mind." In Boston there were ample opportunities for recreation. The Boston Yacht Club building stood at City Point in South Boston (3); on snowy days, boys coasted on the Common (4) as they had for centuries; members of the Boston Athletic Club worked out in a well-equipped gymnasium(5). Tennis was introduced to the United States in 1874, and the first tournament was played in Nahant two years later. Below, Mount Holyoke girls are shown playing the new game(6).

5

6

Sporting Types

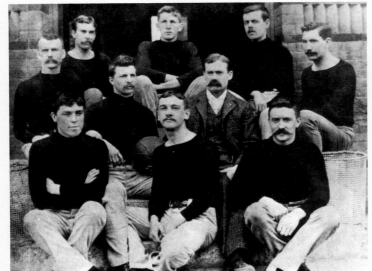

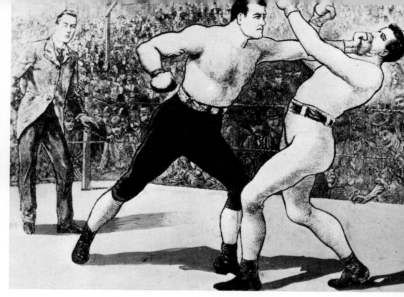

4

The Boston Baseball Club, with its characteristic red stockings, was formed as early as 1871. At the other end of the state, at American International College in Springfield, a new sport, basketball, was invented. The sport's first team is shown here (1), along with Holy Cross's 1877 baseball team (2), and a women's gymnastic group at Smith (3). The great boxer John L. Sullivan was born in Boston and got his start doing exhibition boxing in a Boston theater in 1877, taking on all comers, promising $25.00 to anyone who could last one round against him. When he won the national championship in 1882, he became the idol of Boston. Above (4) he is shown, a decade later, losing the championship to James Corbett. Another, though less famous, idol was the baseball player Mike Kelly (5). Below (6) is a group of athletic heroes: the baseball team known to fans of an earlier generation as the Boston Braves.

Good Food

In the 1880s Worcester could boast of a fine confectionery shop selling Viennese-style sweets. Among Boston's hundreds of dining places were French, Italian, and German restaurants. The food distribution center for much of New England was the Quincy Market (1) in Boston; neighboring streets were clogged with wagons carrying supplies for grocers and restaurants. Fellner's Old Elm Restaurant (2) on Tremont Street, Boston, featured German-style food and sold beer at ten cents a mug in 1892. The decoration on an 1884 menu from the Hotel Brunswick in Boston (3) seemed to promise a medieval banquet, and the hotel's guests could dine on soufflé of goose livers or croquette of game. The Parker House Hotel (4) was famous for its fine French restaurant and wine cellar; and the S. S. Pierce Company (5) provided Bostonians with fine candy and other foods. Ober's restaurant—still in operation under the name of Locke-Ober—proudly advertised its wine cellar (6).

1   2

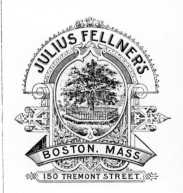

260

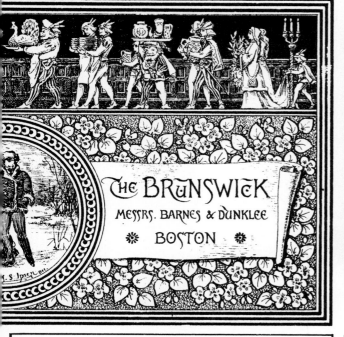

A Tradition of Good Music

The Boston Symphony Orchestra, one of the world's great orchestras, owes its founding in 1881 to the philanthropist Henry Lee Higginson (1), who imported musicians from Europe and paid them out of his own pocket. Annually the Symphony treated Boston to a full schedule of twenty-four programs. At lower left is the ornate cover of the program for the ninth season (2). At first the orchestra played at the Music Hall, a concert hall that was also used for dog shows and wrestling matches. The building of Symphony Hall (3) was begun in 1900. Higginson's chief aide in bringing European musicians to Boston was the conductor Wilhelm Gericke (4). One of Gericke's most notable successors was Karl Muck (5), who was forced to leave Boston during World War I because of anti-German sentiment. The New England Conservatory of Music (6) had been established in 1867 and in a few years became one of the country's foremost music schools.

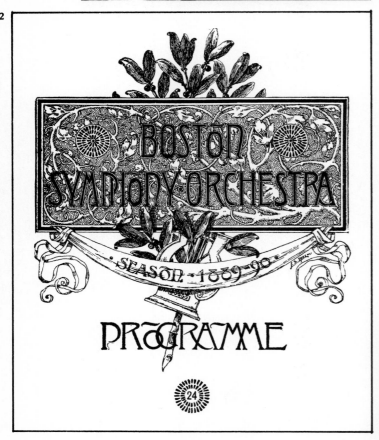

4

5

6

263

1

2

3

4

Entertainment

With the waning of the Puritan tradition, theaters began to open in Boston. By the middle of the nineteenth century several fine large theaters had been constructed. The Grand Museum in the South End (1) was advertising a performance of *Rip Van Winkle* when this photograph was taken around the end of the nineteenth century. Programs of the Hollis Street Theatre, showing the stage (2), and the Boston Museum (3), date from the 1880s. The characters in a farce, *Skipped by the Light of the Moon,* appear in an illustration from an 1888 theater program (4); the play was so successful that it enjoyed runs in two Boston theaters within a few years. More sober entertainment was provided by a panorama of the battle of Gettysburg (5), exhibited for years in a South End building. Outside the big city people, like this New Bedford crowd photographed around the turn of the century (6), were entertained by traveling circuses.

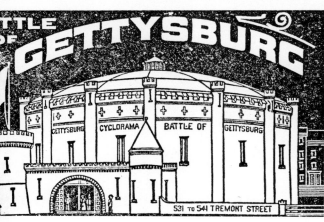

5

6

Faces of the Past

"Every description of photographs," the photographers advertised. "Colored, in the most artistic manner." Amateur photography was uncommon; people went to photographers' studios to sit for formal portraits. Most of the photographs on these pages date from the 1880s and were taken in Worcester. Several show members of the Smith family: a long-haired child named Chetwood Smith (1); J. L. Smith, a girl holding roses alongside a boy who may be her brother (3); and the same girl again (5) at the right with another girl. Both the distinguished-looking bearded man (6) and the elderly woman (8) were named Kinnicutt. Other pictures show three generations of one family (2); a boy named Ralph Williams (4); a mother and daughter named Clark (7); and a belle photographed in Worcester in 1895 (9).

2   3

Women's Lives

The vast majority of women spent their days at home, working hours at a cast-iron stove like that shown at left in "The Kitchen" (1), by the Boston lithographer Louis Prang. But there were many women who led less ordinary lives. Among them was Marie Zakrzewska (2), a Polish immigrant doctor who founded the New England Hospital for Women and Children, established the first nurses' training school in America, and fought for the admission of women to medical schools. Equally notable and even more controversial was Mary Baker Eddy (3), who is revered as the founder of the Christian Science church. Oddly enough, probably the best-known Massachusetts woman of the period was a criminal—the Fall River murderer Lizzie Borden (4) who, as a verse about her says, "took an ax and gave her mother forty whacks." The cause of women's suffrage attracted many, and Boston and Cambridge were pioneers in giving women the vote in municipal elections. Below, Boston women vote in 1888 (5).

Beacon Hill and the Back Bay, Brookline and Milton in the winter and in the summer North Shore watering places such as Nahant (1) and the Masconomo Hotel in Magnolia (2) were the resorts of Boston's high society. Although far less ostentatious and far less rich than comparable society in New York, it was equally self-assured. At the Somerset Club (3), one of Boston's most important, members were involved in high finance, but they had an equal interest in public service and in learning. Oliver Wendell Holmes (4), the great Supreme Court Justice, and Abbott Lawrence Lowell (5), the president of Harvard, were as representative of Boston society as were the bankers and trustees of State Street. Much less typical was the adventurous sportswoman Eleonora Sears, who is shown in profile at lower right (6). Charities and institutions devoted to learning and the arts owed a great deal to the Boston Brahmins, although the eastern half of Massachusetts felt their usually benign influence far more than the western half did.

Isabella Stewart Gardner had a reputation as a showy, extravagant society woman who indulged herself by collecting paintings and building a Venetian-style palace on the Fenway in Boston where she could live like royalty. Actually Mrs. Gardner, whose portrait by John Singer Sargent is displayed in the Gothic Room of the Gardner Museum (1), was a brilliant patron of the arts, who knew which artists to sponsor, which experts to consult, and which paintings to buy. Her palace was always intended to be, as her will states, "a museum for the education and enjoyment of the public forever." The four-story-high great courtyard (2), at the palace's center, is surrounded by rooms displaying great works of art. John Lowell Gardner (3), Isabella's husband, shared his wife's interest in art. Her protégé Bernard Berenson (4), a Jewish immigrant to Boston, became, thanks to her, one of the greatest art scholars of the century. Among her favorite contemporary painters were Sargent (5) and James McNeill Whistler (6).

A Venetian Palace

3

2

5

4

6

1

2

Ayer's Hair=Vigor

Das Beste Haarwasser. Bewahrt die Schön-
heit, Stärke und Farbe des Haares.

In the 1880s Boston was the nation's second largest port of entry. In one year 58,000 foreigners arrived in the city. Many headed directly west; others stayed to settle. Pictures and relics from the period show the immigrants' varied origin. A sea chest painted by a Portuguese seaman depicts New Bedford (1). Below it is the Home for Scandinavian Sailors and Immigrants in East Boston (2). One section of Lowell was so crowded with French Canadians that it was known as Little Canada (3). A page from an 1884 Boston directory (4) shows the names of Chinese who established laundries throughout the city; the 1880 census listed 237 people of Asian descent in Massachusetts. Above is an advertisement from a German almanac published in Lowell (5). Below are Polish immigrants in Lowell around 1900 (6).

LAUNDRIES. 341

BARRETT & BROTHER, 52 Temple pl.
Blanding Lucy M. 96 Tyler
Bradley George E. 1253 Wash.
Brennan S. 85 Green
Callahan Mary Mrs. 185 Pleasant
CAMBRIDGE LAUNDRY, Soden st. Cambridgeport, Boston office, 385 Wash. (see p. 577)
Carr S. Mrs. 589 Main
Charley & Co. 478 Tremont
Charlie Sing, 1138 Washington
Charlie & Co. 33½ Howard
CHELSEA DYE HOUSE AND LAUNDRY, 12 Temple place
Chin Chung, 334 Hanover
Chin Toy, 6 City square, Chsn.
Chung Lee, 65 Shawmut av.
Chung Lee & Co. 49 Portland
City Laundry and Dye House, 98 Lenox, office 1 Avon
Dickson M. E. Miss, 48 Melrose
Dix M. S. & Co. 375 Tremont
Ferdinand E. F. 40 Charles
Flamand Jeann,26 and 49 Buckingham (French)
Fong Hang, 900 Washington
Glen Laundry, S.K.Poore, 160 Dudley
Graham Robert, Green, J. P.
GRIFFITH'S STEAM LAUNDRY, A. W. Griffith & Co. props. 154 Dudley
Groves Fergus O. 38 Hudson
Hadaway D. C. 140½ Court
Harkins Mary, 34 Fayette
Hi Loy, Castle, cor. Wash.
Hing Lee, 1068 Washington
Hing Wah, 136 Saratoga
Home Laundry, 1485 Wash.
Hong Lee, 365 Hanover
Hong Sing, 189 North
Hong Wah, 221 North
Hop Ching, 16 Meridian
Hop Hing, 136 Meridian
Hop Kee & Co. 817 Sumner, E. B.
Hop Lee, 39 Clark
Hop Long, 41 Howard
Hop Sing, 27 Howard
Hop Sing, 65½ Essex
Hop Wah, 126 Main
Hop Yuen, 39 Howard
Hugly Louise Miss, 38 Buckingham (French)
Joe S. 616 East Broadway
Joe Tang Gee, 450 W. Broadway
Kee Chong, 107½ Leverett
Kee Hain, 163 Main
Kee Hop King, 312 W. Fourth
Kee Horp, 50 Leverett
Kee Quong See, 585 Shawmut av.
Kee You, 184 West Eighth

Lee Sing, 12 Bulfinch
Lee Soe, 23 Union-park street
Lee Sooe, 1343 Tremont
Lee Wing, 361 Shawmut av.
Lee Yuen, 50 Beach
Ling Wong, 85 Bunker Hill
Loome R. 968 Tremont
Lum Ah, 231 W. Broadway
Lung Sam, 126 W. Canton
Lung Sam, 1013 Tremont
Lung Sang, 103 Cambridge
Lung Wah, 28 Derne
Martin O. H. 37 Edinboro'
McCabe Lizzie, 23 Chapman
McDonough M. Miss, 54 Fayette
McManus M.A.Mrs. r. 242 Hanover
Meskill Mary, 549 Dorch. ave.
Moon Lee, 336 Main
Murphy Catharine Mrs. 44 Bennington
Quong Chong, 343 Tremont
Quong Kee, 83 Meridian
Quong Lee, 27 La Grange
Quong Lung, 60 Shawmut av.
Quong Sing, 36 Bunker Hill
Quong Wing Chong, 113 Pleasant
RIVERSIDE STEAM LAUNDRY CO. 31 Beach
Rose C. H. & E. L. 75 Essex
Sam Chong, 56 East Canton
Sam Hing, 214 Hanover
Sam Kee & Co. 217 Shawmut ave.
Sam Lang, 304 Sumner, E. B.
Sam Lee, 168 Salem
Sam Lee, 55 Pleasant
Sam Lee, 379 Meridian
Sam Moy, 809 E. Fourth
Sam Sing, 136 Eliot
Sam Toy, 79 Prince
Sam Wah, 157 Eliot
Sam Wah Sing, 56 Eliot
Sam Wing, 105 Warren, Rox.
Sam Wing Kee, 329 Hanover
Sam Wing, & Co. 1268 Wash.
Sam Wo Long, 343 Meridian
Sang Sing, 5 Howard
Sargent's Steam Laundry, 1868 Washington
Scripture Isaac F. 291 Dorchester and 27½ Eliot
Scripture's SteamLaundry,75 Kilby
Sing Kee, 179 Hanover
Sing Lee, 110 Harrison avenue
Sing Lung, 134 Sumner, E. B.
Sing Soden, 291 Harrison av.
Sing Sun, 36 Main
Sing Wah, 163½ Shawmut av.
Sing Wah, 75 Cambridge
Sing Wing, 156 W. Broadway
Sing Wo, 558 Shawmut av.
Sing Yee, 6 Cross
Sing Yee, 132 W. Broadway

Italians and Jews

1

2

Migrations beginning in the 1880s brought to the state two groups that had an immense influence: Italians and East European Jews. Boston's North End (1), shown in an 1899 magazine illustration, became a center of Italian life. Immigrants in the district were introduced to Boston's good schools, like the classroom opposite in the kindergarten of the North End Industrial Home (2). In turn they impressed their own stamp on the area. An Italian cigar manufacturer and a Jewish tailor set up shop in Paul Revere's house in the North End (3). When the East European Jews arrived, German Jews were already well established. By 1893 the German Jewish temple Ohabei Shalom, now in Brookline, could issue a medallion (4) commemorating its fiftieth anniversary. In Boston many Jews settled in the West End (5); they read, in the year 1892, the recently established *Jewish Chronicle* (6).

Catholics

M·H·GERRITS
CLERICAL TAILOR
ST JOHN'S SEMINARY.
BRIGHTON, BOSTON, MASS.

As Boston's Catholic population grew, a new cathedral (1) was constructed. Among the foremost Catholic leaders was the poet John Boyle O'Reilly (2). Clergy were trained at St. John's Seminary (3) and at Holy Cross and Boston College. Most were Irish, like Father George Reardon (4) of Brighton, born in the Irish enclave of East Boston and serving mostly Irish parishioners at a church named after an Irish saint, Columbkille. A few were not: James A. Healy (5), Holy Cross's first graduate, was America's first black bishop. For decades William Henry Cardinal O'Connell (6) was religious leader of Boston's Catholics. Among social leaders were the wife and daughter of Mayor John F. Fitzgerald of Boston (7). Fitzgerald's daughter, at right, is better known as Rose Kennedy.

The Poor

In Boston's slums, like those of Hamburg Street in the South End (1), and in rundown wooden tenements in the mill towns, lived the poor, many of them immigrants or the children of immigrants. Most struggled to maintain family life, although the threat of unemployment or eviction hung over them; at left an 1893 magazine illustration shows a Boston family being evicted from its home (2). Institutions and societies were founded to aid the poor, with funds established for impoverished musicians, for aged women, for German immigrants, and for destitute Catholic children. In Boston tramps could take baths at the Wayfarer's Lodge in the North End (3). Poor young girls were taught the craft of making bouquets of dried flowers at Andover House (4), one of several settlement houses in the city.

There were 1,783,085 inhabitants of Massachusetts in 1880. Towns and cities, like the busy county seat of Dedham (1), had expanded mightily in the decades after the Civil War. Fine houses, like John Anderton's on Court Street, Chicopee Falls (2), appeared in every town, adorned with mansard roofs and carved decorations. A row of wooden houses in South Boston (3), although somewhat older than the 1873 Anderton House, also displays gingerbread carving. By 1880 apartment houses were common. Worcester's first substantial apartment block was the Salisbury Building, whose facade and floor plan are shown opposite (4, 5). At the turn of the century, thousands of wooden three-decker houses were built throughout the state, a form of mass housing characteristic of New England; the one shown here (6) is in South Boston. Larger municipal buildings were required. Opposite are Fall River's remodeled city hall (7) and Wellesley's new town hall (8), shown in a drawing made for its 1887 dedication ceremony.

1

2

3

6

7

8

Rapid Transit

1

3

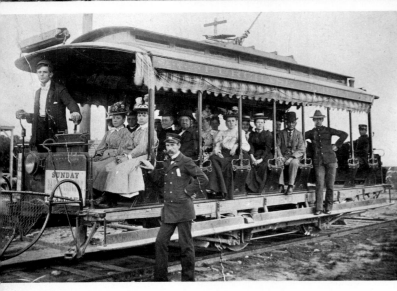

2

4

The growth of transportation made the growth of cities possible. Instead of living crowded in tenements close to work, people could dwell more comfortably in suburbs. Horse cars, such as those seen on page 174 carrying passengers from Boston out to Brookline, gave way to electric trolleys as the nineteenth century progressed. Opposite are trolleys traveling along Washington Street, Boston (1), and the open-sided trolley that took excursionists from New Bedford to Fort Rodman (2). At upper left is the junction of Main and Front streets in Worcester (3). By 1891 the Boston region had 245 miles of trolley track. But increasing congestion inspired the building of a subway, the nation's first. At left is an 1892 drawing of a proposed subway station with double-decker cars (4). Above is the entrance to the subway tunnel built at the edge of the Public Garden (5); below is an elevated section (6).

6

1

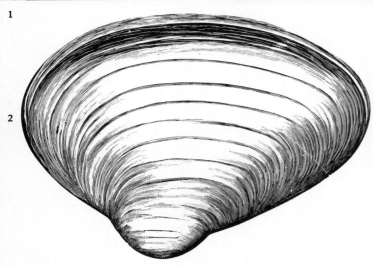

2

As the urban population grew and transportation improved, beach resorts sprang up near the big cities. In the 1890s Maurice Prendergast painted a group of women among the rocks at Beachmont (1). At Nantasket Beach, visitors could dine at the Ocean House for fifty cents on baked clams, chowder, bluefish, and perch; the clam shell at left is the back of the Ocean House menu (2). The most famous beach in America was the L Street Beach in South Boston, where nude bathing was the custom—as it still is—but the most popular was Revere Beach (3), the first beach ever to be set aside as a public park near a great city. Other seaside amusement places were scattered along the coast. One of the busiest was Lincoln Park in Dartmouth, near New Bedford, where this band was photographed around the turn of the century (4).

3

4

WING COTTAGE.
LAGOON HEIGHTS.

M. E. TABERNACLE.

STEAMBOAT LANDING & SEA VIEW HOUSE.

PROSPECT HOUSE.
LAGOON HEIGHTS.

BATHING SC

THE CASINO.

SEA VIEW AVENUE LOOKING SOUTH EAST.

W. F. YOUNG'S COTTAGE

CHRISTOPHER LOOK'S COTTAGE

SUMMER RESIDENCE OF
OF INDIAN

SUMMER RESIDENCE BUILT BY HON. OLIVER AMES,
EX GOV. OF MASSACHUSETTS.

Plans can be had at Boston Office
or of Real Estate Agents at Cottage City.
ESTIMATES OF
BUILDING AND FURNISHING COTTAGES
Can be had by applying to
Office, 53 State Street, Boston.

PLAT & ENVIRONS OF
LAGOON HEIGHT
COTTAGE CITY, MASS.
SHOWING
PROPERTY OWNED BY THE LAGOON HEIGHTS LAND CO., 53 STATE ST., BOSTON

610 EXCHANGE B

D. H. BAILEY & CO., ENG & LITH. BOSTON.

UNION TABERNACLE

SUMMER RESIDENCE OF HON. P.A. CORBIN AT NEW BRITAIN, CONN.

AGASSIZ SUMMER INSTITUTE.   HIGHLAND HOUSE.   PUMPING STATION.
(COTTAGE CITY WATER WORKS.)

DR. TUCKER'S COTTAGE.

NOT OWN A SUMMER COTTAGE
AT
LAGOON HEIGHTS,
Which is Acknowledged to be
E MOST CHARMING SPOT
ON THIS ISLAND OF THE SEA?

Island of the Sea

Soon after the Civil War a small town of gingerbread cottages sprang up on Martha's Vineyard around a Methodist camp meeting ground. The town, dignified with the name of Cottage City, soon outgrew its religious roots and became a full-fledged seaside resort, where even drinking was allowed. Excursion boats sailed to Cottage City from Providence, New Bedford, Boston, and from as far as Bridgeport in Connecticut. A trolley line was built, along with a casino and several hotels. Enterprising real estate developers purchased a large tract of land behind Cottage City, christened it Lagoon Heights, and laid it out ambitiously with streets, parks, and almost a thousand house plots. They advertised it as "the most charming spot on this island of the sea," but their advertisements did not bring in enough customers to put Lagoon Heights on the map. Indeed, even the name of Cottage City disappeared from the map. Today the town is called Oak Bluffs. A lithograph advertising Lagoon Heights shows building plots neatly laid out along broad avenues. Cottage City is at the right side of the picture and Vineyard Haven is at upper left beyond the lagoon. At the top and bottom are small pictures showing the sights of the region including, second from left at top, the Methodist Tabernacle that started it all.

1

1

2

Boston Common (1), shown in Childe Hassam's painting, was a busy city park in the last decades of the nineteenth century. The construction of a subway under it would require the cutting down of the fine row of elms on Tremont Street Mall. A painting of Copley Square (2), with Trinity Church at left, and the old Museum of Fine Arts at right, shows the trolleys that were omnipresent in Boston during the period. As the Back Bay was built up, many of the city's major institutions established their headquarters there or moved further out to the newly developed Fenway region. The downtown area, much of which had been destroyed by the great fire of 1872, became given over to tall office buildings constructed on sites where old dwellings and business premises had stood. The Ames Building (3), seen towering over the Old State House, was the first skyscraper in Boston.

3

CHARLES RIVER

At the Turn of the Century

A richly detailed lithograph provides a bird's-
eye view of Boston as it appeared in 1899. The
Common can be seen at left center and above it
the Charles, with the mud flats of Cambridge
beyond. The river had not yet been dammed; it

was still salty and affected by the tides. A complex network of railroad tracks funneled into the two new union terminals, North Station, visible at the upper right near the bridges connecting Boston to Charlestown, and South Station, at bottom, near the bridges to South Boston. Dozens of wharves ringed the harbor, but Boston's days as one of the world's greatest ports had almost come to an end.

When the Sacred Cod (1) which hangs in the State House was made in 1760, replacing an earlier carving, fishing was one of the state's major industries. The growth of manufacturing soon made it less important. Still, at the end of the nineteenth century, the Boston Fish Pier (2) and fish piers in other seaside towns brought in considerable wealth, as they still do. Around 1900 New Bedford whalers could still be photographed cutting into a sperm whale (3). The New Bedford fleet which annually sailed to the Arctic was caught in the ice at Herschel Island in 1894. The men of the fleet were painted playing football on the ice, at left, and baseball, at right (4). A minor sea-based industry, run by the Mashpee Indians, was making artificial pearls from the scales of alewives caught in the brooks of Cape Cod. Opposite, alewife pearls hang on a drying rack (5).

5

By around 1900 factories were moving out of small towns for the great industrial centers. Some factory towns—Melrose, Hanover, Hingham, Stoneham— became increasingly residential, while others, like North Adams (1), retained their character. Lynn had traditionally relied on shoe manufacturing. The shoe workers shown at upper right and opposite were photographed around 1895 inside a factory (2, 3) and leaving work (4). But with the growth of a great General Electric plant there, Lynn diversified. Textile cities were not so fortunate. As the center of American population and the markets moved farther away from New England, it became more difficult for Massachusetts textile producers to compete. Factories moved south, closer to the cotton and to the customers. The bitter Lawrence textile strike of 1912 (5) was just one episode in the long decline of the state's textile industry.

The Twilight of the Simple Life

By 1900 Massachusetts's population had grown to 2,500,000 and was increasingly concentrated in cities. But in small towns and in rural areas, and even in the medium sized cities, life went on much as it had for decades. Although the railroad had given the population mobility, the horse was still the main means of transportation. With its hitching posts and elms, County Street, New Bedford (1), was typical of hundreds of streets throughout the state—a dirt road on which the autumn leaves fell and remained undisturbed except by the wind and by the passing of an occasional horse and buggy. The peddler with his wagon on a road outside New Bedford(2), the farm in Marlborough (3), and the Nantucket woman (4), shown with her cow on one of the stereoscopic views that were so popular during the period, were typical of an era that would soon pass away.

The Automobile Age

The automobile revolutionized life in Massachusetts. It brought about a profound change in the landscape, fostering the growth of suburbs where there had been farmland or woods; it tied one end of the state to the other, enabling the Boston Symphony Orchestra to be as much at home in Tanglewood as in Boston. Charles and Frank Duryea of Springfield were the first to operate an American-made automobile with success. The car (1) ran along the streets of Springfield in September 1893. In 1896 the Duryeas' company was responsible for the first automobile sale ever made in America. By 1900 the Stevens-Duryea Company of Chicopee Falls was one of twelve automobile-manufacturing companies in the nation, along with another company in Newton which made a steam-operated car, the "Stanley Steamer." Advertisements for Stevens-Duryea cars in 1910 (2) and the 1920s (3) appear below. In 1906 a proud New Bedford group posed sitting in an automobile (4). A 1912 photograph of Revere Beach (5) shows, at right, an automobile which has been driven over the sands.

Stevens-Duryea

Model "Y," 40 H.P. Six-Cylinder Touring Car

VER ten years of continuous success account for every feature of Stevens-Duryea motor cars.

The principle of the Unit Power Plant supported on Three Points, of the Multiple Disc Clutch and the Six-Cylinder Motor, is inseparably woven around the Stevens-Duryea name. These alone would be irrefutable arguments for Stevens-Duryea preference. To them are added refinement of design, true comfort and positive durability.

1910

Stevens-Duryea Company, Chicopee Falls, Mass.
Licensed under Selden Patent.

Stevens-Duryea

"Nearly a Quarter Century of Leadership"

Stevens-Duryea Closed Cars have set a new standard of luxury, refinement and social distinction.

Limousines and Berlines, $5750 to $6200

Stevens-Duryea Company
Chicopee Falls Mass
"Pioneer Builders of American Sixes"

4
5

World War I

THE
UNITED
STATES
ARMY

ARMY RECRUITING STATION,
POST-OFFICE BUILDING,
LYNN, MASS.

OR
3 TREMONT ROW (SCOLLAY SQ.)
BOSTON, MASS.

PUBLIC LIBRARY

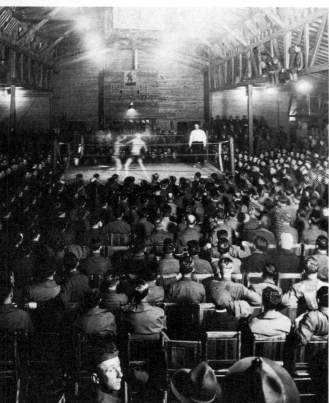

Even before the United States became involved in World War I, thousands of young men read recruiting brochures such as the one shown here (1) and joined up to defend America. In 1916, a "preparedness" parade marched along Beacon Street, Boston, before a reviewing stand set up in front of the State House (2). Not long afterward, a group of New Bedford draftees was photographed marching off to war, still dressed in civilian clothes (3). Draftees at Camp Devens amused themselves by watching a boxing match (4), an appropriately military display. With its China trade, its strong ties to England, and its high percentage of foreign-born citizens, Massachusetts had always had an international orientation; American involvement in the affairs of Europe did not require much adjustment for the people of the state. Nevertheless, after the war was over, sentiment against international entanglements was strong. Massachusetts's influential senator, Henry Cabot Lodge, shown in a caricature above (5), was successful in his battle to keep the country out of the League of Nations.

4

Coolidge and Curley

3

4

Calvin Coolidge's firm handling of the Boston Police Strike of 1919, when guards were posted to prevent looting (1), won him the vice presidency in 1920. When President Warren G. Harding died, Coolidge became president. Opposite are an official portrait of the president (2) and a museum model showing his wife Grace wearing her Inaugural Ball gown (3). James Michael Curley, shown at left with his son riding up Beacon Hill in a 1917 Evacuation Day parade (4), was a fixture in Massachusetts politics for decades. The crowds waiting in the rain (5) for his first inauguration as mayor of Boston in 1913 expected a reform mayor after the graft-ridden administration of John F. Fitzgerald, John Kennedy's grandfather. But during Curley's various terms as mayor and governor of Massachusetts, he freely spent the taxpayers' money on dubious projects. A 1924 cartoon (6), published when Curley was running for governor, shows him examining the State House.

THE MASSACHUSETTS SHOP
ALL KINDS OF POLITICAL GOODS

I GUESS I'LL TAKE IT!

CURLEY

FULLER

STATE HOUSE

GOVERNORSHIP 1924

"NORMAN"

6

5

305

1

2

The immigrant Boukis family posed for a portrait in 1917 (1). At right is Euterpe Boukis, the mother of the state's first governor of Greek descent, Michael Dukakis. Both sons, shown in the almost contemporary picture of a Jewish immigrant family, the Hyfers of Chelsea (2), became doctors; and when Abraham Kaplan (3), a Jewish peddler, was photographed before his Chelsea tenement house, his son was a student at Harvard. Dr. Varazted Kazanjian (4), an Armenian immigrant, became a noted professor at Harvard Dental School. Immigration slowed but did not stop in the 1920s. Below, Irish immigrants arrive in Boston in 1921 (5). Immigrants often met bitter hostility. It reached a climax when two Italians, Niccolo Sacco and Bartolomeo Vanzetti, were executed in 1927 for a crime they probably did not commit. Ben Shahn's satirical painting (6) shows them in coffins beneath the impassive gaze of establishment figures.

The Twenties

Boston's genteel literary tradition frowned on strong emotion and strong language; indeed books with language too strong were banned. Upton Sinclair is shown below (1) selling an expurgated copy of one such book, his novel *Oil*. In 1925 Boston was hit by a disaster unique in history, a great molasses flood more than twenty feet high, caused by the explosion of a storage tank; the flood (2) knocked down buildings and drowned twenty-one people. The decade was one of prosperity. College girls—the ones shown here are from Wellesley (3)—could afford fur coats. Boston's financial institutions prospered in the shadow of the city's tallest building, the Custom House Tower (4). But in textile towns the story was different. Between 1919 and 1935 textile production fell by one fourth in New Bedford. In Lawrence, where the Wood Worsted Mills (5) were located, the population dropped by more than ten percent between 1920 and 1940.

1

4

5

309

1

2

The hard times of the 1930s were felt throughout the state. Many farms were abandoned; the one shown above (1) is in Savoy near North Adams. City slums were crowded with the often jobless poor, like those portrayed by the painter Jack Levine in Boston's South End (2). Some jobs were provided by public works projects, including the building of the enormous Quabbin Reservoir (3). When the devastating hurricane of 1938 struck, it caused unprecedented damage, ruining houses and flooding streets, like this one in Ware (4). The decade saw a great revival of interest in Massachusetts's colonial heritage. New buildings, such as Lowell House at Harvard (5), were constructed in the colonial style. Notable houses throughout the state were photographed and measured as part of a government survey, and one, The Lindens of Danvers (6), was picked up in its entirety and reerected in Washington.

3

4

6

5

With German submarines prowling off the coast-line, with frequent air raid alerts, and with the entire population mobilized for the war effort, the Second World War had a profound effect on the Commonwealth. College campuses were requisitioned to train military men, and women. At upper left, Navy Waves march at the Smith College campus in Northampton (1). At the Gillette razor factory in South Boston (2), and in plants across the state, machines that had been used for civilian production were altered to make war materiel, and women were hired to run the machines. Foods were rationed. The blackboard at a Hood Milk dispatching center in Springfield

World War II

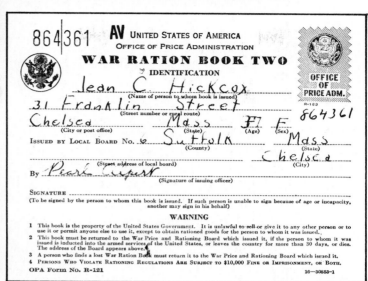

864|361 **AV** UNITED STATES OF AMERICA
OFFICE OF PRICE ADMINISTRATION

WAR RATION BOOK TWO

IDENTIFICATION

Jean C. Hickcox
(Name of person to whom book is issued)

31 Franklin Street
(Street number or rural route)

Chelsea   Mass   F F
(City or post office)   (State)   (Age) (Sex)

864361

ISSUED BY LOCAL BOARD NO. 6   Suffolk   Mass
(County)   (State)

Chelsea
(City)

By Pearl _____
(Signature of issuing officer)

SIGNATURE _____
(To be signed by the person to whom this book is issued. If such person is unable to sign because of age or incapacity,
another may sign in his behalf)

WARNING

1 This book is the property of the United States Government. It is unlawful to sell or give it to any other person or to use it or permit anyone else to use it, except to obtain rationed goods for the person to whom it was issued.
2 This book must be returned to the War Price and Rationing Board which issued it, if the person to whom it was issued is inducted into the armed services of the United States, or leaves the country for more than 30 days, or dies. The address of the Board appears above.
3 A person who finds a lost War Ration Book must return it to the War Price and Rationing Board which issued it.
4 PERSONS WHO VIOLATE RATIONING REGULATIONS ARE SUBJECT TO $10,000 FINE OR IMPRISONMENT, OR BOTH.

OPA Form No. R-121   16—30853-1

(3) listed, for the drivers' information, not only the price of butter but the number of ration stamps that had to be collected for each pound. Every civilian had a ration book; the one at upper right (4) belonged to a minister's wife in the city of Chelsea. The U.S.S. *Massachusetts* (5), a World War II battleship that saw action at Leyte Gulf, is now moored at Fall River. Postwar America was set on a continuing course of involvement abroad when General George C. Marshall, the Secretary of State, at right (6), announced the Marshall Plan to aid the economic recovery of Europe at a Harvard commencement in June 1947.

6

1

2

3

4

314

A Center of Modern Architecture

In towns where the highest structure had been a church steeple or a tall flagpole, lofty, modern apartment buildings rose after World War II, a result of the change in living styles and the increased population. Boston's traditional skyline, with the State House dome atop Beacon Hill and a few tall buildings reaching to the sky, became modified as numerous starkly designed skyscrapers rose in the downtown area and in the Back Bay (1), built in an international style that paid little attention to the city's own traditions. A few of the new structures, like the Christian Science Center (2) and the new Boston City Hall (3), were widely acclaimed as major works of modern architecture. Extraordinary buildings—among them the School of Design at Harvard (4)—rose on campuses throughout the state, and M.I.T., with its strong interest in architecture, constructed many particularly notable buildings. The once provincial center of Worcester could boast of a skyscraper (5) with glass that reflected the sky around it.

The Education Industry

In the post–World War II period, education, which had always played an important part in Massachusetts life, became one of the state's major industries, bringing economic benefits and an influx of young people, many of whom became permanent residents after graduation. At upper left, a Tufts student works in a chemistry laboratory (1); below her are two M.I.T. students with a model of an RNA molecule (2). With their need for new buildings, expanding universities stimulated the construction industry. At the University of Massachusetts (3), skyscrapers now dominate Amherst's once-rural landscape. The Rabb Graduate Center (4) was constructed at recently established Brandeis University. Along the Charles are the campuses of three universities: Boston University (5) on the Boston side, and in Cambridge, M.I.T. and Harvard (6).

3

4

5

6

John Kennedy

1

2

3

4

One sign that the great Irish Catholic immigration of the nineteenth century had been thoroughly assimilated came with the election of John F. Kennedy (1) to the presidency in 1960. Kennedy's enthusiastic welcome at the 1960 Democratic Convention (2) was echoed by the country as a whole once a close election against Richard Nixon and another Massachusetts man, Henry Cabot Lodge (3), had been won. His inauguration (4) seemed to bring new youth to the country. Kennedy and his wife, Jacqueline—a museum model shows her in her Inaugural Ball gown (5) —were young and appealing. Their presence in the White House, their optimism and energy— and their warmth toward Harvard professors, artists, and stars such as the world champion Boston Celtics shown below in the White House in 1963 (6), lifted national spirits. Before the luster could wear off, John Kennedy was assassinated in 1963.

The Alternate Culture

The character of the state, like that of the nation, changed radically in the 1960s. The tone of the times had been set by a group of postwar writers, the "Beat Generation," among them Jack Kerouac of Lowell (1). Young people, attracted to the Boston area by its universities, seemed to be taking over Beacon Hill (2), the Back Bay, and Cambridge. Rock music was their hallmark. A local rock group, appropriately named the Beacon Street Union, was photographed at a concert on Cambridge Common in 1971 (3) and posing for a publicity shot (4). An advertisement for a service led by an Indian mystic (5) at the Arlington Street church in Boston would have appealed to Emerson and Thoreau, who shared with the generation of the sixties and seventies an interest in Eastern religion, nature, radical politics, and unorthodox living arrangements, not too different from those advertised in Boston's *Real Paper* in 1975 (6).

6

2M, 1F seek 1F for friendly, supportive Porter Square household. Our interests include socialism/feminism, radical theology, art, old movies, plants and cornbread. Rent including utilities about $55. call 876-8630.

4th roommate wanted 25+. 2W, 1M. Midpoint between Harvard/Central Sqs. Non-smoker, available now. $70 + utilities. 868-1837.

2F, 1M seek congenial male to complement spacious, clean and peaceful Somerville apt. Desire mid-twenties, non-smoker. Will share meals. Own room, good parking. Avail Apr. 15. $85/mo. heated. 628-0348.

Female roommate wanted to share three bedroom apartment with same. $75 heated. Near Harvard - Inman - Central Squares. On busline. Call 625-8503 between 3:00 - 8:00 p.m.

Arlington. 2F seek same for lovely 6-room duplex. May-Sept. (flexible). Own sunny room, garage, yard, porches. $83 plus util. 646-1377.

Fresh Pond. 2 males, late 20's and dog seeking easy-going roommate for nice apt. on quiet tree-lined street off Huron Ave. Avail. May 1. Share $275 & util. 492-0925.

One male, one female seek congenial third - share meals, thoughts, music in large, sunny, cooperative, Watertown house with best view in New England. Parking, transportation, April 15. $110+. Evenings 923-0375.

Cambridge - Central Square. Roommates wanted to share lrg. 4 bdrm apt., cooking, chores, friendly low key conversation and occasional crazies. Semi-veg., non-sexist. 492-2043.

2M & 1F looking for ezgoing people to share large country home, 20 min. from Boston. We're into music, yoga & photo. $80.00 per month + util. 861-8057 after 11 a.m.

Spacious Cleveland Circle apartment with fireplace needs one housemate $79 including heat, plus deposit. Non-smokers preferred. 277-4044 or Jeff Newman 969-0100 extension 2150. Vegetarians are welcome.

Roommate(s) wanted for large 5 bedroom Brookline apartment near Coolidge Corner. 3F; 1 student, 2 working. Porch and old piano. Near MBTA $83, includes heat. 2 months sec. deposit. 566-7274.

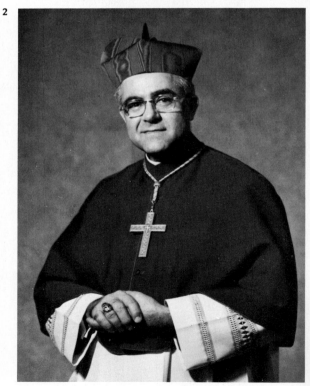

Ethnic Groups

Divisions among Massachusetts ethnic groups have traditionally been bitter, but in recent decades hostility has lessened. Ancient rivalries, like those between the Italians of Boston's North End and the Irish of Charlestown, have all but disappeared. The new spirit is symbolized by the ABC Pizza House in Boston (1), which sells Italian, Greek, and Syrian style food and has a Spanish-language poster pasted beside its window. The appointment of a Portuguese, Humberto Medeiros (2), as Archbishop of Boston, a post that had recently been held by Irishmen, was another symbol of change. But relationships are still far from ideal. Police had to stand in front of Bunker Hill Monument to protect black students when Charlestown High School was integrated in 1975 (3). The previous year, police had to escort school buses carrying black children from Roxbury into South Boston (4). At South Boston High School and elsewhere in Boston, blacks and whites attend school together (5), but the peace between them is an uneasy one.

The Presence of History

Throughout Massachusetts, old buildings, museums, churches, and streets serve as reminders of the state's rich past. Sometimes entire towns such as Deerfield (1) and Old Sturbridge Village, with its old-fashioned general store (2), are museums. Almost every town contains a building or room where historic relics are displayed; the Wampanoag Indian Museum in Mashpee (3) houses artifacts used or made by the Cape Cod Indians. At the Springfield Armory Museum (4) is the site of the first government arsenal. Boston is particularly rich in relics of the past. The Park Street Church and the Old Granary Burying Ground, where Paul Revere lies buried (5), are in the middle of the city. A subway goes underneath the Old State House (6) and skyscrapers tower above it; but the building remains almost as it was when the Boston Massacre took place beneath its windows.

Suggested Reading

There is no satisfactory history of Massachusetts, but a great deal has been written about Boston and about various aspects of the state's history. The founding of the Plymouth and Massachusetts Bay Colonies is best described in the words of their governors: *Of Plymouth Plantation, 1620–1647, by William Bradford,* edited by Samuel Eliot Morison(New York, 1952) and *Winthrop's Journal, "History of New England," 1630–1649,* edited by James Kendall Hosmer in *Original Narratives of Early American History.* Other contemporary narratives of Plymouth were reprinted in number 480 of *Everyman's Library, Chronicles of the Pilgrim Fathers,* with an introduction by John Masefield. *The Diary of Samuel Sewall, 1674–1729,* edited by Milton Halsey Thomas (New York, 1973) gives a firsthand account of Boston life in those years. *The Book of Abigail and John, Selected Letters of the Adams Family, 1762–1784* (Cambridge, 1975) gives insights by distinguished participants into the Revolutionary period.

Many studies of the history of colonial Massachusetts have been published. Particularly noteworthy are Bernard Bailyn, *The New England Merchants in the Seventeenth Century* (Cambridge, 1955) and *The Ordeal of Thomas Hutchinson* (Cambridge, 1974); Thomas Wertenbaker, *Puritan Oligarchy* (New York, 1947); Carl Bridenbaugh, *Cities in the Wilderness, The First Century of Urban Life in America, 1625–1742* (New York, 1955) and *Cities in Revolt, Urban Life in America, 1743–1775* (New York, 1955); and Darrett Bruce Rutman, *Winthrop's Boston, A Portrait of a Puritan Town, 1630–1649* (Chapel Hill, 1965). Of the many highly readable works of the historian Samuel Eliot Morison, the following particularly concern the

early history of Massachusetts: *Builders of the Bay Colony* (Boston, 1930); *The Story of the "Old Colony" of New Plymouth, 1620–1692* (New York, 1956); *The Intellectual Life of Colonial New England* (New York, 1956); *Three Centuries of Harvard* (Cambridge, 1936); *The Maritime History of Massachusetts* (Boston, 1921); and *Harrison Gray Otis, The Urbane Federalist, 1765–1848* (Boston, 1969).

Clifford K. Shipton, *New England Life in the Eighteenth Century* (Cambridge, 1963) is a selection of biographies of eighteenth-century New Englanders, chiefly natives of Massachusetts, who attended Harvard College, selected from his *Sibley's Harvard Graduates,* of which fourteen volumes, covering the classes of 1690 to 1771, have been published. The larger work amounts to a biographical dictionary of colonial Massachusetts in its literate aspects; the sketches are vivid. Ola Elizabeth Winslow, *Samuel Sewall of Boston* (New York, 1964), Esther Forbes, *Paul Revere and the World He Lived in* (Boston, 1942), and Carl Seaburg and Stanley Paterson, *Merchant Prince of Boston, Colonel T. H. Perkins, 1764–1854* (Cambridge, 1971) are outstanding biographies of three very different natives of Massachusetts.

The four volumes of *The Memorial History of Boston,* a collaborative work edited by Justin Winsor (Boston, 1882), are a mine of information concerning the first two and a half centuries of the city. *Fifty Years of Boston, A Memorial Volume,* published by the city in 1932, carries Winsor through the 1930 Tercentenary. For other aspects of Boston, see David McCord, *About Boston* (New York, 1948); Howard Mumford Jones and Bessie Zaban Jones, *The Many Voices of Boston, A Historical An-*

thology, *1630–1975* (Boston, 1975); Walter Muir Whitehill, *Boston, A Topographical History* (2nd ed., Cambridge, 1968), *Boston in the Age of John Fitzgerald Kennedy* (Norman, Okla., 1966), and *Boston as Engraved on Wood by Rudolph Ruzicka* (Boston, 1975). Five biographies by Louise Hall Tharp (all published by Little, Brown and Company in Boston) recreate very different types of local residents: *The Peabody Sisters of Salem* (1950); *Until Victory, Horace Mann, and Mary Peabody* (1953); *Three Saints and a Sinner, Julia Ward Howe, Louisa, Annie and Sam Ward* (1956); *Adventurous Alliance, The Story of the Agassiz Family of Boston* (1959); and *Mrs. Jack, a Biography of Isabella Stewart Gardner* (1965).

On the literary side, the following will suggest lines of further reading: Perry Miller, *The New England Mind, The Seventeenth Century* (New York, 1939), *The New England Mind, From Colony to Province* (Cambridge, 1953), *The American Puritans, Their Prose and Poetry* (New York, 1956); and Van Wyck Brooks, *The Flowering of New England, 1815–1865* (New York, 1936), and *New England: Indian Summer, 1865–1915* (New York, 1940).

Oscar Handlin, *Boston Immigrants* (Cambridge, 1959) is the best account of the nineteenth-century changes in population, and Martin Burgess Green, *The Problem of Boston: Some Readings in Cultural History* (New York, 1966) is a provocative analysis of the decline in Boston's literary influence. Federal Writers' Project, *Massachusetts: A Guide to its Places and People* (Boston, 1939) and Historical American Buildings Survey, *Massachusetts Catalog,* edited by John C. Poppeliers (Boston, 1965) are useful guides to the state's past. A remarkable photographic record of the appearance of Massachusetts is contained in the books of Samuel Chamberlain (all published in New York). Among them are *Beyond New England Thresholds* (1938); *Historic Salem in Four Seasons* (1938); *Gloucester and Cape Ann* (1938); *Lexington and Concord* (1938); *Old Marblehead* (1940); *Martha's Vineyard* (1941); *Historic Cambridge in Four Seasons* (1942); *Salem Interiors* (1950); *Old Sturbridge Village* (1951); *Cape Cod* (1953); *Nantucket* (1939, 1955); *The Berkshires* (1956); *The Book of Boston* (3 volumes, 1960–1964, text by Marjorie Drake Ross); and *Historic Deerfield* (1965).

Picture Sources

The pictorial material relevant to the history of Massachusetts is extraordinarily rich, particularly in light of this volume's aim of interpreting history in the broadest sense. Here the immigrant factory worker in Lawrence is given as much attention as the soldier at Bunker Hill. Certain picture collections individually contain enough material for dozens of volumes as comprehensive as this. Notable among them are the Massachusetts Historical Society, the American Antiquarian Society, the Boston Public Library, the Boston Athenaeum, the New York Public Library, and the Library of Congress. Smaller, but still distinguished, collections exist at the Peabody Museum and the Essex Institute in Salem, at the Bostonian Society and the Society for the Preservation of New England Antiquities in Boston, the Old Dartmouth Historical Society in New Bedford, the Museum of the American China Trade in Milton, the Merrimack Valley Textile Museum in North Andover, and in the New-York Historical Society.

The photographic archives of Boston photographer George Cushing are a valuable repository of material. Equally valuable are the book and print shops which sell old books, engravings, and memorabilia. The Holman Print Shop, Goodspeeds, and the Brattle Book Store, all in Boston, were especially useful in this respect.

The files of certain nineteenth-century magazines have been extremely useful; these are *Ballou's Pictorial Drawing-Room Companion, Gleason's Pictorial Drawing-Room Companion, Frank Leslie's Illustrated Newspaper, Harper's Weekly, Scribner's Monthly,* and *Scribner's Magazine.* Moses King's 1878 *Guide to Boston* and *King's Handbook of Boston,* published in 1883, provided both pictures and information, as did various editions of the *Boston Almanac,* published in the nineteenth century. *American Heritage Magazine,* and the five-volume *Album of American History* published by Scribner's, were rich secondary sources.

Following is a list of abbreviations used in the picture credits:

AAS	American Antiquarian Society, Worcester
BA	Library of the Boston Athenaeum, Boston
Ballou's	*Ballou's Pictorial Drawing-Room Companion*
Barber	Barber, John Warner, *Historical Collections of Massachusetts,* Worcester: Dorr, Howland, and Company, 1840
BPL	Boston Public Library, Boston
CSS	Charles Scribner's Sons
EI	Essex Institute, Salem
GBCC	Greater Boston Chamber of Commerce
Gleason's	*Gleason's Pictorial Drawing-Room Companion*
HABS	Historic American Buildings Survey, Washington, D.C.

HM	*Harper's Monthly*
HW	*Harper's Weekly*
ILN	*Illustrated London News*
King's	*King's Handbook of Boston*
LC	Library of Congress, Washington, D.C.
Leslie's	*Frank Leslie's Illustrated Newspaper*
MDCD	Massachusetts Department of Commerce and Development, Division of Tourism
MFA	Museum of Fine Arts, Boston
MHS	Massachusetts Historical Society, Boston
MMA	Metropolitan Museum of Art, New York
NYHS	New-York Historical Society, New York
ODHS	Old Dartmouth Historical Society and Whaling Museum, New Bedford
PM	Peabody Museum, Salem
SM	*Scribner's Magazine*
SPNEA	Society for the Preservation of New England Antiquities
WAM	Worcester Art Museum, Worcester

20–21 1. Surf, Cape Cod. Photo: John F. Waters. 2. Menemsha Hills Reservation, Martha's Vineyard. Trustees of Reservations. 3. Sand dune, Cape Cod. Photo: John F. Waters. 4. Hog Island, Cornelius and Mine S. Crane Wildlife Refuge, Essex. Trustees of Reservations. **22–23** 1. Woods, Marlborough. Photo: Irv Shaffer. 2. Sudbury River. Photo: Irv Shaffer. 3. Housatonic reflections at Bartholomew's Cobble, Ashley Falls. Trustees of Reservations. 4. Monument Mountain, Great Barrington. Trustees of Reservations. **24–25** Deerfield River Valley. CSS Art Files. **26–27** 1. Marriage certificate of William Bradford and Dorothy May. Pilgrim Hall, Plymouth. 2. *Governor Edward Winslow,* artist unknown, 1651. Pilgrim Hall, Plymouth. 3. *Mayflower* Compact. Bradford, William, *Of Plymouth Plantation. Signatures.* Winsor, Justin, *Narrative and Critical History of America,* vol. III, 1884. 4. *Map of Plymouth Harbor.* de Champlain, Samuel, *Voyages,* 1613. 5. Plymouth Rock. MDCD. 6. Marginal notes and drawings. *Connecticut Magazine,* vol. 5, 1899. **28–29** 1. Pilgrim village, reconstruction. Plimoth Plantation. Plymouth. 2. Harlow House, kitchen. Pilgrim Hall, Plymouth. 3. Elder Brewster armchair, ash and other woods, 1660–1680. Pilgrim Hall, Plymouth. 4. Iron pot of Myles Standish. Pilgrim Hall, Plymouth. 5. Peregrine White's cradle. Pilgrim Hall, Plymouth. **30–31** 1. Bradford, William, *Of Plymouth Plantation.* From original manuscript in the Mass. State Library, Boston. 2–4. Visscher, Nicolaum, *Novi Belgii,* detail, ca. 1650. NYPL, Prints Division, Eno Collection. 5. Second Meeting House, Plymouth, 1683, engraved for the Colonial Society of Mass. from a drawing of unknown date.

Pilgrim Hall, Plymouth. 6. John Alden House, Duxbury, 1653. MDCD. 7. Burial Hill, Plymouth. MDCD. **32–33** 1. Smith, John, Captain, *A Description of New England: or The Observations, and Discoveries, of Captain John Smith (Admirall of that Country), in the North of America, in the year of our Lord, 1614,* London, Humfrey Lownes for Robert Clerke, 1616. NYPL. 2. Restoration of English wigwams as constructed at Mass. Bay in 1630. SPNEA. 3. English wigwam, interior. SPNEA. 4. Bark houses, pioneer village. Photo: Paul J. Weber. 5. Pioneer village. EI. **34–35** 1. Charter of Massachusetts Bay Company, 1629. State House, Boston. 2. *John Winthrop,* school of Van Dyck. AAS. 3. *William Pynchon,* artist unknown, 1657. EI. 4. *John Endecott,* artist unknown. Frick Art Reference Library, collection, State House, Boston. 5. Governor John Endecott's chair. Mass. State Library, Boston. 6. Governor John Endecott's sword. Mass. State Library, Boston. 7. Wood, William, *New Englands Prospect,* London: John Bellamie, 1634. **36–37** 1, 2. Old Ship Church, Hingham. Photos: Dorothy Abbe. 3. *The Bay Psalm Book,* title page, printed by Stephen Daye, Cambridge, 1640. NYPL. 4. *Reverend Richard Mather,* woodcut by John Foster. Princeton Univ. Library. 5. *Genevan Bible,* title page, *Imprinted at London by the Deputies of Christopher Barker, printer to the Queenes most Excellent Majestie, 1599.* MHS. 6. Winthrop Communion Cup, embossed silver with engraving and figures in relief, 11¾″ high, 16 oz., date unknown. Trustees, First Church in Boston. 7. Gravestone of John Foster, Dorchester, artist unknown, 1681. Alan Ludwig. **38–39** 1. Fairbanks House, Dedham, 1636 (?). Halliday Historic Photograph Co. 2. Parson Capen House, Topsfield, 1683. HABS. 3. House of the Seven Gables (Turner–Ingersoll House), Salem, 1662. EI. 4. Browne House, Watertown, ca. 1663. SPNEA. 5. Capen House, Topsfield, 1683, reproduction of kitchen. MMA. 6. Table, oak and maple, Essex County, 1675–1700. MMA, gift of Mrs. J. Insley Blair, 1951. 7. Wainscot chair, oak, ca. 1670–1685. EI. 8. Paneled pine chest, late 17th century. MMA, gift of Mrs. J. Insley Blair, 1945. **40–41** 1. *A Map of New England,* engraved on wood by John Foster. Hubbard, Reverend William, *A Narrative of the Troubles with the Indians in New England,* Boston, 1677. 2. Danforth, Samuel, *An Almanack for the Year of Our Lord, 1647,* printed by Matthew Day, Cambridge, 1647, NYPL. 3. Danforth, *Almanack,* text page. NYPL. 4. Massachusetts pitch marks. *Record of the Governor and Company of Massachusetts Bay in New England, 1628–86,* Boston, 1853–54. Yale Univ. Press. 5. Tide mill, Hingham, 1643. *Old-Time New England,* April 1935. 6. Broad axes and hewing hatchets. SPNEA. 7. Town pound, Westwood, 1700. **42–43** 1. Charcoal kiln, Pelham, late 17th century. HABS, LC. 2. Rolling Mill Iron Works, Saugus. MDCD. 3. Printing press. Vermont Historical Society, Montpelier. 4. Saugus pot. Original in Lynn Public Library. Photo: Chief S. Craft Scribner and Officer Richard P. Jenkins, Lynn Police Dept. 5. Pine Tree shillings. MHS. 6. Self-portrait, Thomas Smith, ca. 1690. WAM. **44–45** 1. *Rebecca Rawson,* artist unknown, ca. 1674. New England Historic–Genealogical Society. 2. *Margaret Gibbs,* artist unknown, 17th century. WAM. 3. *Ann Pollard,* artist unknown, 1721. MHS. 4. *Mrs. Freake and Baby Mary,* artist unknown, 1674. WAM. 5. Abraham Browne, Jr., House, Watertown, kitchen, ca. 1663. SPNEA. 6. Stephen Daniel House, Salem, kitchen. HABS, LC. 7. Sampler, Mary Hollingsworth, ca. 1675. EI. **46–47** 1. *Governor John Leverett,* artist unknown. EI. 2. Charter of Ancient and Honorable Artillery Company. Courtesy, Major Charles T. Cahill, Boston. 3. *Major Thomas Savage,* perhaps by Thomas Smith. WAM. 4. Flag of Ancient and Honorable Artillery

Company. Courtesy, Major Charles T. Cahill, Boston. 5. *A Prospect of the Colledges in Cambridge in New England,* line engraving after William Burgis, 1726. NYPL, Stokes Collection. 6. *Charles Chauncy,* perhaps by McKay. Fogg Art Museum. 7. *Increase Mather,* artist unknown. MHS. **48–49** 1. *A Mapp of New England,* detail. Sellers, John, *Atlas Maritimus,* 1675. LC. 2. *John Eliot,* artist unknown. Henry E. Huntington Library and Art Gallery, San Marino. 3, 4. *The Massachusetts Psalter,* B. and J. Green, Printer, Boston, 1709. BA. 5. Signature from a deed of land in Taunton. BA. 6. *Josiah Winslow,* artist unknown. Pilgrim Society, Pilgrim Hall Museum. 7. Stebbins House, Deerfield. Pocumtuck Valley Memorial Assn., Greenfield. **50–51** 1. Mather, Cotton, *The Wonders of the Invisible World,* 1693. NYPL, Rare Book Division. 2. *Samuel Sewall,* from a portrait by Nathaniel Emmons, ca. 1720. MHS. 3. *William Stoughton.* Harvard Univ. 4. Memorial Petition of Mary Easty. From original manuscript preserved in the court files of Essex County, Salem. 5. Rebecca Nurse House, Danvers, 1678. SPNEA. **52–53** 1. *A Mapp of New England,* detail. Sellers, John, *Atlas Maritimus,* 1675. 2. Marshfield, North River. Photo: Irv Shaffer. 3. *Simon Bradstreet.* Mass. State Library Boston. 4. Address to Sir Edmund Andros, April 18, 1689. Byfield, Nathaneal, *An Account of the Late Revolution.* NYPL. 5. Frary House, Deerfield, 1704. MDCD. **54–55** 1. *View of Boston,* engraved by William Burgis, 1722. NYHS. 2. "Pasters" to be added to William Burgis, *View of Boston.* British Museum. 3. *The Town of Boston in New Englande,* John Bonner, 1722. NYPL, Stokes Collection. **56–57** 1. Faneuil Hall, Boston, engraved by Samuel Hill. *Massachusetts Magazine,* March 1789. NYHS. 2. Southwest view of the State House, Boston. *Massachusetts Magazine,* July 1793. NYPL, Stokes Collection. 3. Weathervane, copper Indian, Shem Drowne, ca. 1750. MHS. 4. Weathervane, grasshopper, Faneuil Hall, Boston. American Airlines. 5. Christ Church, Boston, interior, 1723. MDCD. **58–59** 1. *Bethel,* artist unknown, 1748. PM. 2. *Boston Light House,* engraving by William Burgis. Mariners' Museum, Newport News. 3. Isaac Royall House, Medford. HABS, LC. 4. *Family of Isaac Royall,* Robert Feke, 1741. Harvard Law School. 5. Advertisement. *Boston Gazette,* Sept. 22, 1767. **60–61** 1. Rubbing of tombstone of Silas Bigelow, Paxton, 1769. Ann Parker and Avon Neal, North Brookfield. 2. *Jonathan Edwards,* Joseph Badger. Yale Univ. Art Gallery. 3. Edwards, Jonathan, *A Sermon: Sinners in the Hands of an Angry God,* 1741. NYPL, Rare Book Division. 4. Edwards, *Treatise Concerning Religious Affections,* 1746. NYPL, Rare Book Division. 5. Holden Chapel, Cambridge. Harvard Univ. News Office. 6. Broadside, Boston enlistment regulations of 1755. LC. **62–63** 1. Highboy, japanned decoration, ca. 1700. MMA, 1940, Joseph Pulitzer bequest. 2. High chest, walnut (or butternut), 725–40, Henry Francis DuPont Winterthur Museum, Winterthur, Delaware. 3. Orne House, Marblehead, interior, ca. 1730. MFA. 4. Silver tray, Thomas Edwards, Boston, 1740–50. Henry Francis DuPont Winterthur Museum, Winterthur, Delaware. 5. Benjamin Pickman silver grace cup, William Swan, Boston, 1749. 6. Silver plate, detail, John Coney, Boston, early 18th century. MFA. 7. Silver candlesticks, Jacob Hurd, Boston, 1740–50. MMA, bequest of A. T. Clearwater, 1933. **64–65** Shumway House, Fiskdale, interior, ca. 1740. MFA. **66–67** 1. *A View of Louisburg in North America, taken near the Light House when the city was besieged in 1758,* engraved by P. Canot. NYPL, Stokes Collection. 2. *A Prospect of the City of Lewisbourg,* engraved by B. Cole, 1745. NYHS. 3. *A Prospect of the City* *of Lewisbourg,* detail, engraved by B. Cole, 1745. NYHS. 4. *Sir William Pepperell.* EI. 5. Howe Monument, Belfry Tower, Westminster Abbey. Copyright, Warburg Institute, London. 6. Bill of two pence, 1744. MHS.   **68–69** 1. Tapestry, Chandler Wedding in Old South Church, Boston, 1756. AAS. 2, 3. *A Prospect of the Colledges in Cambridge in New England,* detail, line engraving after William Burgis, 1726. NYPL, Stokes Collection. 4. *A Canon of 6 in One with a Ground: The Words by ye Rev. Dr. Byles, set to music by W. Billings,* engraved by Paul Revere, 1770. Clements Library, Univ. of Michigan. 5. *A few lines on Magnus Mode . . . ,* Boston, 1767. NYPL, Rare Book Division.   **70–71** 1. Major John Vassall House, Cambridge. MDCD. 2. Jeremiah Lee Mansion, Marblehead, stairway and wallpaper, 1768. EI. 3. Side chair, Chippendale, mahogany, 1765–75. MMA, gift of Mrs. Paul Moore, 1939. 4. Designs for parlor chairs. Manwaring, Robert, *Cabinet and Chairmaker's Real Friend and Companion,* London, 1765, plate 9. 5. Secretary desk, Chippendale, Salem, 1760–80. EI.   **72–73** 1. Windmill, Eastham. HABS, LC. 2. Grist Mill, Boxford, early 18th century. HABS, LC. 3. Shoemaker's Shop, Boxford, mid-18th century. HABS, LC. 4. Sawmill, Boxford, early 18th century. HABS, LC. 5. Figure of Mercury, gilded pine, Simeon Skillin the Elder; also attributed to John Skillin. National Gallery of Art, Washington. 6. Original bill of ferry operator, 1709. Chicago Museum of Science and Industry, Dunbar Collection. 7. Bull used by Jonathan Andrews as tannery sign. EI. 8. Tavern, Swansea, late 18th century. HABS, LC. 9. Old gaol, Nantucket, early 18th century. HABS, LC.   **74–75** 1. *Paul Revere,* John Singleton Copley, 1768–70. MFA. 2. Teapot, silver, Paul Revere. MMA, collection of A. T. Clearwater. 3. Sugar bowl and creamer, silver, Paul Revere. MMA, collection of A. T. Clearwater. 4. Liberty bowl, silver, Paul Revere, 1768. MFA. 5. Advertisement. *Boston Gazette,* Dec. 1768.   **76–77** 1. *View of Harvard College,* engraved by Paul Revere, 1770. Harvard College Library. 2. *Royal American Magazine,* January 1774. NYPL, Spencer Collection. 3. Trade card, Andrew Barclay Book Bindery, Boston. AAS. 4. *New England Primer,* Boston Edition, 1767. NYPL, Rare Book Division. 5. *Benjamin Franklin,* J. S. Duplessis. MMA. 6. Wheatley, Phillis, *Poems on Various Subjects,* London: A. Bell, 1773. NYPL.   **78–79** 1. *The Savage Family,* Edward Savage, ca. 1790. WAM. 2. Self-portrait, Robert Feke. Henry Wilder Foote and MFA. 3. *Mr. and Mrs. Isaac Winslow,* John Singleton Copley, 1774. MFA. 4. *Governor and Mrs. Thomas Mifflin,* John Singleton Copley, 1773. Historical Society of Pennsylvania, Phila. 5. *Mrs. Thomas Boylston,* John Singleton Copley, 1766. Fogg Art Museum. 6. *Mrs. John Winthrop,* John Singleton Copley, 1773. MMA, Morris K. Jesup Fund, 1931.   **80–81** *Copley Family Portrait,* John Singleton Copley, 1776–77. National Gallery of Art, Washington, D.C., Andrew W. Mellon Fund.   **82–83** 1, 2. Exchange table, detail, engraved by Peter Hurd, 1778. AAS. 3. Brooks, *Quaint and Curious Advertisements,* Boston, 1886. 4. Union Fire Engine, Salem, 1748. Smithsonian Institution. 5. School Street, Salem, drawing by Dr. Orne, ca. 1765. EI. 6. Samuel Gott House, Rockport, 1710. MDCD. 7. *Vessels in New England Ports,* drawings by Ashley Bowen, 1739–49. Property of Marblehead Historical Society, PM.   **84–85** 1. Stamp used under the Stamp Act. NYPL, Emmett Collection. 2. Receipt, 1766. MHS. 3. Announcement of repeal of the Stamp Act, 1766. NYPL. 4. Stamp Act engraving. NYPL, Print Room. 5. *A View of the Obelisk erected under Liberty Tree in Boston on the Reforcings for the Repeal of the Stamp Act,* Boston, engraved by Paul Revere, 1766. AAS.   **86–87** *A View of Part of the Town of*

Boston in New England and British Ships of War Landing Their Troops, 1768, facsimile of engraving by Paul Revere, 1770. NYPL, Stokes Collection.   **88–89** 1. *A Prospective View of Part of the Commons,* facsimile of watercolor drawing by Christopher Remick, 1768. NYPL, Stokes Collection. 2. *Plan of the Scene of the Boston Massacre, used at the Trial of Captain Preston and Soldiers,* Paul Revere. BPL, Chamberlain Collection. 3. *The Boston Massacre,* engraved by Paul Revere, 1770. NYPL, Stokes Collection.   **90–91** 1. *Boston Tea Party.* NYPL, Picture Collection. 2. Chinese tea chest, 18th century. On loan from Boston Tea Party Chapter, DAR, to DAR Museum, Washington, D.C. 3. *The Bostonians Paying the Excise-Man, or Tarring and Feathering,* 1773. Halsey, *Boston Port Bill,* 1904. NYPL, Prints Division. 4. *The Bostonians in Distress,* 1774. Halsey, *Boston.* NYHS. 5. *The Wicked Statesman, or the Traitor to his Country, at the Hour of Death.* Gleason, Ezra, *The Massachusetts Calendar; or an Almanack for the Year of our Lord Christ,* 1774. Harvard College Library.   **92–93** 1. *The Battle of Lexington, April 19, 1775,* engraved by Amos Dolittle after Ralph Earle, 1775. NYPL, Stokes Collection. 2. *A View of the Town of Concord,* engraved by Amos Dolittle, 1775. NYPL, Stokes Collection. 3. *The Engagement at the North Bridge in Concord,* engraved by Amos Dolittle, 1775. NYPL, Stokes Collection. 4. Flag of Bedford Minutemen. MDCD. 5. Broadside, list of provincials killed and wounded. John Carter Brown Library, Brown Univ.   **94–95** 1. *Sketch of the Burning of the Houses on Dorchester Neck, by our Troops who went and returned upon the Ice, 14th January 1776.* Robertson, Archibald, *Sketches of America,* ms. 66, 1762–1780. NYPL, Spencer Collection. 2. *View of Boston Showing the heights of Dorchester taken from Mount Whoredome, 24th January 1776.* Robertson, *Sketches.* NYPL, Spencer Collection. 3. Medal. MHS. 4. *ChasTown in Ruines, Bunker's hill, Noodles Island and that part of the Town called North End and New Boston, 7th March 1776.* Robertson, *Sketches.* NYPL, Stokes Collection.   **96–97** 1. *Plan of the Town of Boston with the Attack on Bunkers Hill in the Peninsula of Charlestown, the 17th of June, 1775.* Murray, James, *An Impartial History of the Present War in America,* 1778. 2. Handbill sent among the British troops on Bunker Hill. MHS. 3. *An original sketch of the Burning of Charlestown and Battle of Bunker Hill, taken by an English officer from Beacon Hill, Boston.* NYPL, Emmett Collection. 4. *An Exact View of the Late Battle at Charlestown,* engraved by Bernard Romans. NYPL, Prints Division. 5. *Attack on Bunker Hill, with the Burning of Charles Town,* artist unknown, ca. 1783. National Gallery of Art, Washington, D.C., gift of Edgar W. and Bernice Chrysler Garbisch, 1953.   **98–99** *The Battle of Bunker Hill,* John Trumbull. Yale Univ. Art Gallery.   **100–101** 1. *French Squadron anchored off Nantasket,* wash drawing by Pierre Ozanne, 1778–79. LC. 2. Broadside, Great Encouragement for Seamen, March 29, 1777. EI. 3. *Judah Alden,* pen and ink sketch by Tadeusz Kosciusko, 1777. Drake, Francis S., *Memorials of the Society of the Cincinnati of Massachusetts,* p. 210. 4. *Deborah Sampson,* published by H. Mann, 1797. LC. 5. *Dr. William Glysson,* Winthrop Chandler, ca. 1780. Ohio Historical Society, Campus Martius Museum, Marietta. 6. Powder House, Attleboro, mid-18th century. HABS, LC.   **102–103** 1. *John Hancock and his Wife, Dorothy Quincy Hancock,* Edward Savage, ca. 1788. Corcoran Gallery of Art, Washington, D.C., bequest of Woodbury Blair. 2. *John Adams,* Eliphalet Frazer Andrews. Negative Number 23939, Architect of the Capitol. 3. *Samuel Adams,* John Singleton Copley, ca. 1770–72. MFA, deposited by the city of Boston. 4. *General Joseph Warren,* John Singleton Copley, 1775.

MFA. 5. *Join or Die,* engraved by Paul Revere. *Massachusetts Spy,* 1774. **104–105** 1, 2. *A Southwest View of State House in Boston,* Samuel Hill. *Massachusetts Magazine,* July 1793. NYHS. 3. *Looking east from Denny Hill,* Ralph Earl. WAM. 4. *View of the Triumphal Arch and Colonnade erected in Boston in honor of the President of the United States, Oct. 24, 1789. Massachusetts Magazine,* Jan. 1790. NYHS. 5. Facsimile of Massachusetts cent of 1787. Drake, Samuel A., *Old Landmarks of Boston,* 1873. NYPL. 6. Presentation bowl, Paul Revere, 1787. Yale Univ. Art Gallery, Mabel Brady Garvan Collection. **106–107** 1. *Silhouette of Captain Paul Cuffe* [or Cuffee], 1812. ODHS. 2. *Elizabeth Freeman,* Susan Sedgwick. MHS. 3. Broadside. AAS. 4. Silver cup of Moses Michael Hays, Paul Revere. Mark Bortman and MFA. 5–8. Advertisements. *Columbian Centinel,* Boston, July 26, 1794. **108–109** 1. *Charles Bulfinch,* George B. Matthews. Negative Number 716, Architect of the Capitol. 2. State House, 1795. GBCC. 3. *Elevation and Plan of the Principal Story of the New State House in Boston,* Charles Bulfinch. NYPL, Stokes Collection. 4. Tontine Crescent (Franklin Place), after a drawing by Charles Bulfinch, 1793. *Massachusetts Magazine,* Feb. 1794. MMA. 5. Tontine Crescent (Franklin Place), ca. 1850. BA. 6. University Hall, Charles Bulfinch, 1815. Harvard Univ. News Office. **110–111** 1. Thomas, Robert B., *The Farmer's Almanack,* 1794. NYHS. 2. *Elkanah Watson,* engraving. NYPL. 3. Watson, Elkanah, *History of Agricultural Societies,* 1820. 4. Gold medal awarded by the Massachusetts Society for Promoting Agriculture, 1802. Humphreys, David, *The Miscellaneous Works of David Humphreys,* 1804. 5. Farm wagon, Tyngsborough, ca. 1750–1800. Edison Institute, Dearborn, Michigan. 6. *View of the Seat of the Honorable Moses Gill of Worcester County. Massachusetts Magazine,* Nov. 1792, frontispiece. NYHS. **112–113** 1. *View of the Bridge over Charles River,* engraved by S. Hill. *Massachusetts Magazine,* Sept. 1789. NYHS. 2. The Devens Tankard, silver, Benjamin Burt, ca. 1786. MFA, M. & M. Karolik Collection. 3. *A Bridge over the Merrimack River in the Commonwealth of Massachusetts.* Drayton, John, *Letters Written During a Tour Through the Northern and Eastern States of America,* 1794. NYHS. 4. N. Jewett's Bridge, Pepperell, early 19th century. HABS, LC. 5. Milestone, Wayland, 1768. HABS, LC. 6. Milestone, Milton, 1823. HABS, LC. 7. Advertisement, Nov. 24, 1810. Source unknown. 8. Worcester Turnpike corporation certificates, 1807. AAS. **114–115** 1. *Crowninshield's Wharf, Salem,* George Ropes, 1806. PM. 2. *The Launching of the ship "Fame" at the Crowninshield Wharf,* George Ropes, 1802. EI. 3. *George Crowninshield,* Samuel F. B. Morse, 1816. PM. 4. Ship Chandler's Shop, Salem, late 18th century. HABS, LC. 5. Bowditch, Nathaniel, *The New American Practical Navigator,* 1802. U.S. Coast and Geodetic Survey, Washington, D.C. **116–117** 1. *Elias Hasket Derby,* James Frothingham. PM. 2. *The Letter-of-Marque Ship "Mount Vernon" of Salem, Captain Elias Hasket Derby, Jr., Escaping from a French Fleet off Naples,* Corné, 1799. PM. 3. Salem Marine Society certificate of membership, 1797. EI. 4. *Ship "Grand Turk" at Canton,* 1786. EI. 5. Elias Hasket Derby's Summer House, now in Danvers, William C. Endicott estate. EI. 6. Ezekiel Hersey Derby House, Salem, interior, 1799. Phila. Museum of Art, given by George Horace Lorimer. **118–119** *Salem Common on Training Day,* George Ropes, 1808. EI. **120–121.** 1. Pierce-Nichols House, Salem, Samuel McIntire, 1782. Photo: Wayne Andrews. 2. Gardner (White–Pingree) House, Salem, Samuel McIntire, 1804–05. Photo: Wayne Andrews. 3. Figurehead, Samuel McIntire. PM. 4.

Governor John Winthrop, wooden bust, Samuel McIntire, 1798. AAS. 5. Sofa, Sheraton style, Samuel McIntire, ca. 1800. Bayou Bend Collection, Houston. **122–123** 1. *Elbridge Gerry,* engraved by J. B. Longacre from a drawing by Vanderlyn. 2. The Gerrymander. Winsor, Justin, *The Memorial History of Boston,* vol. III, p. 212. 3. *America,* Corné. PM. 4. American seaman's protection paper, signed by William R. Lee, Collector of the Port of Salem, January 19, 1811. EI. 5. *The Town of Sherburne in the Island of Nantucket. The Port Folio,* Jan. 1811. 6. *The Hartford Convention, or Leap no Leap,* etching by William Charles, 1815. NYHS. **124–125** 1. *John Adams,* bust, John Henri Isaac Browere, 1825. New York State Historical Association. 2. *Mrs. John Adams,* Gilbert Stuart. National Gallery of Art, Washington, D.C., gift of Mrs. Robert Homans, 1954. 3. *John Quincy Adams,* engraved by Asher B. Durand, 1826, after a painting by Thomas Sully. LC. 4. *Mrs. John Quincy Adams,* Charles Bird King. National Collection of Fine Arts, Smithsonian Institution, Adams Clemont Collection. 5. The Old House, Adams National Historic Site, Quincy. Photo: Fasch Studio, Milton. 6. Burial place of John Quincy Adams, Quincy. LC. 7. *Death of John Quincy Adams, at the U.S. Capitol,* Feb. 23, 1848, lithograph by Nathaniel Currier, 1848. LC. **126–127** 1. Signals of Salem merchants, 1835. PM. 2. *"Levant" and "Milo,"* unidentified Chinese artist, 1830. PM. 3. House of Augustine Heard and Co., Shanghai, unidentified Chinese artist, 1849. PM. 4. Tray, lacquered and painted decoration; view of Canton showing foreign factories or "hongs," ca. 1825. MMA, Rogers Fund, 1941. 5. Grand chop, or Chinese customs clearance, from Canton for the ship *Astrea,* Thomas Handasyd Perkins supercargo, 1789. MHS. 6. Chinese export porcelain, plate made for Elias Haskett Derby. MFA. **128–129** 1. First Parish Church, Wayland. MDCD. 2. Church and Town Hall, Carlisle, 1811. MDCD. 3. Christopher Wren Church, Sandwich. American Airlines. 4. Town Hall, Pelham. MDCD. 5. Congregational Church, Oldtown. HABS, LC. **130–131** 1. *North-east View of Webster,* 1839. Barber, p. 614. 2. Tenement house, Chelmsford Glass Works, Lowell, late 18th century. HABS, LC. 3. *Francis Cabot Lowell,* Courtesy, Mrs. Harriet Ropes Cabot. 4. *John Lowell,* G.P.A. Healy. Ralph Lowell, Trustee of the Lowell Institute. Photo: MFA. 5. *East View of Lowell,* 1840. Barber. 6. Trade card, Merrimack Manufacturing Co., Lowell. AAS. 7. *Abbott Lawrence.* Contemporary engraving. Source unknown. 8. *Amos Lawrence,* Chester Harding. National Gallery of Art, Washington, D.C., given in memory of the Rt. Rev. William Lawrence by his children, 1944. **132–133** *View of Iron Works, Canton,* John Hidley. MFA, M. & M. Karolik Collection. **134–135** 1. Granite Railway, Quincy. HABS, LC. 2. Quincy Railway, lithograph by David Claypoole Johnston. WAM. 3. Railroad car. HABS, LC. 4. Wharf. HABS, LC. 5. *Study of Bunker Hill Quarry and Monument,* Alvan Fisher. MFA, M. & M. Karolik Collection. 6. Monument at Bunker Hill, engraving. Meyer, Hermann, *Meyer's Universum,* N.Y., 1850. **136–137** 1. First train on Boston and Lowell Railroad, 1835. Railway and Locomotive Historical Society, Inc., Boston. 2. Advertisement. Smithsonian Institution. 3. Plan of Locomotive Engine for the Saratoga and Schenectady Railroad, 1833, lithograph by J. H. Bufford. Smithsonian Institution. 4. Lock keeper's house, Wilmington. HABS, LC. 5. Narragansett Bay, Boston survey map, 1831. National Archives. **138–139** Milbert, J., *Itinerairie Pittoresque du Fleuve Hudson . . . ,* Paris, 1828, vol. III. NYPL. **140–141** 1. *Beacon Hill, from the present site of the Reservoir between Hancock and Temple streets,* from a drawing made on the spot by J. R. Smith in

1811, lithograph by J. H. Bufford, 1858. LC. 2. *The Honorable Josiah Quincy,* Gilbert Stuart. MFA, gift of Eliza Susan Quincy. 3. Boston Fire, 1832. Firefighting Museum of the Home Insurance Company. 4. *Police Quick Step,* a Boston Policeman, 1840, lithograph by Thayer after a painting by W. Lydston. AAS. 5. *The National Lancers with the Reviewing Officers on Boston Common,* engraved by F. H. Lane, 1837, after an original painting by C. Hubbard, lithograph by Moore. NYPL, Stokes Collection. 6. State Street, Boston, 1839. NYPL.   142–143 1. Wm. H. Ladd's Eating House, Boston, ca. 1820. AAS. 2. Tremont House, Boston. Eliot, W. H., *A Description of Tremont House,* 1830, frontispiece. NYHS. 3. *The Tea Party,* Henry Sargent, ca. 1820. MFA, gift of Mrs. Horatio A. Lamb in memory of Mr. and Mrs. Winthrop Sargent.   144–145 1. *The Dinner Party,* Henry Sargent. MFA, gift of Mrs. Horatio A. Lamb in memory of Mr. and Mrs. Winthrop Sargent. 2. *North-American Review and Miscellaneous Journal,* Boston: Wells and Lilly, 1815. NYPL. 3. Antiquarian Hall, Worcester, ca. 1839. Barber. 4. *Nathaniel Bowditch,* Charles Osgood, 1835. PM. 5. *Edward Everett,* Samuel F. B. Morse. Detroit Institute of Arts. 6. *Family of Samuel Morse.* U.S. National Museum, Smithsonian Institution.   146–147 1. Half of New Bedford Meeting House being moved, drawing by Charles Lesueur, 1816. AAS. 2. *William Ellery Channing,* Washington Allston. MFA, gift of William Francis Channing. 3. *South View of Courthouse, Dedham.* Barber. MHS. 4. Unitarian Church, East Boston. *Boston Almanac,* 1854. 5. *Plan of the First Family, Harvard,* George Kindall, July 1836. Fruitlands Museum, Harvard.   148–149 1. Ralph Waldo Emerson, Photo: Southworth and Hawes. George Eastman House, Rochester. 2. Henry David Thoreau, from a daguerreotype by Maschain, Worcester, 1858. CSS Art Files. 3. Walden Pond. Photo: Irv Shaffer. 4. Thoreau, Henry David, *Walden,* Boston, 1854, title page. NYPL, Rare Book Division. 5. Amos Bronson Alcott. Bettmann Archive. 6. Alcott House, Concord. MDCD.   150–151 1. *Nathaniel Hawthorne,* Charles Osgood. EI. 2. *Margaret P. Fuller.* NYPL, Picture Collection. 3. The Brook at Brook Farm, West Roxbury. CSS Art Files. 4. Henry Wadsworth Longfellow, Boston, March 1, 1851. CSS Art Files. 5. John Greenleaf Whittier. Photo: F. Gutekunst, Phila. CSS Art Files. 6. Ralph Waldo Emerson and Oliver Wendell Holmes, Public Garden, 1857. BA. 7. *Philosophers' Camp,* 1858, made from Gleason's glass-plate of painting by William J. Stillman, 1903. Concord Free Public Library.   152–153 1. Dorothea Lynde Dix. By permission of the Houghton Library, Harvard Univ. 2. Mary Lyon. Mount Holyoke College, South Hadley. 3. *Boston Almanac,* 1854. 4. *The Temperance Offering,* Salem, 1846, frontispiece. LC. 5. Dining Room, Deer Island. *Ballou's,* Sept. 20, 1856. 6. Female Hospital, Deer Island. *Ballou's,* Sept. 20, 1856. 7. Nursery, Deer Island. *Ballou's,* Sept. 20, 1856.   154–155 1. *The Ancient Oak, Brighton. Gleason's,* July 9, 1853. 2. West Part School, Pittsfield, early 19th century. HABS, LC. 3. Oread Institute for Girls, Worcester, woodcut. *Gleason's,* March 19, 1853. 4. Pike, Nicholas, *Arithmetic,* Newburyport, 1788. 5. Horace Mann, daguerreotype. LC. 6. The Emerson School, daguerreotype by Southworth and Hawes, 19th century. MMA, gift of I. N. Phelps Stokes, Edward S. Hawes, A. M. Hawes, M. A. Hawes, 1937.   156–157 1. *Harvard University—Commencement Day.* Quincy, Josiah, *History of Harvard University,* frontispiece. 2. *Class-Day Celebration, Harvard—Ceremonies Under the Old Elm, College Green. Leslie's,* July 19, 1856. 3. *The Match between Sophs and Freshmen—The Opening,* engraved by Winslow Homer. HW, Aug. 1, 1857. 4. Astronomical Ob-

servatory, Cambridge. *Gleason's,* 1851. 5. Original Seminary Building, from a Currier print. Mount Holyoke College. 6. *Western View of Williams College and Other Buildings.* Barber.   158–159 1. *The Oxbow,* Thomas Cole, 1846. MMA, gift of Mrs. Russell Sage, 1908. 2. Springfield, from the Longmeadow Road. *Ballou's,* Aug. 26, 1854. NYPL, Picture Collection. 3. *Old View of Court Square, Springfield.* Barber. 4. Northampton in 1840. Willis, Nathaniel P., *American Scenery,* 1840. 5. *Western View of Pittsfield (central part).* Barber. MHS.   160–161 1. View of the town of Marblehead. *Ballou's,* June 17, 1854. NYPL, Picture Collection. 2. *View of Newburyport (from Salisbury),* lithograph after Fitz Hugh Lane. NYPL, Stokes Collection. 3. *The Harbor of Newburyport and the mouth of Merrimack River,* drawn by P. Anderson, 1826. National Archives. 4. *Fishing Grounds, Provincetown,* 1838. Barber. 5. Athenaeum, Nantucket. MDCD. 6. American Airlines.   162–163 1. Crew list of Acushnet, Dec. 30, 1840. ODHS. 2. Frederick Douglass. CSS Art Files. 3. Abolition Church, Boston, 1806. HABS, LC. 4. Israelite Synagogue, Warren Street. *Boston Almanac,* 1854. 5. *The Shoemakers' Strike—The Strikers' Locomotive Demonstrations at Lynn,* from a sketch by C. A. Barry. *New-York Illustrated News,* March 10, 1860.   164–165 1. *Irish Emigrants Leaving Home—The Priest's Blessing.* ILN, May 10, 1851. 2. *Emigrants' Arrival at Cork—A Scene on the Quay.* ILN, May 10, 1851. 3. *Emigrants' Arrival at Constitution Wharf,* Boston. *Ballou's,* Oct. 31, 1857. 4. Church of St. Peter and St. Paul, Broadway. *Boston Almanac,* 1854, 5. St. Augustine's Chapel, early 19th century. HABS, LC.   166–167 1. *Bishop Jean Louis Lefebvre de Cheverus,* Gilbert Stuart. MFA, bequest of Mrs. Charlotte Gore (Greenough) Hervoches du Quillion. 2. Cathedral of the Holy Cross, Boston, Charles Bulfinch, 1859. BA. 3. Ursuline Convent, Charlestown. Drake, Samuel A., *Old Landmarks of Middlesex,* Boston, 1876, p. 91. 4. View of Somerville, from the Ruins of the Ursuline Convent. *Ballou's,* May 13, 1854. NYPL, Picture Collection. 5. *Boston Pilot,* May 25, 1844. American Catholic Historical Society, St. Charles Seminary, Phila. 6. *Orestes Augustus Brownson,* George Peter Alexander Healy. MFA, gift of Mrs. Louisa Healy.   168–169 1. Trumbull, H., *Western Emigration: Journal of Doctor Jeremiah Simpleton's Tour to Ohio,* Boston, 1819. AAS. 2. New England Emigrant Aid Company stock certificate, April 14, 1855. Kansas State Historical Society, Topeka. 3. Advertisement. *Boston Almanac,* 1857. 4. Advertisement. AAS. 5. *A Company of Swedish Emigrants Passing our Office, Bound to the West,* wood engraving. *Gleason's,* Oct. 30, 1852. LC. 6. *William Cullen Bryant,* engraved by H. B. Hall, 1878. NYPL, Picture Collection. 7. Self-portrait, Samuel F. B. Morse, miniature on ivory. National Academy of Design.   170–171 1. Boston, view from State House, 1856. BPL. 2. *View of the Water Celebration on Boston Common, Oct. 25, 1848,* lithograph by F. Rowse after drawing by B. F. Smith, Jr., 1849. LC. 3. Custom House, Boston, ca. 1848, built 1837–47, Ammi B. Young. Sears, Robert, *Pictorial Description of the United States,* N. Y., 1848. 4. Suffolk Bank, Boston, erected 1834, Isaiah Rogers. Source unknown. 5. *A Nightmare Dream of a Patriotic Politician of the Interior,* lithograph by David Claypoole Johnston, ca. 1840. AAS.   172–173, 174–175 *Grand Panoramic View of Tremont Street, Boston, East and West Sides, from Court Street to the Common. Gleason's,* 1853. NYPL, Picture Collection.   176–177 1–6. *Boston Almanac,* 1858. 7. *Boston Almanac,* 1857.   178–179 1. *Missionary Packet "Morning Star" passing Boston Light,* lithograph by Bufford. LC. 2. *Launch of the Clipper Ship "Flying*

Cloud," at East Boston, built by Donald McKay, 1851. *Gleason's.* PM. 3. *Clipper Ship "Sovereign of the Seas." Gleason's,* Sept. 3, 1853. 4. *Donald McKay, builder of the "Great Republic,"* engraved by W. G. Jackman. CSS Art Files. 5. Advertisement. *Boston Almanac and Directory,* 1884. **180–181** 1–3. *Boston Almanac,* 1857. 4. James French and Co. Building. *Boston Almanac,* 1858. 5. *Ballou's,* masthead, Oct. 31, 1857. 6. *Peter Denies Christ. The Child's Pictorial History of the Bible,* Boston: J. V. Pierce, 1845. **182–183** 1. *Jamaica Pond, West Roxbury,* lithograph by Bufford, 1859. LC. 2. *Sleigh Riding on the Neck, Boston. Gleason's,* January 28, 1854. 3. *An Evening Party in Boston. Ballou's,* 1855. **184–185** 1. *Class-Day Celebration at Harvard College—Dance at Harvard Hall. Leslie's,* July 19, 1856. 2. *Preparing the Chowder—Expectant Groups,* from a sketch by E. Champney. *Leslie's,* April 7, 1860. 3. *Fourth of July Picnic at Weymouth Landing,* Susan Merrett, 1845. Art Institute of Chicago, bequest of Elizabeth Vaughan. **186–187** 1. *The Proposal,* ca. 1830. ODHS. 2. *The Hollingsworth Family,* George Hollingsworth, 1840. MFA, M. & M. Karolik Collection. **188–189** 1. *Lynnfield Hotel, Newburyport Turnpike, South Lynnfield,* Frank Poole. Wakefield Historical Society. 2. *View of South Reading from Cowdrey's Hill,* Frank Poole, after 1845. Wakefield Historical Society. 3. *South Reading Common, looking southwest down Main Street,* Frank Poole, 1840. Wakefield Historical Society. 4. *The Second Meeting House of the First Baptist Church,* Frank Poole. Wakefield Historical Society. 5. *Seven-story wood building of Wakefield Rattan Company,* Frank Poole. Wakefield Historical Society. **190–191** 1, 2. *Salem.* NYPL, Prints Division, Stokes Collection. 3. *New Bedford,* drawn and engraved by J. F. A. Cole. NYPL, Prints Division, Stokes Collection. **192–193** 1. *Southeastern View of New Bedford,* Barber. 2. The Seamen's Bethel, New Bedford. MDCD. 3. *The Navigator.* ODHS. 4. Figurehead of Whaleship *Awashonks.* ODHS. 5. Log of bark *Mary and Susan,* 1878–79. ODHS. **194–195** 1. Whaling fleet. ODHS. 2. *Lancing a Sperm Whale,* Raleigh, Charles, *Panorama.* ODHS. 3. *Chewing up the Boat,* Raleigh, *Panorama.* ODHS. **196–197** 1. *New England Farmer,* masthead, April 14, 1849. Quincy Hall, Boston. 2. *View of the Plowing Match at Worcester, 1841, Boston Cultivator.* EI. 3. *Bird's-eye View of the Grounds at the Great National Horse Exhibition at Springfield. Gleason's,* Nov. 12, 1853. 4. Fancy matched horses. *Gleason's,* Nov. 12, 1853. 5. *Western View of Brighton (central part),* Barber. NYPL. **198–199** 1. *Back Bay, Boston,* 1844, drawn by J. W. Barber, engraved by A. Willard and J. W. Barber. BA. 2. *The Express Train,* 1842, published by Currier and Ives. The Old Print Shop. 3. Boston and New York Central Railroad Co. stock certificate, March 24, 1854. AAS. 4. Railroad Station, Lynn. *Ballou's,* Jan. 10, 1857. 5. *New Map of Boston Comprising the Whole City, with the New Boundaries of the Wards.* Engraved expressly for the *Boston Almanac* for 1853 by G. W. Boynton. **200–201** 1. *View of Lowell,* William S. Pendleton, 19th century. WAM, Goodspeed Collection. 2. *View of the Boott Cotton Mills at Lowell. Gleason's,* May 29, 1852. 3. *The Westerly Part of the Grounds of the Atlantic Cotton Mills,* Jan. 1849. Merrimack Valley Textile Museum. 4. *View of the Dam from the second Pier of the Bridge,* May 22, 1847. Merrimack Valley Textile Museum. 5. *Boiling Room of Waltham Bleachery. Gleason's,* Dec. 17, 1853. 6. *Falling of the Pembreton Mills. Leslie's,* Jan. 28, 1860. **202–203** 1. *View of Appleton, Tracy and Co.'s Watch Manufactory, Waltham. Ballou's,* Oct. 2, 1858. 2. Watch, 1854. Waltham Watch Co. 3. Sewing Machine, Elias Howe, Jr,

April 1845. United States National Museum. 4. *Hunt and Webster's Sewing Mach. Mfy., Exhibition and Sales Room, Boston,* engraved by John Andrew. *Ballou's,* July 12, 1856. 5. *Turner's Falls on the Connecticut River. Ballou's,* Aug. 26, 1854. NYPL, Picture Collection. 6. Stone Quarry, Quincy, from unpublished sketchbook by T. K. Wharton, Oct. 18, 1853. NYPL. **204–205** 1. *The Shoemakers' Strike in Lynn. Leslie's,* March 17, 1860. NYPL, Picture Collection. 2. *Shoemakers' Strike in New England, view of Central Square. New York Illustrated News,* March 10, 1860. 3. Strikers in factory. *Leslie's,* March 17, 1860. 4. Railroad shop, South Framingham, interior, ambrotype, ca. 1860. AAS. 5. *Lazell, Perkins and Company Iron Works, Bridgewater,* lithograph by J. P. Newell, ca. 1860. Yale Univ. Art Gallery, Mabel Brady Garvan Collection. **206–207** 1. Daniel Webster, from a daguerrotype by T. DeBourg Richards. 1846. Photo: F. Gutekunst, Philadelphia. CSS Art Files. 2. *Daniel Webster delivering his "Reply to Hayne" before the Senate,* G. P. A. Healy. City of Boston, Art Commission. 3. Edward Everett. U.S. Signal Corps photo No. 111–B–1413 (Brady Collection) in the National Archives. 4. Honorable Edward Everett in the Assembly at Albany. *HW,* April 18, 1857. 5. *Diagram of the Senate Chamber.* Commonwealth of Massachusetts, *A Manual for the Use of the General Court,* Boston: Wright and Potter, 1863. 6. *Massachusetts Senate,* lithograph by Winslow Homer, 1856. LC. **208–209** 1. William Lloyd Garrison, 1865. LC, Brady–Handy Collection. 2. *The Liberator,* April 23, 1831. 3. *Antislavery Meeting on the Common. Gleason's,* May 3, 1851. 4. Broadside, July 8, 1854. Source unknown. 5. *Charles Sumner,* Walter Ingalls. Negative number 24411, Architect of the Capitol. 6. *William Lloyd Garrison's Meeting in Tremont Temple, Boston. HW.* **210–211** 1. *The Grand Review at Camp Massachusetts, Near Concord,* Sept. 9, 1859. *HW,* Sept. 24, 1859. 2. *Massachusetts Volunteers, Jersey City. HW,* May 4, 1861. 3. *Attack on the Massachusetts 6th at Baltimore,* April 19, 1861. LC. 4. *Recruiting Office, Boston, 9th Massachusetts Battery, Summer, 1862,* drawing by C. W. Reed. LC. 5. Advertisement. *Boston Almanac,* 1862. **212–213** 1. Haverhill editor tarred and feathered. *Leslie's,* Aug. 31, 1861. 2. Filling cartridges, engraved by Winslow Homer. *HW.* 3. Salem Common, artist unknown, 1863. MFA, M. & M. Karolik Collection. 4. *Governor John Andrew,* engraved by Alexander H. Ritchie. NYPL, Picture Collection. 5. Clara Barton. CSS Art Files. **214–215** 1. *Commissary Department, Encampment of the Massachusetts 6th Regiment of Volunteers at the Relay House near Baltimore, Md.* Lithograph by J. H. Bufford, from a sketch by Alfred Ordway, 1861. 2. *Charge of First Massachusetts Regiment on a Rebel Rifle Pit Near Yorktown,* sketched by Winslow Homer. *HW,* May 17, 1862. NYPL. 3. *Colonel Paul J. Revere.* Winsor, Justin, *The Memorial History of Boston,* Boston, 1881, vol. III, p. 319. 4. *Colonel Robert Gould Shaw.* Winsor, *The Memorial History,* vol. III, p. 321. 5. *Officers of the First Massachusetts Cavalry at Army of the Potomac Headquarters,* Petersburg, Va., Aug. 1864. LC. 6. General Ben F. Butler. War Department Collection. 7. *Funeral of Captain Christopher S. Hastings,* Sept. 15, 1863. William Benton Museum of Art, Collection of Mr. and Mrs. Peter Tillou. **216–217** 1. Senator Charles Sumner and Henry Wadsworth Longfellow, J. W. Black and Co., Boston, 1895. CSS Art Files. 2. William Dean Howells in his library. CSS Art Files. 3. John G. Whittier. Photo: Thomas, Newburyport. CSS Art Files. 4. Louisa May Alcott. CSS Art Files. 5. Edward Everett Hale and Oliver Wendell Holmes in Dr. Holmes' study, May 1893. CSS Art Files. 6. Emily Dickinson. NYPL, Picture Collection.

7. Authors' Group, Noteman Photo Co., Boston, ca. 1882. Concord Free Public Library. **218–219** 1. *Newburyport Marshes*, Martin J. Heade. MFA, bequest of Maxim Karolik. 2. *Medford Marshes*, George Loring Brown. MFA, M. & M. Karolik Collection. 3. *Neponset River*, Benjamin Smith Rotch. MFA, gift of Misses Aimee and Rosamund Lamb. 4. *Lighthouse at Nantucket Beach*, Thomas Doughty. MFA, bequest of M. Karolik. 5. *Bash-Bish Falls, South Egremont*, John Frederick Kensett. MFA, M. & M. Karolik Collection. **220–221** 1. *The Chinese in New England, North Adams*, from a sketch by Theo. R. Davis. *HW*, July 23, 1870. NYPL, Picture Collection. 2. New England Factory Life, *Bell-Time*, Washington Mills, Lawrence, Winslow Homer. *HW*, July 25, 1868. 3. *Employees at Blake Brothers, Playing Ball at Hamilton Park*, July 31, 1869, sketched by J. R. Spencer. MFA. 4. Broadside. A Factory Operative's Appeal to the President of the United States, 1869. LC, Rare Book Room. **222–223** 1. The Richardson Manufacturing Company's Works, Prescott Street, Worcester. *Worcester Illustrated Business Guide*, 1880. 2. Advertisement. *Providence Directory*, 1860. 3. Advertisement. *Worcester Illustrated Business Guide*, 1880. 4. South Boston Iron Co.'s Works. *King's*, 1878. 5. T. K. Earle Manufacturing Company. *Worcester Illustrated Business Guide*, 1880. 6. Textile sample of Pacific Mills. Merrimack Valley Textile Museum. 7. Mills of Nonotuck Silk Company, Florence, Mass., 1844. Brockett, L. P., *The Silk Industry in America*, 1876. **224–225** 1. Union Passenger Station, Worcester. *Worcester Illustrated Business Guide*, 1880. 2. Boston and Maine Railroad Depot, Haymarket Square. *King's*, 1878. 3. Old Colony Railroad Depot, Kneeland St. *King's*, 1878. 4. State Street as decorated for the Railroad Jubilee, 1851. NYPL, Picture Collection. 5. Hoosac Tunnel Entrance. *HW*, Dec. 5, 1868. 6. The *"Bristol," Fall River Line—New York and Boston*, engraved by J. A. Lowell and Co., Boston. *King's*, 1878. **226–227** 1–3. *King's*, 1878. 4. *Charles Francis Adams*. *SM*, vol. IV, Oct. 1888, p. 487. 5. *Opening of the New Merchants' Exchange on Waltham Street—Scene in the Reading Room*, sketched by E. R. Morse. NYPL, Picture Collection. 6. *Merchants' Exchange, State St. King's*, 1878. **228–229** 1. *Corn Husking at Nantucket*, Eastman Johnson, ca. 1875. MMA, Rogers Fund, 1907. 2. General view of Massachusetts Agricultural College, Amherst. *Scribner's Monthly*, vol. XII 1876, p. 841. 3. *Stables of Winthrop W. Chenery at Belmont*, after a drawing by T. Marsden. *HW*, July 21, 1860. 4. Advertisement. *Providence Directory*, 1860. 5. *Picking and Sorting Cranberries*. *HM*, June 1875. NYPL, Prints Collection. **230–231** 1. Bark *Massachusetts* of New Bedford, 1868. ODHS. 2. Advertisement. *Boston Almanac*, 1858. 3. Drying fish, Little Harbor. *HM*, 1874. NYPL, Picture Collection. 4. *Ship-building, Gloucester Harbor*, engraving by Winslow Homer. *HW*, Oct. 11, 1873. 5. *Gloucester from Brookbank*, Fitz Hugh Lane. MFA, M. & M. Karolik Collection. **232–233** 1. The Boston Fire of 1872. *King's*, 1878. 2. Advertisement. *Worcester Illustrated Business Guide*, 1880. 3. The Summer Street Fire, Boston, Nov. 9 and 10, 1872. Panorama from New P. O. Building, stereoscopic view. CSS Art Files. 4. Ticket, World's Peace Jubilee and Int'l Musical Festival, Boston, June 1872. Lithograph by Armstrong and Co. 5. The Boston Water-works. *King's*, 1878. **234–235** 1. View of steeple of Arlington Street Church. Bryant, William Cullen, *Picturesque America*, New York, 1872. 2. David Sear's plan for Back Bay development, June 4, 1849. BA. 3. John Souther's steam shovel loading gravel for the Back Bay, Needham. BA. 4. Commonwealth Avenue and Dartmouth Street, Boston, 1872. BA. 5. Charles River and the Back Bay, Boston.

Detroit Photographic Co. **236–237** 1–6. *King's*, 1878. 6. *The Old Museum—The Lawrence Room*, Enrico Meneghelli. MFA, gift of M. Knoedler and Co. **238–239** 1. *Wonderful Experiments with the Telephone by Professor Graham Bell*. *Daily Graphic*, March 6, 1877. 2. Garret in the building at 109 Court St., Boston. Bell Telephone Laboratories. 3. First telephone—June 3, 1875. New York Museum of Science and Industry. 4. Original Telephone Exchange Switch Board, May 1877. Floyd L. Darrow. CSS Art Files. 5. Worcester Switchboard using lamps, 1896. CSS Art Files. **240–241** 1. Advertisement. *Leslie's*, May 31, 1879. 2. Brochure of the Columbia Riding School. Pope Manufacturing Co., Boston. 3. *Opening of the Four Days' Bicycle Contest for the Championship of the World, in Boston, Nov. 5, 1879*, from a sketch by H. R. Burdick. *Leslie's*, Nov. 22, 1879. 4. *Annual Meeting of the League of American Wheelmen, at Boston, May 30, 1881*, from a sketch by Charles Upham. *Leslie's*, June 18, 1881. 5. *Family Tricycle, Bicycle Tournament in Hampden Park, Springfield, Sept. 18–20*, from a sketch by Charles Upham. *Leslie's*, Sept. 29, 1883. **242–243** 1. College of the Holy Cross. *Worcester Illustrated Business Guide*, 1880. 2. Worcester County Free Institute of Industrial Science. *Worcester Illustrated Business Guide*, 1880. 3. Zoology Laboratory, c. 1890. Mount Holyoke College, South Hadley. 4. Wellesley College. *King's*, 1878. 5. Massachusetts Institute of Technology, Boylston St. *King's*, 1878. 6. Amherst College. Source unknown. **244–245** 1. Provincetown schoolhouse. Cape Cod Views, C. H. Nickerson, stereoscopic view. CSS Art Files. 2, 3. Stebbins, L., *Eighty Years Progress in the U.S. by Eminent Literary Men*, Worcester, 1861. NYPL. 4. The High School. *Worcester Illustrated Business Guide*, 1880. 5. Groton School Chapel. MDCD. 6. Verdi Hall. Courtesy, St. Columbkille's Church, Brighton. **246–247** 1. *President Charles William Eliot*. *Scribner's Monthly*, vol. XII, 1876, p. 351. 2. *Quadrangle, Harvard College*. Drake, *Old Landmarks*, p. 231. 3. *Memorial Hall, Dining-Room*. *Scribner's Monthly*, vol. XII, 1876, p. 358. 4. *Sanders' Theater, Memorial Hall*. *Scribner's Monthly*, vol. XII, 1876, p. 357. 5. *The Two Hundred and Fiftieth Anniversary of Harvard College—President Cleveland and Governor Robinson Entering the College Grounds at Cambridge—Salute by the Students*. *Leslie's*, 1886. LC. **248–249** 1. Chronicle of facts and events. *Boston Alamanc*, 1883. 2. Henry Adams. MHS. 3. *William James*, ca. 1865, sketch from his medical-school notebook. Houghton Library, James Papers. 4. *Reading Room of the Boston Public Library*, J. J. Harley. *Every Saturday*, January 28, 1871. 5. The Museum of Natural History, 1864. BA. 6. Louis Agassiz. CSS Art Files. 7. *Asa Gray*, engraved by J. J. Cade in *Eclectic Magazine*, 1880. LC. **250–251** 1. Prang's Aids for Object Teaching, *Printer*. L. Prang and Co., Boston. LC. 2. Old Corner Bookstore, 1880. *HM*, Feb. 1881. NYPL, Picture Collection. 3. Little, Brown, & Co., Washington St. *King's*, 1878. 4. Riverside Press, Cambridge. *Daily Graphic*, March 14, 1878. **252–253** 1. *Pilgrims Going to Church*, George H. Boughton, 1867. NYHS. 2. U.S.S. *Constitution*. GBCC. 3. New England Historic–Genealogical Society, Somerset St. *King's*, 1878. 4. Concord Minute Man. MDCD. 5. Robert Gould Shaw Memorial, St. Gaudens, 1897. Architect of stone frame, Charles F. McKim. MDCD. 6. Faneuil Hall, interior. American Airlines. **254–255** 1–4. *King's*, 1878. 5. Harvard Medical School, Boston. Boston and Neighborhood Descriptive Series, stereoscopic view. CSS Art Files. 6. Children's Hospital, 1583 Washington St. *King's*, 1878. 7. Advertisement. *Boston Almanac*, 1862. **256–257** 1. Calisthenics Class, 1865. Mount Holyoke College, South

Hadley. 2. Pioneer Camp of 1885. Worcester Natural History Society, pamphlet, 1890. 3. Boston Yacht-Club House, City Point, engraved by Russell Richardson. *King's,* 1878. 4. Coasting—The Boston Common. *King's,* 1878. 5. The Gymnasium, Boston. *SM,* vol. XVIII, July 1895. 6. Lawn Tennis at Mount Holyoke Female Seminary, May 1884. Mount Holyoke College, South Hadley. **258–259** 1. First Basketball Team. Springfield College. 2. Baseball Club of 1877. Holy Cross. 3. Women's Gymnastic Group. Smith College. 4. Sullivan–Corbett Fight, Sept. 7, 1892. The *Ring* Collection, NYPL, Picture Collection. 5. Mike Kelly. BPL. 6. Boston Baseball Team (Braves), 1892. Photo: Elmer Chickering. BPL. **260–261** 1. Quincy Market, Boston. *America Illustrated,* Boston and Suburbs, stereoscopic view. CSS Art Files. 2. Advertisement. Temple Programme, Feast of Purim, March 10, 1892. Temple Adath Israel, Boston. CSS Art Files. 3. The Brunswick, Menu, Jan. 17, 1884. CSS Art Files. 4. Parker House, School St. *King's,* 1878. 5. Advertisement. Boston Symphony Orchestra program, week of April 20, 1890. CSS Art Files. 6. Advertisement. *King's,* 1878. **262–263** 1. Henry Lee Higginson, B. L. Pratt, 1908. Boston Symphony Orchestra. 2. Boston Symphony Orchestra Season Programme, 1889–1890, cover. CSS Art Files. 3. Symphony Hall, Boston. MDCD. 4. Wilhelm Gericke. Photo: Falk. NYPL, Music Room. 5. Karl Muck. Photo: Geis. NYPL, Music Room. 6. Advertisement. Boston Symphony Orchestra Season Programme, 1889–1890. CSS Art Files. **264–265** 1. The Grand Museum, Dover and Washington sts. CSS Art Files. 2. Hollis St. Theatre, Program, ca. 1880. Lux Engraving Co., Stebbing Photo. CSS Art Files. 3. Boston Museum, Program, ca. 1880. CSS Art Files. 4. "It's Funny, Very, Very, Very Funny!" *Skipped By the Light of the Moon,* Program, Mechanic Hall, Thursday, April 26, 1888. Under the management of W. W. Fowler and Wm. Warmington. CSS Art Files. 5. Advertisement. Hollis St. Theatre Program, ca. 1880. CSS Art Files. 6. Circus, New Bedford. ODHS. **266–267** All: CSS Art Files. 1. Chetwood Smith. Photo: C. R. B. Claflin, Worcester. 2. Infant, mother, grandmother. Photo: Davis, Worcester. 3. J. L. Smith and boy, 1884. Photo: C. R. B. Claflin, Worcester. 4. Ralph Williams. Photo: Ritz and Hastings, Boston. 5. J. L. Smith and girl, 1885. Photo: Everett's Studio, Worcester. 6. F. H. Kinnicutt. Photo: C. R. B. Claflin, Worcester. 7. Mrs. B. C. Clark and Alice N. Clark, 1891. Photo: C. F. Conly, Boston. 8. E. W. Kinnicutt. Photo: Fitton. 9. Girl, June 1895. Photo: Schervee. **268–269** 1. Prang's Aids for Object Teaching, Trades and Occupations. *The Kitchen.* L. Prang and Co., Boston, 1874. LC. 2. Marie E. Zakrzewska, M.D. Boston Medical Library, Francis A. Countaway Library of Medicine. 3. Mary Baker Eddy. First Church of Christ, Scientist, Boston. 4. Lizzie Borden. Fall River Public Library. 5. *Women Voting at Municipal Election in Boston on Dec. 11,* drawn by Henry Sandham. *HW,* December 5, 1888. **270–271** 1. *The Cliffs at Nahant.* Grant, Robert, *American Summer Resorts, The North Shore of Massachusetts,* New York: Charles Scribner's Sons, 1896, p. 11. Illustrated by W. T. Smedley. 2. *Pavilion at "The Masconomo."* Grant, Robert, *American Summer Resorts,* p. 31. 3. Somerset Club House, Beacon St. *King's,* 1878. 4. Justice Oliver Wendell Holmes. LC. 5. Abbott Lawrence Lowell. Harvard Univ. Archives. 6. Mrs. Reginald C. Vanderbilt and Miss Eleanora Sears. Halpert, Stephen & Brenda, *Brahmins and Bullyboys: G. Frank Radway's Boston Album,* Boston: Houghton Mifflin Co., 1973. Reprinted by permission of Houghton Mifflin Company. **272–273** 1. The Gothic Room. Isabella Stewart Gardner Museum. 2. North Court. Isabella Stewart Gardner Museum. 3. *John Lowell Gardner,*

Antonio Mancini. Isabella Stewart Gardner Museum. 4. Bernard Berenson, ca. 1887. Isabella Stewart Gardner Museum. 5. John Singer Sargent, Uffizi Gallery, Florence. Art Reference Bureau and Frick Art Reference Library, permission of Alinari Brothers. 6. *James McNeill Whistler,* Henri Fantin-Latour. Smithsonian Institution, Freer Gallery of Art, Washington, D.C. **274–275** 1. Sea Chest of Manoel E. De Mendonca, ca. 1865. ODHS. 2. Scandinavian Sailors and Immigrants Home, East Boston. Postcard. CSS Art Files. 3. *Little Canada. SM,* vol. XIII, March 1893, p. 366. 4. *Boston Almanac and Directory,* 1884, p. 341. 5. Advertisement. *Ayer's Deutcher Almanach,* Lowell, 1897. CSS Art Files. 6. Polish immigrants, Lowell, ca. 1900. Carpenter Center for Visual Arts, Harvard Univ. **276–277** 1. *The Italian Quarter,* 1899. *HM,* November 1899. NYPL, Picture Collection. 2. *The Kindergarten in the North Industrial Home, Boston,* from a sketch by Chas. Upham. *Leslie's,* June 4, 1881. LC. 3. Paul Revere's home, Boston. CSS Art Files. 4. Souvenir, fiftieth anniversary of Temple Ohabei Shalom, 1843–1893. *American Jewish Archives,* Hebrew Union College, Cincinnati. 5. *The Jewish Quarter,* 1899. *HM,* November 1899. NYPL, Picture Collection. 6. Advertisement, Temple Programme, Feast of Purim, March 10, 1892. Temple Adath Israel, Boston. CSS Art Files. **278–279** 1. Cathedral of the Holy Cross, Boston. LC. 2. John Boyle O'Reilly. *The Pilot.* 3. St. John's Seminary. Courtesy, St. Columbkille's Church, Brighton. 4. Father Reardon. Courtesy, St. Columbkille's Church, Brighton. 5. Reverend James A. Healey. BPL. 6. William Henry Cardinal O'Connell. Halpert, Stephen and Brenda, *Brahmins and Bullyboys: G. Frank Radway's Boston Album,* Boston: Houghton Mifflin Co., 1973. Reprinted by permission of Houghton Mifflin Company. 7. Rose Fitzgerald and mother. Halpert. Reprinted by permission of Houghton Mifflin Company. **280–281** 1. *Hamburg St., from Harrison Ave. near Andover House. SM,* vol. XIII, March 1893, p. 393. 2. *The Ejectment—Commerce St.,* drawn by Walter Shirlaw, engraved by W. B. Witte. *SM,* vol. XIII, March 1893, p. 361. 3. *Tramps at Wayfarer's Lodge, Hawkins St.,* drawn by Walter Shirlaw, engraved by C. I. Butler. *SM,* vol. XIII, March 1893, p. 368. 4. *Flower Meeting in Back Parlor of Andover House. SM,* vol. XIII, March 1893, p. 357. **282–283** 1. Dedham, aerial view, detail, Edwin Whitefield, 1877. AAS. 2. Residence of John Anderton, Chicopee Falls, ca. 1879. *History of the Connecticut Valley in Massachusetts,* vol. II, Phila.: Louis H. Everts, 1879. 3. Wooden houses, South Boston, 1936. Photo: Walker Evans. Fogg Art Museum, gift of Mr. John McAndrew. 4. Salisbury Building, engraved by C. F. Jewett Co. *Worcester Illustrated Business Guide,* 1880. 5. Floor plan of Salisbury Building. *Worcester Illustrated Business Guide,* 1880. 6. Three-decker house, South Boston. Photo: Irv Shaffer. 7. City Hall, Fall River, ca. 1877. Peck, Fredrick M., and Earl, Henry H., *Fall River and Its Industries,* New York: Atlantic Publishing and Engraving, 1877. 8. New Town Hall, Wellesley. Programme, Juvenile Entertainment at the New Town Hall, Wellesley, May 21, 1887, by the children of the Episcopal Sunday School. CSS Art Files. **284–285** 1. Washington St., Boston, looking north. CSS Art Files. 2. Fort Rodman Trolley, New Bedford. ODHS. 3. Worcester, ca. 1900. CSS Art Files. 4. *Proposed Subway Station, Boston,* drawn by Otto H. Bacher, engraved by W. B. Witte. *SM,* vol. XI, June 1892, p. 753. 5. *The Descent to the Subway, Public Gardens. HM,* Nov. 1899. NYPL, Picture Collection. 6. *The Elevated Railway, Boston,* 1899. *HM,* Nov. 1899. NYPL, Picture Collection. **286–287** 1. *Low Tide, Beachmont.* Maurice Prendergast. WAM. 2. Ocean

House Menu, Nantasket Beach. CSS Art Files. 3. *Bathing at Revere Beach. SM,* vol. XXIII, June 1898, p. 679. 4. Lincoln Park, Dartmouth. ODHS. **288–289** Plat and Environs of Lagoon Heights, showing property owned by the Lagoon Heights Land Co., Cottage City, lithograph by O. H. Baily and Co., Boston. BPL. **290–291** 1. *Boston Common at Twilight,* Childe Hassam. MFA, gift of Miss Maud E. Appleton. 2. *Copley Square with Trinity Church and the Old Museum,* K. Calhoun. MFA, gift of George H. Edgell. 3. *The Ames Building, Boston,* drawn by E. C. Peixotto. *SM,* vol. XV, March 1894, p. 317. **292–293** Boston, 1899, lithograph by George H. Walker and Co., Boston. BPL. **294–295** 1. Sacred Cod of Massachusetts. David F. Lawlor, from A. Devaney, New York. 2. Boston Fishing Pier. CSS Art Files. 3. Cutting into a Sperm Whale. LC. 4. *Whalers at Herschel Island,* John Bertonchini. ODHS. 5. Pearl Drying Rack, Indian Museum, Mashpee. Photo: Irv Shaffer. **296–297** 1. Eclipse Mill, North Adams. CSS Art Files. 2. Shoe factory worker, Lynn, ca. 1895. Photo: F. B. Johnston. LC. 3. Shoe factory worker, Lynn, ca. 1895. Photo: F. B. Johnston. LC. 4. Shoe factory workers letting off, Lynn, ca. 1895. Photo: F. B. Johnston. LC. 5. Battery A of Boston at Washington Mills Boarding Houses, March 1912. Merrimack Valley Textile Museum. **298–299** 1. County Street, New Bedford. ODHS. 2. Peddler, Horse and Wagon. ODHS. 3. Farm, Marlborough. Photo: Irv Shaffer. 4. Nancy Lee, who lived alone at Nantucket. From a stereoscopic view. SPNEA. **300–301** 1. Duryea Automobile, 1893. Smithsonian Institution, gift to the National Museum by Inglis M. Uppercu in 1920. 2. Advertisement, 1910. Stevens-Duryea Company, Chicopee Falls. 3. Advertisement, ca. 1920. Stevens-Duryea Company, Chicopee Falls. 4. Joseph D. Roberts at wheel of automobile, 1906. ODHS. 5. Revere Beach, 1912. BPL. **302–303** 1. United States Army recruiting brochure cover. CSS Art Files. 2. World War I Preparedness Parade, Beacon St., 1916. BPL. 3. Draftees after one week's training, New Bedford. Photo: F. W. Dresser. 4. Boxing Match in auditorium, Camp Devens. CSS Art Files. 5. *Senator Henry Cabot Lodge,* Cesaré. Gilbert, C. W., *Mirrors of Washington,* N.Y.: G. P. Putnam's Sons, 1921. **304–305** 1. Boston Police Strike, 1919. BPL. 2. Calvin Coolidge. U.S. Bureau of Engraving and Printing. 3. Mrs. Grace Goodhue Coolidge. Smithsonian Institution. 4. Mayor James Michael Curley and son leading Evacuation Day Parade up Beacon St., 1917. BPL. 5. James Michael Curley—first inauguration as mayor of Boston, Mechanics Hall, 1913. BPL. 6. James Michael Curley running for governor. "Norman" cartoon, 1924. BPL. **306–307** 1. Boukis Family in U.S.,

1917. Mrs. P. S. Dukakis, Chestnut Hill. 2. Hyfer Family, Chelsea. Collection of the author. 3. Abraham Kaplan, Chelsea. Collection of the author. 4. Dr. Varazted Kazanjian. Harvard Univ. 5. Irish immigrants who landed in Boston on S.S. *Vedig,* March 2, 1921. UPI. 6. *The Passion of Sacco and Vanzetti,* Ben Shahn. Whitney Museum of American Art, gift of Edith and Milton Lowenthal in memory of Juliana Force. **308–309** 1. Upton Sinclair selling a figleaf edition of his book, *Oil,* to Florence L. Leiscomb in Boston. UPI. 2. Great Molasses Flood, Atlantic Avenue, Boston, 1919. BPL. 3. Wellesley College. 4. Custom House Tower. *SM,* vol. LXXV, June 1924. 5. Wood Worsted Mills, Lawrence. American Woolen Company. **310–311** 1. Deserted farm house, Savoy Mountains, 1941. LC. 2. *Street Scene #1,* Jack Levine. MFA. 3. Quabbin Reservoir. MDCD. 4. Flood in Ware, Sept. 1938. New England Western Electric. 5. Lowell House Tower. Harvard Univ. 6. The Lindens, Danvers. Now in Washington, D.C. HABS, LC. **312–313** 1. U.S. Navy. 2. LC. 3. Standard Oil Company, N.J. 4. Courtesy, Jean C. Hickcox, South Yarmouth. 5. U.S.S. *Massachusetts,* Fall River. MDCD. 6. Harvard Univ. Archives. **314–315** 1. John Hancock Mutual Life Insurance Co. 2. Christian Science Church Center, Boston. Photo: Gorchev and Gorchev, Winchester. Cossutta and Ponte, Architects and Planners. 3. Boston City Hall. GBCC. 4. Gund Hall, School of Design. Harvard Univ. News Office. 5. Bank Building, Worcester. Photo: Irv Shaffer. **316–317** 1. Tufts Univ. 2. MIT Historical Collections. 3. Univ. of Mass., Amherst, News Bureau. 4. Brandeis Univ. 5. Boston Univ. Photo Service. 6. Harvard Univ. News Office. **318–319** 1. John F. Kennedy. U.S. Bureau of Engraving and Printing. 2. Wide World Photo. 3. United Nations. 4. Wide World Photo. 5. Jacqueline Bouvier Kennedy. Smithsonian Institution. 6. Boston Celtics. **320–321** 1. Wide World Photo. 2. MDCD. 3. The Beacon Street Union. Cambridge Common, Cambridge, 1971. Photo: Wayne Ulaky, Windham. 4. The Beacon Street Union. MGM Records. 5. Advertisement. *Real Paper,* April 9, 1975. 6. Classified advertisements. *Real Paper,* April 9, 1975. Reprinted with permission of *Real Paper,* Cambridge. **322–323** 1. ABC Pizza House. Photo: Irv Shaffer. 2. Humberto Cardinal Medeiros. Archdiocese of Boston. 3–5. UPI. **324–325** 1. Main Street, Deerfield. Historic Deerfield. 2. Miner Grant's General Store. Old Sturbridge Village, Sturbridge. 3. Wampanoag Indian Museum, Mashpee, interior. Photo: Irv Shaffer. 4. Springfield Armory Museum, Springfield. MDCD. 5. Park Street Church, Boston. MDCD. 6. Old State House, Boston. GBCC.

Index

The index to this book serves as a guide to both textual and pictorial material. The contents of the pictures themselves are indexed in a great many cases, as explained in the introductory note, *This Book and Its Uses,* on page vii. The following system of references is used:

180   reference to the text only or to both text and pictures on page 180

180:3   not mentioned in the text but depicted in picture number 3 on page 180

180:**3**   depicted in picture number 3 on page 180 and mentioned in the accompanying text

The number preceding the colon is the page number; the number following the colon is the picture number. When only one picture appears on a two-page spread, as on pages 108–109 or 288–89, the indication 108–109:1 or 289:1 is given for pictorial references not mentioned in the text. When the identification of a subject is not obvious, an explanation of its position appears in parentheses following the page and picture number: e.g. Mill Dam, view of, 96–97:3 (lower right). When it seems desirable, dates are given to place a subject in its proper time frame.

Ashley Falls, Massachusetts, 23:3
Asians, *see also* Mongolians
    census of 1880 and, 275
astrological symbols, 40:3
Athenaeum, Boston, 12, 13, 14
    pictures from, *see list of picture sources*
Atheneum, Nantucket, 161:5
athletics, *see* sports
Atlantic Cotton Mills, Lawrence, 200:3
Atlantic Ocean, 20, 29
    North, French dominance of in 18c., 67
Attleboro, Massachusetts, 128
    powder house, 101:6
auditoriums:
    Lyceum Hall, Salem, 238:1
    Tremont Temple, Boston, 1853, 209:6
Auerbach, Red, 319:6 (at Kennedy's right)
autographs, *see also* handwriting
    of William Bradford, 26:1, 27:3
    of Dorothy May, 26:1
    of Mayflower Compact signers, 27:3
    of King Philip, 49:5
    of Isaac Royall, 60:4
automobiles, 300–301
    on Revere Beach, 1912, 301:5
    c.1970, 325:6
awnings, c.1808, 118–19:1
axes, 17c., 41:6

Back Bay, *see* Boston, Back Bay
ballot box, 1888, 269:5
Ballou's Pictorial Drawing-Room Companion (earlier
    known as *Gleason's Pictorial Drawing-Room
    Companion*), *see also Gleason's*:
    masthead of, c.1857, 181:5
    pictures from, *see list of picture sources*
Baltimore, Maryland, Massachusetts militia attacked
    at, 1861, 210–211:3
balustrades:
    carved, 70:2
    roof, 36:1, 70–71:1, 76:1, 96–97:3, 120:1,2, 311:6
    in Salem, c.1765, 82:5
bands:
    Beacon Street Union, c.1965, 320–21:3,4
    at Lincoln Park Casino, c.1900, 287:4
    at Weymouth picnic, 185:3 (lower right)
banking and banks, 11, 12, 13, 226–27
    Maverick National Bank, Boston, 19c., 226:1
    Pittsfield, c.1839, 159:5
    Springfield, c.1839, 159:3 (at left)
    Suffolk Bank, Boston, 1834, 171:4
Baptists, 6
bar bells, 256:1
Barber, John Warner:
    drawings by:
        of Dedham, 146–47:3
        of Pittsfield, 159:5
    engravings after, *see list of picture sources*
Barclay, Andrew, bookbindery of, 76:3

bark used for siding in wigwams, 32–33:4
barns, 24–25, 299:3
Barnstable, Massachusetts:
    founding of, 4
Barnstable Bay, *see* Cape Cod Bay
Barnstable County, Jews in, 9
Barnum and Bailey Circus, 265:6
barrels:
    cracker, 184:2
    making of, *see* cooperage
    whale oil, 230:1
        number of extracted per whale, 193:5
Bartholomew's Cobble, Ashley Falls, 23:3
Barton, Clara, photograph of, 213:5
baseball:
    Boston Baseball Club, 259
    Boston Braves, 19c., 259:6
    Holy Cross team, 1877, 258:2
    Readville laborers playing, 1869, 221:3
Bash-Bish Falls, South Egremont, Massachusetts, by
        John Frederick Kensett, 219:5
basket, for eggs, 268–69:1
basketball:
    Boston Celtics at White House, 1963, 319:6
    first team, at American International College, c.1870,
        258:1
bathing, *see also* beaches
    hot water for, in water heater, 268–69:1
    at L Street Beach, 286
    tramps, at Wayfarer's Lodge, Boston, 280:3
bathing suits, 1897, 287:3
battles, 48:1, 210–11:3, 265:5
    of Bunker Hill, 8, 20, 94, 96:1–97:5, 98–99:1
    Lexington and Concord, 92:1–93:5
    naval, 43:6 (upper left)
beaches, 286, 288
    Beachmont in 1890s, watercolor by Maurice Pren-
        dergast, 286:1
    Cape Cod, 21:3
    Martha's Vineyard, 20:2, 289:1 (top center)
    Provincetown, 1826, 160:4
    Revere Beach, 287:3, 301:5
Beachmont, Massachusetts, watercolor by Maurice
        Prendergast, 1890s, 286:1
beacon, on Beacon Hill, 46:3 (upper left), 54:1 (top
        center), 88:1
Beacon Hill, *see* Beacon; Boston, Beacon Hill
Beacon Street Union (rock group), 320–21:3, 321:4
"Beat generation," 321
beaver, detail from Dutch map, c.1650, 30:2
Bedford, Massachusetts:
    flag of militia, 1775, 93:4
    list of soldiers killed from, 1775, 93:5
beds:
    hospital, 153:6
    nursery, 153:7
beer mug, 1892, 260:2
belfry, *see also* cupolas; steeples, 36:1
Belknap and Hall (printers), 110:1
Bell, Alexander Graham, 238–39
    portrait of, 238:1
Bellotti, Francis X., 17
Bell Time by Winslow Homer, 220–21:2

dog, in engraving of Boston Massacre by Revere, 89:3
Dollar, Emanuel, 107:7
dolls, 80
Dorchester, Massachusetts, 36
    branding mark, 41:4
    founding of, 4
    gravestone of John Foster at, 37:7
Dorchester Heights, Massachusetts (now South Boston), 8
    annexed to Boston in 1805, 139
    British burning every shelter at, 94–95:1
    sketch of, by British officer, 1776, 94:2
    toll bridge between Boston and, opened 1805, 138–39:1
dories, 190–91:3
Doughty, Thomas, painting of *Lighthouse at Nantasket Beach,* 218–19:4
Douglass, Frederick, photograph of, 162:2
Dover, Massachusetts, branding mark, 41:4
Drowne, Shem, sculpture by, 56:3
drumlins, 20:4
Dudley, Massachusetts, 101
Dukakis, Michael, 17, 307
Dunster, Rev. Henry, 6
Durand, Asher B., engraving of portrait of John Quincy Adams, 124:3
Durant, Henry Fowle, 13
Duryea, Charles and Frank, 300
dustpan, 19c., 268–69:1
Dutch:
    census of 1790 and, 8–9
    map, c.1650, of Plymouth Colony, 30–31:2–4
    marriage certificate, 26:1
Duxbury, Massachusetts, 101
    founding of, 4
    house built in 1653, 31:6

Earl, Ralph, *Looking East from Denny Hill* by, 104–105:3
Earle Company, T. K., 223:5
easel, 180:2
East Boston, Massachusetts:
    Scandinavian Home, 274:2
    shipbuilding at, 179
    Unitarian church, 19c., 147:4
    wharves, 1899, 293:1 (lower right)
East Chelmsford, Massachusetts, *see also* Chelmsford, 10
Eastern Line, 199
Eastham, Massachusetts, windmill, 72:1
Easty, Mary, affidavit re witchcraft arrest, 51:4
Eaton, Francis, autograph of, 27:3
Eclipse Mill, North Adams, c.1900, 296–97:1
economy, *see also* banking and banks; manufacturing; textile industry; trade
    of Massachusetts Bay colony, 5
    post-Revolutionary, 8
    19c., 9–11
    20c., 11, 316

Eddy, Mary Morse Baker, *see also* Christian Science, 16
    photograph of, 268:3
Edgartown, Massachusetts, 192
education, *see also names of individual institutions;* schools, 3–4, 11–12, 13–14, 17, 154–57, 242–47, 271, 316–17
    agricultural, 228:2
    Puritans and, 3–4, 14, 46
Edwards, Jonathan, 60–61
Edwards, Thomas (Boston silversmith), tray by, 63:4
egg basket, 268–69:1
Eisenhower, Dwight D., 318–19:4 (far left)
elephants, 115
elevated train, *see* subways
Eliot, Charles W., portrait of, 246:1
Eliot, John:
    Indians and, 49
    portrait of, 48:2
Eliot family, 12
elm trees, 159:3, 290–91:1, 298:1
    on Boston Common, 88:1
    in Pittsfield, 110:3
embroidery, *see* needlework
Emerson, George B., schoolmaster, 154:6
Emerson, Ralph Waldo, 16, 17, 145, 149, 151, 166, 181, 253
    camping in Adirondacks, 1858, 151:7
    photographs of, 148:1, 151:6 (at left), 217:7
Emerson School, Boston, 155:6
emigration, 168
    tract to discourage, 19c., to Ohio, 168:1
Emma Isadora (ship), c.1850, 168:4
Endecott, John, 35
    portrait of, 35:4
England and English:
    American Revolution and, 92–99
    Boston Massacre and, 88, 89:3
    Britain, symbolized as griffin, 103:5
    cartoon re Boston Port Bill, 91:4
    cartoon re Boston Tea Party, 90:3
    governing Massachusetts colonies, 6–7, 52
    Indians and, 49, 52
    industrialization in, 9
    locomotive, 1835, 136:1
    Massachusetts settlements named for towns in, 4
    prerevolutionary taxes of, 7, 84, 87, 91
    rivalry with France, 67, 84, 101
    as settlers of Massachusetts, 3–5, 6, 8, 9, 32, 107:8
    troops in Boston, 87, 88, 94–95:1, 95:4
    War of 1812 and, 123
engraving, 180:2
    tools, 74:1
entertainment, *see also* sports, theater
    camping, 151:7, 256:2
    circus, 19c., 265:6
    dance, 156:2
    fairs, 40:3, 111, 196–97:3
    horseback riding, 68–69:2
    parades, 46:3 (upper left), 118–19:1, 141:5, 215:7, 241:4, 302–303:2, 305:4
    parties, 143:3, 183:3
    picnics, 184:2, 184–85:3
    singing, 69:4

George III, 1812 cartoon and, 123:6
Gericke, Wilhelm, photograph of, 263:4
Germans:
    almanac published in Lowell, 275:5
    census of 1790 and, 9
    census of 1900 and, 9
    during World War I, 262
    in post–Civil War work force, 220
Gerry, Elbridge, portrait of, 122:1
gerrymandering, 122:2
Gettysburg, battle of, panorama of, 265:5
Gibbs, Margaret, portrait of, 1670, 44:2
Gidney, Bartholomew, 53:4
Gill, Moses, Princeton, farm of, 111:6
Gillette razor factory, World War II and, 312:2
glassblowers, 73, 130
Gleason's Pictorial Drawing-Room Companion (later
        called *Ballou's Pictorial Drawing-Room Com-
        panion*), *see also Ballou's*
    advertisement for, 172 (at bottom)
    pictures from, *see list of picture sources*
Gleason's Publishing Hall, Tremont Street, 169:5,
        174:2
globe, 145:6
    representation of, 37:7
    world, 1861, 244:3
Glory of the Seas (ship), 11
Gloucester, Massachusetts:
    branding mark, 41:4
    census of 1790 and, 9
    founding of, 4
    shipbuilding at, 231:4
    view of, 231:5
Gloucester from Brookbank by Fitzhugh Lane, 231:5
Glysson, Dr. William, portrait of, 101:5
Godkin, E. L., 17
Gott, Samuel, house of, Cape Ann, 1710, 83:6
grace cup, *see loving cup*
Grand Museum, Boston, late 19c., 264–65:1
grandstand at fair, 196:4
Grand Turk (ship), 1786, 117:4
granite, 134–35, 203:6
    railway, 134:1
Grant, Robert (member of commission reviewing
        Sacco-Vanzetti case), caricature of, 307:6
Grant, Ulysses S., labor petition to, 1869, 221:4
grapes, 229:4
grasshopper as weathervane, 57:4
gravestones, *see also* cemeteries; monuments, 31:7,
        92:2, 165:5
    of Silas Bigelow, 60:1
    of John Foster, 37:7
Gray, Asa, portrait of, 249:7
Great Barrington, Massachusetts, 23
Great Seal of Massachusetts, 75
Greeks:
    food, 323
    immigrants, 306:1
Green, B., book printed by, 48:3, 49:4
Green, T., books printed by, 60:3,4
Greenfield, Massachusetts, 171:5
griffin, 103:5
Groton School, 245:4

guards, to protect stores from looters:
    after Boston fire, 1872, 232:1
    during Boston Police Strike, 1919, 304:1
gymnasiums, 256:1, 258–59:3
gymnastic equipment, 256:1

Hadley, Massachusetts, founding of, 6
hair tonic, advertisement for, 275:5
Hale, Edward Everett, photograph of, 217:5 (at left)
Halibut Point, Cape Ann, S. Gott house, 1710, 83:6
Hampden County, Massachusetts, 6
Hampden Park, Springfield, 1883 bicycle tournament,
        241
Hampshire County, Massachusetts, 6
Hampton, New Hampshire, branding mark, 41:4
Hancock, Dorothy, portrait, 102:1
Hancock, John, 7
    enlistment broadside issued by, 100:2
    mansion, 88:1
    name of ship of, 84:3
    portrait, 102:1
    trading wharf, 86–87 (at center marked B)
Hancock, Massachusetts, 10
handwriting, *see also* autographs, 73:6
    17c., 26:1, 27:3,6, 30:1, 31:5, 34:1, 43:6, 46:2, 49:5,
        51:4
    18c., 84:2
    19c., 162:1, 193:5
Hanover, Massachusetts, 132, 297
harbors:
    Boston, *see* Boston, harbor
    Gloucester Harbor:
        shipbuilding at, 231:4
        view of, 231:5
    Marblehead, 160:1
    New Bedford, 190–91:3, 192:1, 274–75:1
    Newburyport, 160:2,3
    Plymouth Harbor, 27:4, 30
    Provincetown, 160–61:4
    Salem, 83, 114–15:1, 114:2, 116:3
Harding, Chester, portrait of Amos Lawrence by, 131:8
Harding, Warren G., 305
harp, c.1820, 124:4
Harper's Weekly, 231
    illustrations from, *see list of picture sources*
    harpoons, 194:2
Harrison, Peter, 6
Hartford, Connecticut, 41
Harvard, John, statue of, 109:6
Harvard, Massachusetts, Shaker settlement, 147:5
Harvard College, 3–4, 6, 13–17, 46–47, 76–77, 145,
        156–57, 246–47, 316–17
    astronomical observatory, 157:4
    class day, 1856, 156:2, 184:1
    commencement procession, 156:1, 313:6
    Dental School professor, 307:4
    Dunster House, 317:6 (at right)
    football match at, 1857, 156:3
    founding of, 3–4, 14, 47:5
    Harvard Hall, 47:5 (at left), 76:1 (center), 156:1
        (with cupola), 156:2

steeples, *see also* belfry; churches; cupolas, 54:**2**, 86–87:1, 96–97:3
stereoscopic views:
  of Harvard Medical School, 255:**5**
  of Nantucket woman, 299:**4**
  of Provincetown school, c.1890, 244:**1**
  of Quincy Market, Boston, 260:**1**
  of spot where 1872 Boston fire began, 232:**3**
Stevens, Nathaniel, 10
Stevens-Duryea Company, Chicopee Falls, advertisements, 300:**2**, 300:**3**
Stevenson, Adlai, 318–19:4 (upper left)
stile, 118–19:1 (next to gate)
Stockbridge, Massachusetts, founding of, 6
stock certificates, 168:**2**, 198:**3**
  detail from, 113:**8**
stone walls, 41:6, 92–93:3, 155:1, 188:3, 215:7, 231:5
Stoneham, Massachusetts, 297
stools, 45:5, 81
stores, *see also* advertisements; signs, 172–75, 284:1,3
  book, 76:3, 181:**4**, 250:**2**, 251:**3**, 276:1 (*libreria*)
  cigar, 276:3
  clothing:
    Charbonneau Hat Store, Worcester, 284–85:3
    Macullar, Williams and Parker, Boston, 232:1
    Modern Clothing Store, Worcester, 284–85:3
    Posner's Clothing Store, Boston, 304:1
    Six Little Tailors, Boston, 284:1
    tailor shop, 276:3
  dairy, 264–65:1
  drug, 204:1 (at left), 212:1 (at left)
  French, James and Company, 181:**4**
  general store, Old Sturbridge Village, 324:**2**
  Hunt & Webster's factory sales room, 202:**4**
  Little, Brown, & Company, 19c., 251:**3**
  music, Boston, 1853, 175
  ship chandler's shop, Salem, 115:**4**
  tea store, 169:5 (at right)
Stoughton, William, 50:**3**, 53:**4**
stoves:
  cast-iron, coal burning, 19c., 268–69:**1**
  for heating, 153:6,7, 325:2
    in factory, 1860, 204:3
  implements related to use of, 268–69:**1**
    broom and dustpan for ashes, 268–69:1 (on rack)
    lifter for raising stove lid, 268–69:1 (on rack)
    shaker for shaking out ashes, 268–69:1 (on rack)
Stratton, Samuel W. (member, commission reviewing Sacco-Vanzetti case), caricature of, 307:6 (at right)
straw, used in construction, 32:3
Strawberry Banke (later Portsmouth, New Hampshire), branding mark, 41:**4**
street-cleaning sprinkler:
  1839, 141:**6**
  1853, 174:1 (in front of Leonard & Co.)
street lighting:
  Boston, 181 (at right), 255:3,6
    c.1830, 142:2
    c.1840, 171:4
    1853, 174.2
    c.1890, 290–91:**1**
    1893, 280:1

1899, 276:1, 277:5
  c.1970, 320:2, 325:6
Revere, 1912, 301:5
Salem, 1840, 115:4
Worcester, 1880, 223:5
Street Scene #1 by Jack Levine, 310:**2**
Stuards Bay, *see* Cape Cod Bay
Stuart, Gilbert, portraits by:
  Abigail Adams, 124:2
  Jean-Louis Lefebvre de Cheverus, 166:1
  Josiah Quincy, 140:2
Sturbridge, Massachusetts, *see* Old Sturbridge Village
suburbs, 300
subways, 291, 324
  Boston, "T" sign for, c.1970, 325:6
  drawing of proposed station, 1892, 284–85:**4**
  elevated, 285:**6**
    at Atlantic Avenue, Boston, 308–309:2
  Public Garden tunnel entrance, 285:**5**
Sudbury, Massachusetts:
  branding mark, 41:4
  founding of, 4
  list of soldiers killed from, 1775, 93:5
Sudbury River, 23:2
Suffolk Bank, Boston, 1834, 171:**4**
Suffolk University, 14
suffrage, women voting in Boston election, 1888, 269:**5**
sugar bowl, silver, by Revere, 75:3
Sullivan, John L., boxing J. Corbett, c.1890, 259:**4** (at right)
Sully, Thomas, portrait of John Quincy Adams by, 124:3
Sumner, Charles:
  photograph of, 216:1 (at left)
  portrait of, 209:5
sun, representation of, 37:7
Supreme Court justices, *see also* Warren, Earl, 17, 271
Swan, William (Boston silversmith), cup by, 63:5
Swansea, Massachusetts, tavern in, 73:**8**
Swedish immigrants heading west, 1852, 169:**5**
Swift, Gustavus, 197
switchboard:
  1877, used in first telephone exchange, 239:**4**
  1896, Worcester, 239:**5**
swords, 46:3, 85:4, 93:4
  of John Endecott, 35:6
symbols, *see also* griffin; Indians; lion; seals; unicorn
  British royal, 84:1
  griffin, 103:**5**
  Tudor Rose, 84:1
Symphony Hall, Boston, c.1900, 262–63:**3**

tables:
  butcher's, 214:1
  empire style, 143:3
  factory, 1860, 204:3
    1875, 250–51:1
  gateleg, 18c., 64–65
  gateleg, oak and maple from Essex County, 39:6
  kitchen, 268–69:1